The Literary
Monster on Film

The Literary Monster on Film

Five Nineteenth Century British Novels and Their Cinematic Adaptations

ABIGAIL BURNHAM BLOOM

McFarland & Company, Inc., Publishers
Jefferson, North Carolina, and London

LIBRARY OF CONGRESS CATALOGUING-IN-PUBLICATION DATA

Bloom, Abigail Burnham.
    The literary monster on film: five nineteenth century British
novels and their cinematic adaptations / Abigail Burnham Bloom.
        p.   cm.
    Includes bibliographical references and index.

    ISBN 978-0-7864-4261-4
    softcover : 50# alkaline paper ∞

    1. Monsters in motion pictures.   2. Monsters in literature.
3. Horror films—History and criticism.   4. English fiction–
19th century—Film adaptations.   5. Film adaptations—History
and criticism.   I. Title.
PN1995.9.M6B56   2010
791.43'67 — dc22   2010023148

British Library cataloguing data are available

Cover information: Robert De Niro as the Creature in the 1994 film
Mary Shelley's Frankenstein (American Zoetrope/TriStar
Pictures/Photofest); (inset) frontispiece to Frankenstein, Colburn
and Bentley, London, 1831 (Engraving by Theodore Von Holst, private collection, Bath, England)

Manufactured in the United States of America

McFarland & Company, Inc., Publishers
    Box 611, Jefferson, North Carolina 28640
    www.mcfarlandpub.com

Table of Contents

Preface

When my son was a teenager, he delighted in watching horror movies. He wanted to see as many as he could, and I frequently accompanied him. I had never watched many before, and I was amazed by the manner in which the monster was an aberration from ordinary life and unconnected with the main characters. Often there was no motive involved in the murders committed by the monster, or the explanation was given so quickly that I didn't get it. In *Child's Play* (1988), Chucky, a "good guy" doll, destroyed those around him without any reason whatsoever. A character like Michael Myers, whose monstrousness stems from insanity, remained unconnected with his victims. Sometimes, as in *Scream* (1996), the explanation for the murders was much more forgettable than the machinations involved. *The Blair Witch Project* (1999) presented disappearances from no coherent cause. Monsters could also be created by scientific mishap, as in *Godzilla* (1998), but the monster remained an outsider, a threat to anyone in its path and unconnected with the protagonist. Then there was *Hostel* (2005), in which the torture and murder was done for the pleasure of torture and murder alone. The monsters in these films are generally unacquainted with the protagonist and drawn to murder a victim for no particular reason. Interest in the film comes not from who is murdered or why, but how and in what manner.

These horror films struck me as completely different from the nineteenth-century horror novels that I read and taught. Within these novels, the monster is a manifestation of the protagonist or intimately connected with him. Frankenstein and his creation are doubles of each other. Dr. Jekyll develops Mr. Hyde as a means of behaving as he likes while maintaining his reputation in society. The monster reflects what is wrong with an individual or even within society as a whole. These monsters reminded me of what kind of person I should and shouldn't be.

I began to watch the films adapted from nineteenth-century horror novels as I wondered if they showed the monster as unconnected to the victim or the protagonist, as in most of the modern films I had seen. I observed that many different means of connecting the monster with another character were used by filmmakers. For example, connections were often made through the parallel

1

placement of actors or by cutting back and forth between characters and actions. Telling the story from the point of view of the monster added to identification with it. However, the identification of monster and protagonist was seldom as sustained as in the novel.

I believe the differences between the portrayal of the monsters in the novels and the films occur for several reasons. People of the nineteenth century had the leisure to absorb the meaning of what they read. Books can be put down and read slowly; readers expected novels to have a moral message that they could apply to their lives. In today's world the movie must deliver an immediate visceral punch. Movies seek to make the viewer react emotionally rather than intellectually. They evoke a relentless fear aroused by watching an unstoppable monster bent on destruction. Whereas readers of horror novels feared they were like the monster, the watchers of horror movies fear they will be the monster's victim. By examining nineteenth-century horror novels and adaptations made from these novels, I seek to examine the monsters within and without ourselves.

Introduction

An uncontrollable creature who slaughters innocent people in his search for revenge, a man who maims and murders for pleasure, an all-powerful and exquisitely beautiful woman with eternal life, a doctor who creates men from animals, and a vampire who has made his home amongst us— all five monsters arouse fear in the reader. This fear may come from many things: surprise, disgust, fear of harm to characters in the novel, and ultimately a threat to our own safety. We fear both becoming the victims of these monsters and that we are these monsters.

During the nineteenth century most people believed in original sin, the sin committed by Adam and Eve in the Garden of Eden, which is transferred to each individual at birth. Since mankind was conceived in sin, each person must be protected from the evil within himself. If all goes well, if a child is restrained and educated correctly, eventually the child will grow up and can overcome, or at least repress, the evil within himself or herself. In the nineteenth century the source for monsters is within the ordinary human. The most frightening part of nineteenth-century novels comes from the discovery of our own similarities to the monster. By the time films were routinely produced in the twentieth century, most people believed that people are basically good and born innocent. In twentieth century films, the monster, for the most part, does not know his victims and seeks to destroy one person rather than another by chance. No longer is the monster intimately connected to his victim. Horror in movies evolves from how different the monsters are from us.

Rationale of This Book

In this work I will examine five British nineteenth-century horror novels: *Frankenstein, Dr. Jekyll and Mr. Hyde, She, The Island of Dr. Moreau,* and *Dracula.* Although *She* is more like an adventure novel, and *The Island of Dr. Moreau* is closer to science fiction, all of the novels contain a monster who disrupts the world of the novel. In each of the five novels, the monster bears a distinctive relationship to the protagonist. In looking at the monsters in nineteenth-century novels, I have chosen to discuss novels that I consider great, that have been read continuously since their publication, and that have been made into numerous cinematic adaptations.

Following my discussion of the novel, I will consider two or three film adaptations of each novel. I look at films which are works of art, are enjoyable on their own, are celebrated by many people, portray an unusual conception of the monster, and were commercially released in theaters rather than being made for television. Within my discussion of each novel and film I will examine the world at the start of the work, the connection between the monster and his victims, the threat the monster creates, the nature of the evil, how the monster is destroyed, and how the world of the novel is returned to normality — if it is. "The World at the Start of" each work details the world before the coming of the monster, the world that is threatened by the monster. I think of this as the normal world, the world that we read about at the beginning of a novel or see on the screen at the start of a film. This world is a given for a particular work of art against which changes can be measured. The second area of discussion, "The Monster Within and Without," presents my reflections on the tendency within the protagonist or his victims towards the monstrous. There is always evil in the world, but it comes to the fore for different reasons. The next section, "The Threat of the Monster," reveals the process by which the monster is created and how he intends to destroy his victims. "The Threat of the Monster" is followed by "The Nature of the Evil," which reveals what is monstrous about each individual monster. Indeed, often it is not the creature initially thought to be the monster that is the true monster of the work. For example, in *The Island of Dr. Moreau*, the Beast Men physically resemble monsters, but the real monster is Dr. Moreau. He longs to be a god and to dominate his own realm. After the monster and his intensions are identified, the monster is defeated, usually through a flaw in itself. The "Monster Destroyed" section chronicles the process of the monster's death. The last section, "Normality Restored," indicates how the characters will continue to live and how their view of the world has changed since the start of the work.

Mary Shelley's Creature from her novel *Frankenstein* (1818) is intimately connected with his creator and is a doppelgänger for Victor Frankenstein. The creature in James Whale's film *Frankenstein* (1931)[1] is the product of an insane scientist, Frankenstein, who is brought back to his senses through the love of his father and fiancée. The presence of an insane scientist or creator in a film suggests that the monster is unconnected with the protagonist, as the insanity, which the viewer does not identify with, is responsible for the monster. Ironically, this film, which shows only an occasional connection between the creator and his monster, has caused confusion about the name Frankenstein — which is sometimes understood to be the name of the Creature itself. Some of the *Frankenstein* adaptations complicate the relationship between the monster and the protagonist. For example, Kenneth Branagh, in his film *Mary Shelley's*

Frankenstein (1994), establishes a connection between the creature and Franken-stein when the Creature is shot and Frankenstein finds a wound corresponding to the Creature's gunshot wound on himself. Frankenstein literally feels the pain of the Creature. In this film, where the Creature is given more voice to tell his own tale, it is Frankenstein who becomes the monster of the work.

Robert Louis Stevenson in *Dr. Jekyll and Mr. Hyde* (1886) created the char-acter Dr. Jekyll, who becomes the monster Mr. Hyde when he drinks a potion. What becomes clear in Stevenson's tale is that each of the major characters in the novel is similar in many ways to Dr. Jekyll. Each engages in hypocrisy in order to keep his reputation untarnished within society; consequently, the novel becomes a condemnation of Victorian society as a whole. The films directed by John S. Robertson (1920), Rouben Mamoulian (1931), and Victor Fleming (1941) all emphasize the division between Jekyll and his friends, and between Jekyll and Hyde. They build up the goodness of Dr. Jekyll so that he has further to fall downwards, showing him as a unique individual unconnected with us.

In H. Rider Haggard's *She* (1887), several of the characters are reincarna-tions, and Haggard continued writing their lives in other books about Ayesha or She-who-must-be-obeyed. Reincarnation is a means of producing a double for a character. But characters also take characteristics from the society in which their authors lived. In part, Ayesha represents the Victorian man's fear of woman's power and the place of Britain within the empire. As with *Dr. Jekyll and Mr. Hyde* and *The Island of Dr. Moreau*, Victorian concerns about evolution and de-evolution are present in the novel. The film adaptations of *She* that I will discuss, Lansing C. Holden and Irving Pichel's film from 1935, and Robert Day's adaptation from 1965, present the unusual image of a beautiful monster and focus on the adventure aspect of the plot. Although the character of She remains very close to that of the novel, in these films her relationships with her victims have been changed, reflecting the attitudes during the eras when the films were made.

The Island of Dr. Moreau (1896), by H. G. Wells, includes creatures who have been formed from animals to become human beings. Wells' novel, based on knowledge of evolution and a sense that all men have evolved from animals, suggests the horror of vivisection in Victorian England and satirizes man's opin-ion of himself as a species. In film adaptations of this novel, the science has changed, as well as the representation of men and animals. *Island of Lost Souls*, directed by Erle C. Kenton (1933), and *The Island of Dr. Moreau*, directed by Don Taylor (1977), indicate everyman's ability to escape from the monstrous and return to a normal life. The conflicts are more complicated in John Franken-heimer's *The Island of Dr. Moreau* (1996), in which all men are capable of behav-ing badly, and some of the Beast Men are more violent than the humans, while others are more moral than the humans.

The title character of Bram Stoker's *Dracula* (1897) comes from Transyl-vania to England, bringing a scourge from the East to the West. The vampire brings out the sexuality of his victims, and in so doing, he reveals the *fin-de-siècle* fear of the New Woman. F. W. Murnau's 1922 film shows vampirism as a plague, coming from the East into Germany, that can be stopped by a person who is pure of heart. In Tod Browning's 1931 adaptation of Stoker's novel, Dracula is a charming foreigner and a threat from outside rather than connected with his victims. At the same time, Dr. Van Helsing is shown as having many parallels with his nemesis, Count Dracula. Francis Ford Coppola's film *Bram Stoker's Dracula* (1992) presents a vampire who feeds on others and a man who seeks eternal love, causing the viewer to connect with his human side while being repulsed by his monstrousness.

The Nineteenth Century

The nineteenth century was the heyday of the genre of the novel. A novel examines the development of a character against the backdrop of a society. It is more than the story of an individual, it is the story of the individual shown against other people. Before one can understand oneself as an individual, one must see oneself in relation to other people and see oneself in other people. Many of the protagonists in nineteenth-century novels are young people who are developing, leading to the mature integration of the self. When the characters look at the people around them, they see some aspect of themselves in others and some aspect of others in themselves. They learn and adapt from their observations. We, as readers, learn from their experiences as well. Through our reading we develop sympathy, empathy, and identity.

The alter ego, or doppelgänger or other, is a complicated psychological as well as literary concept with a basis in folklore and psychology. The novels I am examining concern characters who are so intimately connected with a monster that the monster can be seen as their double or as part of themselves. The monster becomes a doppelgänger, a double who suggests an aspect of the main character. In *Frankenstein* and *Dr. Jekyll and Mr. Hyde* the main characters seem incomplete, and their creations are the part of themselves that lead them to destruction. The characters never become fully integrated themselves, but their experiences may give us, as readers, an idea of how we can live our lives. Nineteenth-century novels generally provide a moral or a meaning for the experiences they relate.

British nineteenth-century society admired nothing so much as an unruffled surface. People sought to be like others, maintaining a calm demeanor and an established routine. No reminder of difference or of non-conformity was openly tolerated. But beneath the surface another reality lay hidden. Within each person was a range of emotion and feeling that might burst out at any time. The ugly thoughts that everyone entertains were repressed until they could not be held back any longer. In the nineteenth-century horror novel these negative emotions are just beneath the facade of each character. At times of crisis, these emotions find a physical embodiment. Because the monsters come from within a person, they are portrayed as intimately connected with that individual. The monsters represent the negative potential of each human being and the ills of society as a whole. They force us to realize that we also harbor within ourselves the ugliest of thoughts and possibilities.

We fear being unlike others, being the outsider, not fitting in, not finding love, not having a fulfilling life. We worry about the reaction that others have to us. We worry about our origins. We fear people will see us as monsters. Being near a monster causes people to feel a physical sensation of horror, and we worry that we will induce this in others. Frankenstein feels faintness, rage, and horror as he sees the creature approach (65). Enfield says of Mr. Hyde, "There is something wrong with his appearance; something displeasing, something downright detestable. I never saw a man I so disliked, and yet I scarce know why. He must be deformed somewhere; he gives a strong feeling of deformity, although I couldn't specify the point" (11). People respond with fear toward monsters because they are abnormal, "disturbances of the natural order." The response to monsters is often caused by what has been called the "interstitial" condition of the monster, that it belongs to no clear group and defies expectations (Carroll 16). There is something abnormal about the monster, something both human and inhuman. They are a hybrid; their humanity makes them believable, but the introduction of something non-human makes them a monster. And this is our fear for ourselves as well.

Horror

As Robin Wood has written, the formula for horror is normality threatened by a monster ("An Introduction to the American Horror Film" 175). Rising from the Gothic tradition, the nineteenth-century novel reveals many elements of horror in the form of monsters who threaten the world at the start of the novel. These monsters contain aspects of the main characters and are often doubles of the main characters. Evil comes from within the individual, seeping outward to destroy society. Monsters are often representations of the problems of society which must be dealt with by the heroes of the novel and by the readers as well: selfishness in the case of *Frankenstein*, the desire for a spotless reputation in *Dr. Jekyll and Mr. Hyde*, the desire for immortality in *She*, the position of man within the Animal Kingdom and evolution in *The Island of Dr. Moreau*, and the fear of the outsider in *Dracula*.

The film adaptations of the novels, for the most part, depict the horror as coming from outside, as separate from the characters. The monster in films becomes an aberration to society. Rather than using the monster to reflect the evil in the characters and in all of mankind, the monsters are an uncontrollable, unrecognizable evil that threatens the characters and their society. Instead of being a doppelganger of the character, the monster is unique and apart from mankind. Because the film adaptations of the nineteenth-century novels were created during a different time, they reflect attitudes of their directors and aspects of the era in which they were made. This monster does not have its source within the characters themselves; consequently, the monster seems less of a threat to us. Ultimately the film characters must defeat the monster in order to reunify society. Frequently the endings of horror films do not contain a moral message, but just the release of triumph over evil.

Films often do not indicate the evil within good characters; they tend to show characters as being more black and white than novels. There are many reasons for this. Ron Bass, a screenwriter, has stated, "Books are about what happens *within* people. Movies are about what happens *between* people" (qtd. in Joslin 3). There is a difficulty in showing interiority in films. A monster, as in the film *Alien* (1979), can be literally within the character, and yet it is just inhabiting the space; it is not connected with the character in any other way. Yet connections are frequently made between monsters and characters in the films. Characters can be doppelgangers, like Van Helsing and Count Dracula in Browning's *Dracula*. The director may cut back and forth between characters or events to create similarities or contrasts between them, as in Murnau's *Nosferatu* or at the mill in James Whale's *Frankenstein*. Characters may find themselves in the same situation, the same place, or sharing the same experience as the monster, as at the end of the 1965 film *She*. In the 1994 *Mary Shelley's Frankenstein* a physical connection is made between the Creature and Victor Frankenstein; while in *Bram Stoker's Dracula* there is a psychic connection between Dracula and Mina Harker. In many different ways, directors have found means to suggest connections between the protagonist or other characters and the film monster.

Although there has been a recent rise in movies with monsters as victims, films rarely show an interconnection between the monster and the victim.[2] Nineteenth-century novels were written to teach a moral lesson that may take the form of a warning against hypocrisy or an attempt to increase the reader's sympathy through identification with the characters. We frequently recognize ourselves in the characters and often in the monsters. The films blame the creation of monsters on an outside or uncontrollable force, such as the insanity of a character or unsafe scientific practices. We, as viewers, enjoy a sense of pleasure resulting from experiencing fear in a controlled environment — watching it on the screen. The monster is far from us and unconnected with our lives. Watching a horror film, we don't have to confront the monster within. We can enjoy the spectacle of something from outside of ourselves threatening the human.

1

Creator and Monster

Frankenstein, by Mary Shelley (1818)

Mary Shelley's *Frankenstein* raises unanswerable questions about the nature of evil and the monstrous. Is the Creature innately evil or does he become so because of his situation and lack of nurturing? Is Frankenstein himself to blame for the evils that the Creature commits? Who is the monster? Thinking about these questions brings out the importance of the intricate connection between Frankenstein and the Creature. In this novel they are doubles whose lives are intertwined. Both Victor Frankenstein and the Creature are narcissistic and think primarily of themselves. They claim to have started life with benevolent intentions, and yet they rail against their situations, blame each other for what has gone wrong, and fail to take responsibility for their own actions. Ultimately both are responsible for disrupting the well-being of society.

In the Introduction to the Third Edition of *Frankenstein* in 1831, Mary Shelley compares herself to Victor Frankenstein. She describes the events leading up to her first thoughts of the novel, which she began writing during the summer of 1816 at a villa near Geneva. Mary Godwin, her future husband Percy Bysshe Shelley, Lord Bryon, and Lord Byron's doctor, John Polidori, read ghost stories to each other and advanced to writing scary stories. She imagined a medical student who created life and then became horrified by what he had done. He sleeps but later is awakened to see the eye of the Creature watching him. Shelley describes her vision:

> His success would terrify the artist; he would rush away from his odious handywork, horror-stricken. He would hope that, left to itself, the slight spark of life which he had communicated would fade; that this thing, which had received such imperfect animation would subside into dead matter; and he might sleep in the belief that the silence of the grave would quench for ever the transient existence of the hideous corpse which he had looked upon as the cradle of life. He sleeps; but he is awakened; he opens his eyes; behold the horrid thing stands at his bedside, opening his curtains, and looking on him with yellow, watery, but speculative eyes [172].

She describes Frankenstein as an artist, a creator much like herself. Her horror at the thought of the Creature is similar to that of her protagonist; but unlike Victor Frankenstein, Shelley seized her subject and wrestled with it in order to create the novel. The scene described above occurs in the novel as Frankenstein awakes to see the Creature looking at him from behind the bedcurtain, "his eyes, if eyes they may be called, were fixed on me" (35). Frankenstein attempts to disallow any humanity to the Creature whatever as he wonders if the Creature's eyes can even be called eyes.

Frankenstein immediately denies his connection with the Creature. He avoids caring for his creation in any way. He refutes the possibility that the Creature has the highest of human attributes. For if the eyes are the window to the soul, and if the Creature does not have eyes, he cannot have a soul. On the other hand, Mary Shelley was aware of her similarity both to Frankenstein and to the Creature.[3]

Like her characters Robert Walton and Victor Frankenstein, Shelley sought fame and reputation for her accomplishment. At the end of the Introduction, Shelley writes, "I bid my hideous progeny go forth and prosper" (173). When Mary Shelley refers to her "hideous progeny," she acknowledges her vision which ignited her creative spark, the Creature that developed in her imagination, and the novel to which she gave birth. The creation of her novel parallels the creation of the Creature by Frankenstein, yet she wants her novel to prosper and sell, while Frankenstein seeks the destruction of the Creature and decides against creating a whole race of monsters. Through the association between Mary Shelley and her characters, and between Frankenstein and his Creature, Shelley indicates a connection with her readers as well. She writes so that we may learn a lesson from their actions which her main characters could not.

Frankenstein's Creature appears monstrous because of his hideous looks, but his creator behaves even more monstrously than the Creature himself. In chapter 1 I will discuss Mary Shelley's Frankenstein and his Creature as doubles who are intimately connected with each other. The film *Frankenstein* (1931), directed by James Whale, shows the creature as external and unconnected with the creator up until the climax of the film. Although the creature acts innocently at first, he creates mayhem with his destruction. Kenneth Branagh's *Mary Shelley's Frankenstein* (1994) shows the connection between the creator and the creation, and comes much closer to presenting the Creature as a monster from within. Ultimately Frankenstein repeats the creative process that made the Creature in order to bring Elizabeth back to life. Through this act Frankenstein becomes more monstrous than the Creature in his selfishness.

The World at the Start of Shelley's Novel Frankenstein

Within a novel that deals with the impossible, Shelley takes care to create a world that is somewhat ordinary. In *Frankenstein* the normal world is present in the frame that surrounds the story of Frankenstein and his creation. This frame consists of letters written from Robert Walton, an explorer, to his sister[4] that tell his own story of finding a ship and sailing north. This world, although fraught with the possibilities of disaster, provides a contrast to the horror of the story that lies ahead. The letters then relay the tale that Frankenstein relates to him, Walton's decision to return to civilization, and finally Walton's own encounter with the Creature.

Walton's letters fascinate, in part, because of their exotic setting in the Arctic waste. Walton and his ship's crew are in danger of having their ship frozen in the ice. Although the situation is hardly normal, it is believable because the nineteenth century was an era of travel and exploration. Amid the solitude, it is startling for Walton to record first the appearance of one sled and then the arrival of Victor Frankenstein on another.

Walton perceives Frankenstein's superiority to other men, particularly through Frankenstein's love of nature:

> The starry sky, the sea and every sight afforded by these wonderful regions, seems still to have the power of elevating his soul from earth. Such a man has a double existence: he may suffer misery, and be overwhelmed by disappointments; yet when he has retired into himself, he will be like a celestial spirit, that has a halo around him, within whose circle no grief or folly ventures [16].

Walton sees a halo around Frankenstein, the sign of an angel. He admires Frankenstein's elevated soul, and believes that Frankenstein lives on a lofty platform from which he is isolated from earthly woes. In fact, the very factor of feeling himself above the rest of humanity has led to Frankenstein's creation of the Creature, which has consequently led to his all too human misery. Following the creation of life, Frankenstein no longer enjoys nature as he did before, which is evidence of his fallen state. Frankenstein, like many Romantic heroes, considers himself above the laws of mankind. He creates new life without thinking about the consequences. Frankenstein's creative power is cut off from moral and social concerns.

Walton's presence in the novel serves two major functions: it makes the story more believable, and it provides a moral lesson for the novel. Walton begins the story in the present; Frankenstein's tale is a flashback to what has already happened. If Frankenstein were to tell his own tale, the reader would have no basis for believing him. Walton verifies Frankenstein, having first seen the two parties arrive on sled, listened to the story from Frankenstein, and then heard it again, confirmed, from the Creature. The basic tale is fabulous and unreal, but it is made believable. Here is a man, Robert Walton, who has seen the Creature from afar and who then transcribes Victor Frankenstein's story. The first application of Frankenstein's story will be as a warning to Walton.

The Monster Within and Without

Frankenstein suffers because of the magnitude of his creative vision coupled with his selfishness, which is a kind of fatal flaw. The subtitle of *Frankenstein*, "The Modern Prometheus," suggests creative genius and the angst arising from it. Prometheus, in Greek mythology, created mankind and gave him fire, and for this was subject to eternal punishment by Zeus. Like Prometheus, Victor Frankenstein has similarly attempted to create a new race and suffers as a result. Frankenstein is a Romantic thinker who attempts to act as god, and he sees himself as punished by his creation or an outside force. In addition to acting as a god, Frankenstein also acts selfishly and does not accept responsibility for his actions.

From his early years, trouble is brewing within Victor Frankenstein from what he refers to as "the birth of that passion, which afterwards ruled my destiny" (21)—his love of natural philosophy. Victor Frankenstein explains to Walton that his early education was not well directed. Frankenstein has an interest in the works of Cornelius Agrippa, and his father tells him not to waste his time on reading Agrippa. Frankenstein believes that had his father more carefully explained to him that the principles of Agrippa had been superseded by more modern science, he would have applied himself to more modern study and have avoided the study which led to the development of the Creature. By blaming his father for his own error, Frankenstein avoids taking responsibility for his actions.

Yet Frankenstein can only see the error of his studies when he looks back. While he is young, his years present a pastoral idyll enhanced by the adoption of Elizabeth into his family and broken by a few occurrences. Before Frankenstein leaves for the university, his mother dies: "an omen, as it were, of my future misery" (24). Frankenstein speaks of this first sorrow in his life as connected with his own unhappiness rather than the sorrow of his father and family, showing a selfish outlook. The death of Frankenstein's mother presages later deaths when other members of his family will be taken from him. But rather than die of disease, they will be murdered by the being Frankenstein creates.

Frankenstein states that he takes upon himself the creation of a new species in order to win the praise of his creation, the blessings of a new species, and to benefit mankind. Through his knowledge, he believes he will "pour a torrent of light into our dark world" (32). But his actions are more selfish than magnificent. It is while Frankenstein is at the university, away from his family and friends, that he discovers the secret of creating life. Frankenstein's isolated situation has led him to a scientific possibility devoid of moral constraints. He hasn't considered the ramifications of his actions. Circumstances come together to lead to the creation and the tragedy it entails. Ultimately Frankenstein loses his brother, his best friend, his fiancée, his father, and his life due to his actions.

When he is young, Frankenstein does not show evil within himself, but he does have unhealthy tendencies. He dwells on his own misery and feels sorry for himself. He denies his guilt and puts responsibility on others. Then his attempt to fulfill his ambitions causes him to fall, making him as monstrous as his own creation. Frankenstein and the Creature are doubles who are bound together throughout the novel; Frankenstein can never escape his own creation.

The Threat of the Monster

In Mary Shelley's novel, the Creature's physical appearance is described in a general way. Because he has made his Creature of a large size in order to work more easily in assembling the parts, the Creature has added stature and strength, and becomes a physical threat to those he encounters. Frankenstein tells how he attempted to create an attractive Creature, but somehow the end result is not what he had anticipated:

> His limbs were in proportion, and I had selected his features as beautiful. Beautiful!— Great God! His yellow skin scarcely covered the work of muscles and arteries beneath; his hair was of a lustrous black, and flowing; his teeth of a pearly whiteness; but these luxuriances only formed a more horrid contrast with his watery eyes, that seemed almost of the same colour as the dun white sockets in which they were set, his shriveled complexion, and straight black lips [34].

The Creature's eyes haunt Frankenstein, frightening him on his first look and also later in the novel. If the eyes are a window of the soul, the creature's eyes, pale and watery, may suggest an incomplete or only partially-formed soul. People judge the Creature by his looks and are immediately afraid of him because there is a radiating sensation of evil emanating from him, stemming from his unique means of creation and the resulting unnaturalness of his appearance. The horror may come from the overwhelming feeling that the Creature is not human or not a human born in the usual manner. The minute Frankenstein sees the "dull yellow eye of the Creature open ... the beauty of the dream vanished, and breathless horror and disgust filled my heart" (34). Frankenstein cannot cope with the reality of the Creature's ugliness and existence. Victor Frankenstein looks normal but behaves outlandishly. The Creature looks different from everyone else but initially does nothing to cause alarm.

After rushing away from the Creature, Frankenstein falls asleep and dreams of Elizabeth. In his dream he kisses her and finds he holds the corpse of his mother.[5] His dream indicates that with the creation of the Creature, Frankenstein's prospects of marrying Elizabeth are at an end. His attempt to find love will bring only death. Although the Creature reaches out to him, Frankenstein runs away and never accepts responsibility for what he has done nor nurtures his creation. He acts with selfishness, attempting to forget what he has done, but Frankenstein's act of creation haunts his dreams and the remainder of his life.

The Creature wants the comfort and compassion of his creator, but cannot find him. This novel can be seen as a kind of creation story, with Frankenstein, as a god, creating mankind. In part, it is a reflection on the relationship between god and man. Victor, like god, has created a species and then taken a step backwards. He has set life in motion and then abandoned it, something that man has often accused his god of doing. Mankind, like the Creature, spends his life seeking communication with his creator. Man is thus left in a deadly chase with his creator, expecting some form of acknowledgement, forever seeking, until exhaustion and death overwhelm him.

On the title page of the novel is a quotation from Adam in John Milton's *Paradise Lost*, asking, "Did I request thee, Maker, from my clay / To mould me man?" He is asking, in effect, "Why was I born?" These could be the words of the Creature as he tries to understand the world, and, of course, the words of almost every teen struggling to come to terms with his or her own existence. Frankenstein can also be seen as the parent who creates and then deserts his child. Having sought fatherhood, he should be there to educate and care for his child rather than abandoning him to the world.

Frankenstein becomes the true monster, for he does not take responsibility for his creation, and he continues to allow others to suffer because of what he has done. Although Frankenstein experiences momentary clarity concerning his guilt, he fails to take action to help others. Frankenstein longs for revenge on the Creature for having killed his brother William, yet he admits, "I, not in deed, but in effect, was the true murderer" (61). Frankenstein also sees the Creature as a dark shadow of himself. Following William's death, Frankenstein describes the Creature as "my own vampire, my own spirit let loose from the grave, and forced to destroy all that was dear to me" (49). Frankenstein and the Creature are completely entwined.

Although the Creature in the novel vows vengeance on all of mankind, he is actually only a threat to people connected with Frankenstein. The one exception (and she is a member of the Frankenstein household) is that he plants the portrait of Mrs. Frankenstein on Justine Moritz, seeking to do her harm because her "smiles are bestowed on all but me" (97). Rejection has led the Creature to desperate measures. The Creature seeks a relationship with Frankenstein and achieves that only through the destruction of Frankenstein's loved ones. The Creature constructs a relationship based on hatred and vengeance rather than nothing at all.

When Justine Moritz is condemned for the murder of William, Frankenstein knows that she is innocent but takes no action or responsibility. He does not attempt to tell his story because Frankenstein fears he will be thought mad and will not be believed. Frankenstein's protestations about being the true murderer and more miserable even than Justine are not the same as accepting responsibility. He verbally acknowledges her innocence, but he does not act to prove it or tell anyone the truth.

Tormented by his own actions, Frankenstein sees himself as evil and damaged. Following Justine's execution, Frankenstein travels with his remaining family to Chamounix in the Alps for the magnificent scenery, but feels horror and despair for himself:

> I wandered like an evil spirit, for I had committed deeds of mischief beyond description horrible, and more, much more (I persuaded myself), was yet behind. I had begun life with benevolent intentions, and thirsted for the moment when I should put them in practice, and make myself useful to my fellow-beings. Now all was blasted: instead of that serenity of conscience, which allowed me to look back upon the past with self-satisfaction, and from thence to gather promise of new hopes, I was seized by remorse and the sense of guilt, which hurried me away to a hell of intense tortures, such as no language can describe [59].

Examining his conscience, Frankenstein sees no way to improve the situation, no way to attempt to make amends or to fix things for the future. Having seen lightning reduce a beautiful oak tree into a "blasted stump" when a child (23), Frankenstein is astonished by the destruction of the stump and seeks to learn more about electricity. As Frankenstein's life progresses, he comes to think of himself as "blasted." According to the *Oxford English Dictionary*, blasted means "stricken by meteoric or supernatural agency, as parching wind, lightning, an alleged malignant planet, the wrath and curse of heaven; blighted." Thus, Frankenstein has removed himself from nature and become cursed after the creation of the Creature. He had "begun life with benevolent intentions" which had somehow gone wrong, and consequently he becomes tortured by guilt. Guilt molds Frankenstein's perceptions about himself and the possibilities available to himself, as well as the world around him. Frankenstein feels guilt but not responsibility. Being "blasted" is something that happens on account of an outside force, whether it be the resulting action of nature or a god. Actually, Frankenstein has brought his misery upon himself.

In the Alps, surrounded by the magnificence and majesty of nature, the Creature finally confronts Frankenstein. As the Creature approaches Frankenstein, Frankenstein reports, "His countenance bespoke bitter anguish, combined with disdain and malignity, which its unearthly ugliness rendered it almost too horrible for human eyes." Frankenstein feels faintness, rage, and horror as he sees the Creature approach (65). He feels himself in the presence of evil. In this case it is the presence of a new race. The Creature is both human, as he is composed of human parts, and not quite human because he was created rather than born. Frankenstein's reaction at the approach of the Creature epitomizes those who have contact with monsters, both in this novel and others. In *Frankenstein* the Creature terrifies himself and then identifies himself as a monster when he sees his reflection in a pool: "At first I started back, unable to believe that it was indeed I who was reflected in the mirror; and when I became fully convinced that I was in reality the monster that I am, I was filled with the bitterest sensations of despondence and mortification" (76). But monstrousness is more than looks.

When the Creature and Frankenstein meet, they question their tie to each other and Frankenstein's duty as a creator. Frankenstein believes that since he has created life, he can also destroy it. The Creature counters that having created life, he cannot play with it — he must respect it. Both Frankenstein and the Creature reveal their suffering to each other. The Creature says, "All men hate the wretched; how, then, must I be hated, who am miserable beyond all living things!" (65). With persuasion and threats, the Creature offers to make a deal with Frankenstein. For the first time Frankenstein feels a sense of duty and compassion towards his creation, and Frankenstein states, "I felt what the duties of a creator towards his creature were and that I ought to render him happy before I complained of his wickedness" (67). The reader, like Frankenstein, is struck by the articulateness of the Creature. Indeed, it is during the Creature's commentary on his life, first to Frankenstein and later to Walton, that the reader, like Frankenstein, develops the sympathy for the Creature that makes this novel so complex and fascinating.

The Nature of the Evil

The Creature develops his own ideas about relationships and punishes those who do not behave as he desires. By watching the interactions of the DeLacey family he has learned what the relationship of father and child should be. Although he has no actual human interactions with them, he feels connected to the DeLacey family and thinks of himself as their protector. At last the Creature reveals himself to the DeLacey grandfather, who is blind. He hopes that he will be heard without the repugnancy inherent in seeing him. However, the rest of the family returns home, and after scaring the Creature away, they quit the area.[6]

Looking at the Creature, everyone assumes that he is evil because he is ugly — they assume his looks are a projection of his inner self. The Creature hopes that someone can get beyond his looks to develop a relationship. When the Creature first sees William, he hopes that William is young enough so that he will be able to "educate him as my companion and friend" (96). People reject the Creature because of his ugliness, causing his natural love to turn to hate. In turn, he seeks to punish others for their rejection of him. The Creature relates his attempt to save a woman's life and how he was shot for his efforts. He views himself as someone innately good who went bad because others rejected him.

Many similarities are revealed between Frankenstein and the Creature in

terms of how they see themselves. The Creature tells Frankenstein, "I was benevolent and good; misery made me a fiend" (66). Frankenstein also believes that
he was innately good until he became "blasted." The Creature calls himself
Adam, as well as Satan, the fallen angel, and appeals to Frankenstein as lord
and king (66). Frankenstein also sees himself as Satan, the fallen angel. Frankenstein says of his life, "Despondency rarely visited my heart [as I once was]; a
high destiny seemed to bear on, until I fell, never, never again to rise" (147).
Both Frankenstein and the Creature have violated the higher laws. Frankenstein
has created life and then neglected it; the Creature has chosen to use his life to
seek vengeance.

The Creature requests from his creator that which everyone wants: the
possibility of love. Frankenstein consents to make the Creature a mate, although
it is against his better judgment. He has been persuaded by his own desire to
be left alone by the Creature and by his sympathy for the Creature. Frankenstein
agrees, although he fears that the Creatures will not cut themselves off from
the rest of the world, that they will bring into the world a new race of monsters,
that the female monster will not find the Creature attractive and will mate with
mankind. Frankenstein is afraid of the mixing of the monstrous with the normal. He is afraid of the unnatural intermingling of the human with monsters.
His ultimate fear is that the monsters may take over the world and destroy
mankind.

The Monster Destroyed

In agreeing to the Creature's demand for a mate, Frankenstein realizes he
has become "the slave of my Creature" (105). His every action is tied to that of
the Creature and he is aware of the Creature watching him. Frankenstein
attempts to break this bond by not completing the mate for the Creature. When
the Creature learns of his decision, he says to Frankenstein, "I shall be with you
on your wedding-night" (116). Frankenstein interprets this to mean that the
Creature will kill him if he goes ahead with his marriage. His thinking is solip-
sistic; he does not consider the Creature's point of view. The Creature will not
allow Frankenstein to have a spouse or a friend if he does not have one. Instead
of Frankenstein, the Creature kills Elizabeth on their wedding night and hearing
this news, Frankenstein's father sickens and dies.

Following the death of Elizabeth, Frankenstein determines to spend the
rest of his life attempting to kill the Creature. The novel has circled back on
itself to return to where it started, with Frankenstein chasing the Creature on
the ice and being rescued by Walton. The Creature seems at his happiest as he
races across the ice with Frankenstein in pursuit of him. All of Frankenstein's
attention is now directed towards him and the Creature even leaves Frankenstein food and other essentials to assure that Frankenstein will continue fol-

lowing him. During the pursuit, Frankenstein and the Creature are closer than they have been previously; their experiences are the same. For once they are focused on each other.

Normality Restored

At the end of the novel, Frankenstein has weakened, although he refuses to turn from his task. He finds the strength to address Walton's men and exhorts them to keep going towards glory. But then Walton decides to head back when faced with the mutiny of his men. With his final words Frankenstein confirms Walton's decision, "Seek happiness in tranquility, and avoid ambition" (152). In the end, Walton decides in favor of the continuance of life rather than glory and renown. He takes a different path from Frankenstein. Frankenstein, after telling his story to Walton and exhorting Walton to kill the Creature, dies. But Walton feels sympathy for the Creature and leaves him to seek his own death.

Walton remains alone to tell the story to his sister, "a sadder and a wiser man," just like the wedding guest in "The Rime of the Ancient Mariner" (1798) by Samuel Taylor Coleridge. There is a stress in this novel towards a higher morality, a morality that involves the suppression of the self in order to bring happiness to others. Walton, for example, renounces fame and fortune for the safety and well-being of his crew. This is evident as well in some of the minor stories in the novel. Walton tells the tale in his second letter of his lieutenant who loves a Russian lady who loves someone else. When the lieutenant discovers the truth of the lady's feelings, he outfits the man of her choice to be her husband and steps away from the situation. Victor Frankenstein's father saves the daughter of his close friend following his friend's death, and later she rewards him by becoming his wife. Felix De Lacey saves the life of Safie's father, a Turk, because he knows he is innocent, with no sense of seeking anything for himself. In this case it backfires in the short term because he and his family are imprisoned, but eventually he wins the love of the man's daughter. These stories set a standard for nobility, kindness, and love in this novel. It is this higher morality that Frankenstein supports with his last breath, and this Walton finally acts upon.

The monstrous in this novel is selfishness, that which makes man act solely for his own purposes. Frankenstein acts alone and secretly in creating the Creature, and behaves selfishly in abandoning him. As he dedicates himself to killing the Creature, Frankenstein's feeling of his own misery becomes supreme. Yet the Creature maintains that his agony is the greater, as he constantly feels remorse for his actions. His behavior is selfish as well, however, for he acts out of anger at his creator and others who wrong him. Together, Frankenstein and the Creature fashion an intricate dance between creator and monster in which they become indistinguishable from each other, and which spirals them both towards increasing misery and death.

In Mary Shelley's novel, Frankenstein and the Creature are intimately connected, and both are involved with monstrous behavior. The monstrous in this novel comes from within; it is not a force external to the characters. Although Frankenstein feels he has been blasted, he is to blame for his own misery. By making connections between herself and her characters, Shelley indicates the universality of her characters. She wants her readers, like Walton, to look within themselves and to follow a path away from selfishness and towards a higher morality.

Mary Shelley's "hideous progeny" has continued to propagate, as shown from the number of adaptations made from this novel. There have been hundreds of films based on the character of Frankenstein and his creation. At moments these films show the intimate connection between Frankenstein and the Creature. Filmmakers have found ingenious and varied means of showing the characters as doubles for each other and as unique with regard to the Creature's appearance.

Because of the nature of the medium, films must begin reimagining *Frankenstein* with the visual aspect of horror. Mary Shelley gave little actual description of the Creature, leaving the details of his look to the imagination of the reader. Each film has had to decide on how the Creature will be shown on the screen. In the 1910 film the monster has long, matted hair and is swathed in bandages, rather like a mummy. His hair and bandages act to accentuate his height and breadth. For the majority of people, the mention of Frankenstein conjures up the image of Boris Karloff as the Monster from the 1931 film directed by James Whale. This image has become a cultural icon. Later films have varied the Creature's looks, in large part because Universal copyrighted the look achieved by Boris Karloff. The Hammer Studio productions, which made seven Frankenstein movies between 1957 and 1973, feature a tall, thin Creature, whose skin has the pallor of death. In *Young Frankenstein* (1974) the Creature is modernized with the addition of a zipper to his neck. Branagh's 1994 *Mary Shelley's Frankenstein* features a clearly sewn-together Creature whose stitches resemble those on a baseball.

One of the very earliest American films was a fifteen-minute silent film, *Frankenstein*, made by the Edison Film Company in 1910 and directed by J. Searle Dawley. The final scene, which takes place in Frankenstein's study, is described in this way in the production notes:

> Monster enters—business of seeing reflection of himself. Original fades leaving the reflection still in glass. Frankenstein enters at door. His reflection takes place over monster's. Monster fades leaving Frankenstein's reflection there. Frankenstein [crosses] room — sinks in chair as bride comes in. Winds up with Frankenstein and bride in each others [sic] arms [Hitchcock 129].

This story contains one important element of the novel in the connection that is made between Frankenstein and the monster, although the use of a mirror to make this connection is new. As the monster fades into Frankenstein, it all can be seen as an hallucination or as a psychological doubling of the two. The possibility that the monster came from Frankenstein's imagination suggests the monster within rather than a force from without. As in many Hollywood versions, the film has a happy ending. Frankenstein can have a happy marriage, having resolved his conflicts with his creation. Such moments of showing the monster and Frankenstein as connected appear in movies, but generally do not constitute the center of the films.

I have chosen to look at two of the available Frankenstein films: James Whale's 1931 *Frankenstein* and Kenneth Branagh's 1994 *Mary Shelley's Frankenstein*. Both pictures contain brilliant scenes and were commercially successful, but do not completely succeed as a whole. Whale's film has been significant because of its influence on the versions that have come after it. Branagh's film imposes modern concerns on the frame of the nineteenth-century work. Both show, to some degree, the connection between Frankenstein and his Creature that is central to Mary Shelley's novel.

Frankenstein (1931)

DIR.: James Whale. PERF.: Colin Clive, Mae Clarke, John Boles, Boris Karloff. Frankenstein: The Legacy Collection, 2004. DVD.

The 1931 movie *Frankenstein* takes the basic idea of a scientist creating or reanimating life from Mary Shelley's novel, but follows a very different path from the book. It is a loose adaptation, dispensing with the framing presence of the Arctic explorer Robert Walton, and changing the relationship between Frankenstein and the monster. The film has become a cult classic for several reasons: the dramatic performance and look of the Monster as portrayed by Boris Karloff and the feeling that the film is not taking itself completely seriously. The horror of the scenario results from Frankenstein's obsession and the Monster's inability to comprehend the world. Interspersed with the horror, moments of humor — derived from the buffoonery of the characters, particularly Baron Frankenstein — punctuate the movie. Although many scenes in the film are haunting and beautifully filmed, parts of the picture seem patched together without an overarching plan. For example, the decision to leave Frankenstein alive at the end, celebrating his much-delayed wedding, seems to have been tacked onto the film.

For the 1931 film the look of the Monster was created by the make-up artist Jack Pierce, in conjunction with Boris Karloff, who played the Creature. This look included a huge head and a large, clumsy body. The Creature seems to have outgrown his suit, as the sleeves are too short for his arms. He wears heavy black shoes, slowing down his walk and giving him a lurching gait which makes his movements unpredictable. Pierce recalled his conception of the Creature's look:

> I didn't depend on imagination. In 1931, before I did a bit of designing, I spent three months of research in anatomy, surgery, medicine, criminal history, criminology, ancient and modern burial customs, and electrodynamics. My anatomical studies taught me that there are six ways a surgeon can cut the skull in order to take out or put in a brain. I figured that Frankenstein, who was a scientist but no practicing surgeon, would take the simplest surgical way. He would cut the top of the skull off straight across like a potlid, hinge it, pop the brain in, and then clamp it on tight. That is the reason I decided to make the Monster's head square and flat like a shoe box and dig that big scar across his forehead with the metal clamps holding it together [qtd. in Nollen 20–21].

In addition to the basically square head, flattened on top, and scars resulting from his brain transplant, Pierce built up Karloff's forehead to suggest a Neanderthal appearance. The heavy brow above his eyes implies primitive intelligence. Karloff increased the strangeness of his appearance by putting white on his eyelids, thus making them thick and heavy and applying black shoe polish to his fingernails. Bolts on the neck indicate the means by which electricity brought him to life, adding to his mechanical and other-than-human look. In the novel, people's reactions to the Creature's looks can be overcome by talking with him; his words bring attention to the intelligence beneath the outward appearance. Whale's Monster cannot speak, but only makes guttural sounds. Consequently, he must make himself understood and attempt to connect to others with his expressions and gestures.

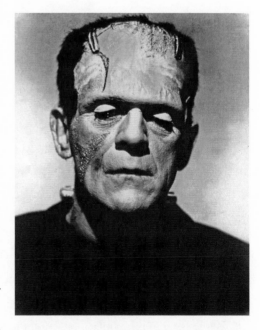

The monster from without, created by man but not connected to him — the Monster (Boris Karloff) in James Whale's Frankenstein (1931) (Universal/the Kobal Collection).

Several changes from the novel were made in the names of characters and in the relationships shown in the film. Because Frankenstein's creation is referred to as the Monster in the credits, I will refer to him as the Monster rather than the Creature while writing about this film. Other names have been changed from the novel for no apparent reason. Victor Frankenstein of the novel has become Henry Frankenstein, perhaps because in the novel Frankenstein's friend was Henry Clerval. In this film, one character, Victor Moritz, has been given the last name of one of the victims in the novel. Victor Moritz is clearly in love with Elizabeth, and happy to wait in line in the hope of supplanting Frankenstein in her affections. Indeed, Frankenstein even meaningfully requests that Moritz take care of Elizabeth should anything happen to him. Whatever the outcome of his experiments, Elizabeth will be able to lead a normal life. In this manner the importance of the continuance of the race is insisted upon, and Frankenstein's experiment becomes less important to the world as a whole. Having a proper husband for the female character is a common concern in Hollywood films, as will be seen in the movies made from *Dr. Jekyll and Mr. Hyde*.

Frankenstein begins with a disclaimer spoken by a suave and ingratiating Edward Van Sloan, the actor who plays Dr. Waldman in the movie. He gives the viewer a "friendly warning" in the form of an opportunity to leave the theater and not watch the movie, although he assumes you will see it anyway, as he ends his talk by shruggingly exclaiming, "Well, we've warned you." Obviously, the intention is to build the viewer's anticipation. He states that the movie deals with a man who sought to "create life in his own image without reckoning upon God," and is concerned with two mysteries of creation, life and death. Although the statement may be true, it is not what we find in the novel or in this movie. In this movie God does not punish Frankenstein; indeed, everything works out well for him.

The World at the Start of Whale's Film Frankenstein (1931)

A horror film must in some way establish a normal world so that the audience may compare that world with the havoc which ensues once the monster has arrived. Henry Frankenstein's father, Baron Frankenstein, personifies the normal world of this film. His is a world of tradition, of wine put away by his ancestor to be consumed at moments of celebration. Above all else, the Baron desires an heir for the House of Frankenstein to continue the family traditions. When his son has been away for too long, the Baron assumes he has a mistress, as that is the only explanation that makes sense to him. Henry Frankenstein feels the pull of the regulating forces of Elizabeth, his fiancée, of his father, and finally of the village itself in the form of the Burgomaster who says that the village wants a wedding. The elevation of the family in society is brought out by the father's rank of Baron and by the Burgomaster's deference to them. He compliments Frankenstein to his father, "such a nice young man" and "the image of his father." "Heaven forbid," replies the Baron, thinking he is joking, but anticipating the distance between Frankenstein and the Monster, who is not the image of his father or creator. A son for the House of Frankenstein becomes not only important to the Baron but to the entire village.

At the start of the film, Henry Frankenstein has removed himself from the world of his father and this traditional German village, and is behaving in an antisocial manner. Experimenting in a watchtower, and attended only by his hunchback assistant Fritz, Frankenstein left the university and isolated himself because he was "ambitious to create life." The resulting Monster, Frankenstein's creation, is a son only in a world of dark and nefarious undertakings. The Monster is not a proper heir to the House of Frankenstein and jeopardizes the possibility of there ever being a son to carry on the Frankenstein tradition.

The Monster Within and Without

Frankenstein is the first of the mad scientists we will look at in this study. Because they are an aberration, they are disconnected from other people, and they are not in control of themselves — they are a force from without. Away from the regulating aspects of home and the university, Frankenstein is tense and driven by his goal. The film begins as Frankenstein starts to assemble the parts for his experiments. The camera focuses on the rope that lowers a coffin into the grave, emphasizing the centrality of death. Frankenstein and his lab assistant, Fritz, watch from outside the cemetery gates while mourners bury their dead. Frankenstein manifests his impulsivity and his nervousness by admonishing his assistant, who sticks his head up, "Down, down, you fool" and then proceeding to stick his head up in exactly the same way. This scene, showing them as doubles and as contrasts, produces a comparison of their faces — Frankenstein smooth and handsome, Fritz strange and deformed.[7] Frankenstein then becomes an opposite of Fritz, although they are closely connected by their actions.

Frankenstein and Fritz become the unnatural elements in the landscape. The mourners at the burial are stark figures who stand out in juxtaposition against the sky. Tombstones loom in the background, and include a huge crucifix and a figure of death as the grim reaper. A minister handles a giant staff, and then all is still. The moon rises as Frankenstein and Fritz hurry to dig up the coffin. As they move in to recover the corpse, the church bells are still tolling, reminding people to pray for the soul of the dead, and reminding the viewer that Frankenstein is disturbing the soul of a dead person. Frankenstein pats the coffin they have removed from the earth and addresses the camera, informing the audience that the contents are "just resting, waiting for a new life to come." In this way Frankenstein justifies his own behavior, making it sound natural and ordinary. Here is a resurrection in this world rather than the next.

Seeking a brain for his Monster, Frankenstein sends Fritz to steal one from the university. Frankenstein has moved from grave robbing to theft. During a lecture on the brain, Professor Waldman compares a normal brain with the degenerate brain of a man whose life was one of "brutality, of violence and murder." When the lecture hall empties, Fritz picks up the normal brain but is startled by an unexplained gong into dropping it; Fritz then leaves with the abnormal brain. This Monster is no blank slate: with a criminal brain, the Monster would seem to have no alternative but to live a life of crime. The film provides a possible reason for the Monster's criminal behavior. Yet the Monster does not act like a criminal. He attempts to be obedient and only acts violently out of innocence or as a reaction to the behavior of others. The criminal brain becomes a dead end in trying to explain the behavior of the Monster.

The initial evil comes from Frankenstein himself. His work at the university has removed him from normal intercourse with other people. His isolation and association with Fritz has led him further afield. The figure of death in the graveyard, and the skeleton and pictures in the lecture hall, form a kind of foreshadowing of the horror that will come from Frankenstein's deeds. Out of disrespect for death will come disaster. These initial scenes of the film graphically reveal the evil and horror of Frankenstein's activities.

In the novel, Frankenstein's concern is not with religion, nor with what religion would say about his activities or his breaking the laws of God or religion by disturbing buried bodies. Indeed, he does not seem to be breaking into hallowed places, like cemeteries, but taking body parts "legally." He justifies his devotion to his task by comparing himself to a religious person as he speaks of the "cell" in which he works. He brings the dedication of the monk to his mission. Frankenstein's tendency towards an evil selfishness has been with him for years; it is not a recent and temporary aberration in his behavior as it is in the film.

The Frankenstein of the 1931 film is obsessed, even insane. This insanity comes from his isolation and will be overcome when he is reabsorbed back into society. Rather than a dedicated researcher and student, the Frankenstein of the 1931 film defies traditional religion and seems, as he begins the process of animating the Monster, to be a mad scientist who is willing to do anything to bring off his crazy scheme. During the film he will come back to a more normal life so that at the end of the movie he will join with others in hunting down the Monster. Finally, he will take his rightful place in the village through marriage. Frankenstein will be able to rejoin society and be redeemed in a way that he is only able to do in the novel through his legacy to Walton and the reader. Frankenstein's deviation in the film is temporary, caused by something outside of himself, possibly part of a breakdown or brain fever or bad period of his life. This goes towards distancing the Monster from Frankenstein, keeping them apart.

In this film, a whole delegation arrives to help Frankenstein. Waldman knows that Frankenstein is dealing with the creation of life, and he agrees to go with Elizabeth and Victor to talk to Frankenstein. Waldman becomes an older, almost father-figure to Frankenstein who attempts to help him control his behavior and come back onto a proper path. These changes made in the adaptation of the novel into the film indicate the temporary nature of Frankenstein's madness and society's role in saving him. Frankenstein's insanity is not endemic to his character but a temporary state.

The contrast in the film between Frankenstein's life and the life he should be leading is shown by the crosscutting from one scene to a contrasting scene. The scenes jump back and forth from Frankenstein's laboratory to the goings-on in the village in a kind of "meanwhile back at the ranch" contrast. For example, the scene shifts from the cold stones of Frankenstein's watchtower to the warmth of Elizabeth's room, where she has his picture on her table. The viewer is constantly reminded of how Frankenstein should be behaving. As Elizabeth talks with Victor Moritz, Frankenstein's picture remains between them, preventing them from getting too close together. This is where Frankenstein belongs, protecting his fiancée from the world. Instead, Elizabeth leads a group to rescue Frankenstein from himself, proving herself a woman of the twentieth century.

The Threat of the Monster

While the creation of the Creature in the novel is barely described, the film takes advantage of the visual impact of the Monster coming to life. Rain pours down, thunder and lightning threatens, and Frankenstein's electrical equipment crackles and flares, making for a tense atmosphere that increases the anticipation of the viewer. Just as Frankenstein and Fritz begin their experiment, Elizabeth, Victor, and Dr. Waldman insist on entering the laboratory. They have come to bring Frankenstein back to the normal world, but they make no attempt to physically interfere with the experiment. Victor accuses Frankenstein of being inhuman and crazy, and Frankenstein justifies himself as a visionary. He says of the Monster, "That body's not dead, it has never lived." He starts the equipments, raises the body to the roof, and then brings it down after much noise and flashes of lightning. The storm makes it seem as though the judgment of God is at work, and the Monster is given life from an external source. As the Monster's hand moves, Frankenstein says, several times, "It's alive," and, "Now I know what it feels like to be God." Frankenstein believes the creation has been a complete success and that he is the god who engineered it.

The horror initially comes from the excitement of the creation and Frankenstein's gleeful insanity, but in the next scene the horror comes from the appearance of the Monster. The audience does not see the Monster immediately, as Frankenstein explains that the Monster is only a few days old and has been kept in the dark. Previously his face was covered by bandages. But suddenly his footsteps are heard and he backs into the room, casting a huge shadow on the wall. He turns slowly around, revealing the now famous face. Although the Monster obeys Frankenstein's simple commands, Frankenstein doesn't treat the Monster as human. He refers to the Monster as "It" rather than "He" and has no sense of giving him a name, even as one would a dog. Like a dog, this Monster understands many words and obeys commands, but lacks language. He makes his feelings known through grunts and groans and gestures.

The Monster immediately seeks the light, showing a predilection for what is good, simple, and life enhancing, and attempts to reach his hands toward his creator. Rejected by his creator, and left in the company of Fritz, the Monster responds to the sadistic behavior of Fritz. Whereas Frankenstein has ignored his creation, Fritz seeks to frighten him first with a whip and then with fire.[8]

The Monster of the film might be destined to be a killer from the start since Frankenstein used the brain of a criminal. After the creation, however, Frankenstein learns of the use of the criminal brain, and he responds that it is only a piece of tissue. The movie takes the viewpoint that evil behavior is learned. Instead of behaving like a criminal, the Monster is innocent and child-like. The Monster murders in self-defense and out of inexperience. The monster's murder of Fritz shows the Monster's instincts for self-preservation. Fritz has tormented the Monster with a torch and a whip. Later on the Monster's innocence and lack of understanding of death lead to the drowning of Maria. Yet because the Monster kills people unrelated to Frankenstein, the connection between creator and creation is lessened. They no longer function as doubles—at least not until one of the final scenes of the film.

The Nature of the Evil

Frankenstein's creation is a monster that must be destroyed. In this film Frankenstein takes responsibility for the Monster, but allows himself to be controlled by his family and friends. Dr. Waldman and Frankenstein agree that the Monster must be killed, although Frankenstein protests that this will be murder. He does not believe that he has the right to destroy what he has created, although he is willing to let Waldman do it for him. However, their plans are interrupted by the arrival of Elizabeth and Frankenstein's father. Elizabeth blames others for Frankenstein's plight: "What have they done to you?" she asks. Although Frankenstein whimpers in response, "It's all my fault," he does not take charge of the situation. Frankenstein lets himself be taken home to recover from his experiences and rejoin his "normal" life by making preparations for his marriage. Although he has suffered temporary insanity, Frankenstein shows no tendency toward evil.

The professor is left to painlessly destroy the Monster. Despite his promise, it doesn't appear as though the doctor is planning to destroy the monster painlessly. Rather, he seems to have been corrupted by Frankenstein and to be undertaking his own experimentations, as he is about to perform an autopsy on a living Monster. As the doctor bends over the Monster, the Monster's hand comes slowly up from behind, grabs the doctor's neck, and strangles him. The Monster murders his second victim, Dr. Waldman, in self-defense.

In a contrasting scene, the social life of the village has an ordinary, happy aspect. Frankenstein and Elizabeth experience an idyllic time which will soon be ended by the appearance of the Monster. Frankenstein's madness has abated, and he remarks, "It's like heaven being with you again," indicating the closeness of his former milieu to hell. Happily, the couple set their wedding date. This scene fades into the traditional orange blossoms for their wedding. Baron Frankenstein explains that these were worn for three generations, and he can only hope that in thirty years they will be worn by another generation. We hear the toast, "A son for the House of Frankenstein,"; bells are ringing, and crowds are celebrating in the street. The wedding brings together the village and the family and their hopes for the future. The mistake of Frankenstein's first creation will be replaced by another, more conventional son.

The Baron dispenses beer in the town, briefly causing goodwill among the citizens. Good comes from without, from the influence of intoxication and a wedding, and so does the evil. Evil arrives through the actions of the Monster, yet the Monster himself does not seem responsible for what he does. The viewer sees little from the point of view of the Monster and consequently cannot identify with him.

While the village is celebrating, the Monster has contact with his third victim. In the novel, the Creature had hoped a child would not be scared of him. However, when he approaches Frankenstein's brother, William is horrified by the appearance of the Creature. In the film, a young girl, Maria, unconnected with Frankenstein, shows no fear of the Monster. The child takes his hand and asks him to play, preferring him to the kitten her father has instructed her to play with. They play with flowers, a symbol of innocence (and a short life, in this case) and a contrast to the Frankenstein orange blossoms which have been in the family for generations. The Monster and Maria throw the blossoms into the water to watch them float. During this brief time the Monster is happy. The appearance of the Monster is in stark contrast with the small girl and the beautiful lakes and mountains behind them. When they run out of flowers, the Monster gets excited and then throws the girl into the water, expecting her to float. Instead, she goes under, and he runs through the woods, frightened by what has happened. This scene was removed from some early release prints of the movie because of its graphic nature. However, it reveals the Monster's innocence, as he has not intended to kill the child, and yet she is dead.

Back in the village, everything is not going smoothly at Frankenstein's wedding, as Elizabeth says she is afraid. Frankenstein dismisses her anxiety, but she insists, "Something is coming between us." As Frankenstein leaves to check the rest of the house, he locks Elizabeth in her room. The action becomes hectic as Frankenstein learns that Dr. Waldman has been murdered and that the Monster is in the house. The Monster comes through the window of the room where Elizabeth waits and approaches her from behind. Her screams alert Frankenstein, who rushes into the room to find her lying across the bed. She looks as though she is dead, adding to the anxious anticipation of the viewer; but she is revealed later to be alive.

In the next scene Maria's father walks into the festivities carrying the body of his drowned daughter. She hangs across his arms with one stocking up and one down, looking as though she has been raped and murdered. Slowly the villagers realize the serious nature of the situation, stop celebrating, and follow behind the peasant to demand action. The Monster of the film kills Fritz and Dr. Waldman in self-defense, drowns Maria, and threatens Elizabeth and Frankenstein. He is a danger to everyone he has contact with, as shown by his unintentional murder of Maria. The evil he spreads has not come from his criminal brain nor from his own nature, only from his lack of understanding. The Monster acts from outside of the community and apart from Frankenstein; he has not been shown to be connected with Frankenstein at this point in the film.

The Monster Destroyed

With the death of Maria and the threat to Elizabeth, all hands conspire to kill the Monster. Frankenstein states that there can be no wedding while the Monster is alive: "I made him with these hands and I'll murder him." As in the novel, Frankenstein is determination to kill the Monster himself, but in this film he is joined by the entire village. The men of the village are divided into three sections and go off with torches, pitchforks, and even hounds to sniff out the Monster. Somehow Frankenstein becomes separated from the men he is leading, and faces his Monster alone. Briefly they are connected with each other, as they are for so much of the novel.

Frankenstein's strength cannot match that of the Monster, and the Monster carries his unconscious creator into an abandoned mill. This scene, the climax of the film, provides a complex look at the characters by showing them as doubles. As Frankenstein wakes up, they look at each other across the spokes of a wheel. Here for a brief moment Frankenstein and the Monster connect, as each of their heads is identically framed in alternate shots within the machinery of the mill. They become united with each other as equals and as alter egos, which is brought out by the manner in which they are shot by the camera. It is a moment where each recognizes the other, but nothing is stated. Then the Monster throws Frankenstein off the mill so that his body hits the arm of the windmill and then falls to the ground. Frankenstein lies as if he is dead. Men carry

Frankenstein (Colin Clive) finally comes face to face with the Monster (Boris Karloff) as the connection between them is revealed in James Whale's *Frankenstein* (1931) (Universal/the Kobal Collection).

Frankenstein back to the village while others torch the windmill. The Monster screams and appears to be pinned under a beam as the structure burns.

Torches, usually a symbol of bringing truth and light into a dark world, take a strange turn in this movie. First they are used by Fritz as a means of tormenting the Monster. In the mob scene they become a way of uniting force, but remain part of the stark and bleak look of the movie. What began as a traditional wedding for the village becomes a mob scene. Although the mob is a potentially evil force, here it acts to kill the Monster who has become a threat to the community. It completes the murder that Frankenstein is not able to do.

Normality Restored

In the final scene of the film the giggling staff brings wine for the recovering Frankenstein, but the Baron drinks it instead, saying, "Here's to a son for the

House of Frankenstein." This repeated line emphasizes the importance of marriage and the continuance of family. Rather than behaving properly, Frankenstein has been spending his time with activities that are outside the range of the normal and do not lead to the benefit of society. With Baron Frankenstein, the emphasis is on tradition — orange blossoms, wine, champagne for the servants, and beer for the townspeople. The film seems to have been intended to end with the fire in the mill and the death of Frankenstein and the Monster. The final scene feels tacked on in order to end the picture on a happy note. With Frankenstein recovered from his insanity and the Monster dead, all threat of evil is over, at least for the present.

The evil depicted in the film occurs as a force from outside the characters and the community. Frankenstein creates the Monster while suffering from temporary insanity, and elements of nature spark the Monster's life. The murders committed by the Monster are done out of innocence and for self-preservation. Only at the climax of the film is the Monster connected with Frankenstein. This allows a suggestion of what might have been, but is not followed up. Back in the bosom of his family, Frankenstein has recovered from his temporary insanity.

The ending also allows for another movie to be made to continue where *Frankenstein* left off. *Bride of Frankenstein* (1935), also directed by James Whale, takes up the process of creating a mate for the Monster. Strangely, the identity of Frankenstein and the Monster is confused in the title of the film, as the bride is created not for Frankenstein himself but for the Monster. *Bride of Frankenstein* begins with the same actress who plays the bride (Elsa Lanchester) playing Mary Shelley, who explains to her husband and Lord Byron that the Monster was not actually destroyed at the mill, thus beginning a tradition of the resurrection of the Monster.

Mary Shelley's Frankenstein (1994)

DIR.: Kenneth Branagh. PERF.: Robert De Niro, Kenneth Branagh, Tom Hulce, Helena Bonham Carter. TriStar, 2000. DVD.

Discussions of adaptations often distinguish between a film being faithful to the letter or the spirit of the original text. An adaptation may attempt to include all of the specific characters and plots of the original — the letter — or it may try to be faithful to the themes of the original — the spirit. In actuality, such a dichotomy cannot be so simply applied, as a multitude of factors influence the message and meaning of a film. Kenneth Branagh sought to remain faithful to the ideas behind the plot and characters of Shelley's novel rather than to the plot alone. Writing about his film, Branagh emphasizes what attracted him to the two central characters, Victor Frankenstein and the Creature: "the prospect of creative life, of a man playing God; and the idea of the noble savage, the disadvantaged creature who through misfortune discovers wisdom and compassion in a way that arrogant and complacent man cannot" (Branagh 9). Although in this statement Branagh focuses on the differences between Frankenstein and the Creature, in his finished film, the two are deeply connected. This connection provides the most satisfying aspect of the picture.

Movies must not be negatively judged because of their distance from their source. *Mary Shelley's Frankenstein* has many similarities to a movie made at the same time and in the same studio, but with a different director — Francis Ford Coppola's *Bram Stoker's Dracula*, which will be discussed in the Dracula chapter of this book. Both movies are dramatic, loaded with acting talent, and very entertaining, but eventually somewhat hollow in terms of delivering a clear and satisfying meaning. The titles of both movies suggest their link with the original novel, and yet both take great liberties with the plot of the original. However, *Mary Shelley's Frankenstein* is at its most intense and interesting where it deviates the furthest from Mary Shelley's novel, *Frankenstein*. *Mary Shelley's Frankenstein* and *Bram Stoker's Dracula* do not disappoint as movies because of their distance from their sources, but because they do not find images or ideas that successfully hold them together. The noisy, dizzying aspect of the films eventually overpowers and detracts from their themes. Yet the intriguing aspect of the films can be seen by the number of awards that they were nominated for. *Mary Shelley's Frankenstein* received an Oscar for Best Makeup and was nominated for many awards by the Academy of Science Fiction, Fantasy & Horror Films, as well as winning several other awards.

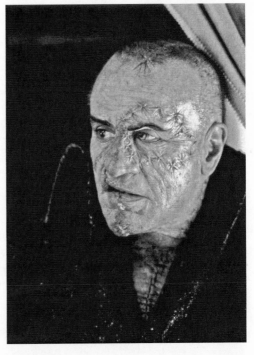

His mismatched eyes suggest his capacity for good and evil, just like that of any man — the Creature (Robert De Niro) in Kenneth Branagh's *Mary Shelley's Frankenstein* (1994) (Tri-Star/American Zoetrope/the Kobal Collection).

In Mary Shelley's novel, the Creature develops the capacity for evil because Victor Frankenstein provides no nurturing for him. Both Frankenstein and the Creature act with selfishness and fail to take responsibility for their actions. In James Whale's 1931 film, Frankenstein becomes temporarily insane when he acts in isolation from society, and the Monster commits murder because of his desire for self-preservation and because of his innocence of the world. The mob which seeks to kill the Creature represents the potential for evil within mankind. For Kenneth Branagh, evil is not something that arises in a person through isolation. The evil within mankind boils to the surface through mob activity in an even more monstrous way than in Whale's film. At two different times in the Branagh film a mob acts with violence, creating more havoc than any character individually.

Mary Shelley's Frankenstein differs from earlier Frankenstein films in the extent of the sympathetic presentation of the monster. The Creature, as he is referred to in the credits (and played by Robert De Niro), is, like every man, born with a capacity for good and evil.[9] Branagh establishes an integral connection between Victor Frankenstein and the Creature. Branagh's treatment of evil is more like Mary Shelley's than that explored by Whale, who presented Frankenstein and the Creature as individuals linked only by Frankenstein's creation of him and Frankenstein's final attempt to kill his creation. Branagh suggests that Frankenstein and the Creature are closely connected throughout the Creature's life; they are similar in many aspects and ultimately they become one in death. They are shown as doubles most clearly through their shared emotions of pain and love. Consequently, this film reveals monstrousness as being part of both Frankenstein and the Creature, as coming from within the characters.

The World at the Start of Branagh's Film
Mary Shelley's Frankenstein

Branagh takes care to immediately establish *Mary Shelley's Frankenstein* as a horror movie. His film begins with a voiceover of Mary Shelley's words from her Introduction to the 1831 edition of *Frankenstein,* which state that with this story she intended "to curdle the blood and quicken the beating heart" (32) of her readers. Shelley's words evoke the presence of the author and give the sense that her imprimatur is on Branagh's work. In his effort to entertain the audience through fright, Branagh will add to the horror of Shelley's original tale.

Branagh uses the arctic adventures of Robert Walton as a frame for his story of Frankenstein and the Creature. Walton functions as a double for Frankenstein. Their similarity is demonstrated in two major ways. First, words on the screen explain that Walton's voyage "would uncover a story to strike terror in the hearts of all who venture into the unknown," words that are not in Mary Shelley's novel. Like Frankenstein, Walton will "venture into the unknown." Second, Frankenstein recognizes his similarity to Walton and tells

Walton, "You share my madness." Here Branagh emphasizes the kinship of Walton and Frankenstein, both of whom are involved in dangerous scientific pursuits of the unknown. By showing their similar tendencies at the start, Branagh can show later how their characters diverge when Walton learns from Frankenstein's mistakes.

Walton also functions as a substitute for the reader, the person who will listen to and learn from Frankenstein's story. Frankenstein tells his story as a means of changing Walton's behavior so that he will save his ship, his men, and himself by not continuing north. Frankenstein directs his story to Walton: "Hear my story, Captain Walton, and be warned." Frankenstein's words imply that there is a moral to be learned from him and that he will reveal this lesson to Walton — and, through him, to the reader. Walton is in charge of his vessel and the destinies of himself and his crew. At the end he safeguards life rather than attempting to fulfill Frankenstein's goal of killing the Creature or proceeding further north.

Frankenstein's story is told in the form of a flashback, contrasting the isolation and danger of the first scenes with the lush scenery, beautiful mansion, and loving family of Frankenstein. In these scenes of Frankenstein's childhood, Branagh accentuates the role of Elizabeth and his mother in Frankenstein's upbringing. Elizabeth has a stronger personality and larger function than in the novel, befitting a woman in the era during which the film was made rather than in the era it portrays. Even at the start, as a child brought into the family, she shakes hands with Frankenstein as his equal. As they grow up, the relationship between Frankenstein and Elizabeth includes a physical passion not explored in the nineteenth-century novel. This portrayal adds to the sensual and romantic flavor of the film and leads to its dramatic climax.

Through the depiction of Frankenstein's childhood, Branagh evokes a normal world where the most horrific event is death at an early age. Frankenstein's experiments with life are shown to develop directly from his reaction to the death of his mother during the birth of Frankenstein's brother, William. The horror of death is revealed by the blood that drenches Frankenstein's father and his ensuing grief over the loss of his wife. The terror of this birth suggests the appeal to Frankenstein of parthenogenesis — reproduction from a single parent — and gives him a motive for his future experiments. Films often provide images that convey the emotions of the actions, as the mother's red blood suggests the horror of birth and death. The events inside the Frankenstein's mansion are complemented by the weather outside. A thunder and lightning storm rages, indicating the natural forces which cannot be tampered with by man; and a tree is struck by lightning, signifying the fragility of life. All of these elements suggest the passion within Frankenstein which will lead him towards the creation of life.

Frankenstein's mother continues to influence him after her death. Even three years later, Frankenstein morosely dwells on his loss: he wants her to be brought back and states that no one should die. Frankenstein's mother has left a journal to be given to Victor "to fill with the deeds of a noble life." The journal becomes an ironic reminder of his potential, as the journal will record his experiments with creation. Left in his coat and found by the Creature, the journal provides the basis for the Creature's understanding of himself and enables him to track down Frankenstein. Frankenstein's journal becomes the Creature's Bible whereby he learns the story of his birth, much as man may learn this story from Genesis or John Milton's *Paradise Lost*. Frankenstein does not live the noble life his mother had imagined for him. His good intentions lead to naught and go against the natural order. His own process of giving birth is more horrific than his mother's and leads to the death of his loved ones and eventually his own death. Although Frankenstein appears a handsome, normal young man, blessed with all that life can offer, he never recovers from the emotional trauma of his mother's death.

The Monster Within and Without

The monster of Branagh's film is the most human of movie monsters, while Victor Frankenstein is the most monstrous of Frankensteins. In pursuit of the creation of life, Frankenstein seeks to study with Professor Waldman, who has traveled the same road that Frankenstein seeks — he has experimented with life. Indeed, while visiting Waldman's home, the unattached and electrified hand of an ape grabs Frankenstein's friend and fellow student, Henry Clerval, and won't release the hold. This scene foreshadows what is to come: the experiment is successful, but the experimenter no longer has control of what he has created. There are unintended consequences in science, and modern science is not far from Frankenstein's experiments. While discussing their experiments, Frankenstein suggests the possibility of heart transplants, not a possibility in 1816, but quite common when the film was made. The idea of a heart transplant also looks toward the climax of Branagh's film in which Frankenstein provides Elizabeth with a new heart and uses his knowledge for even greater evil than the creation of the Creature.

In this film Frankenstein works in the same area of research as Waldman and within the same society. The events in the town they live in provide a scientific backdrop for their experiments. Waldman attempts to administer a smallpox vaccine, a scientific innovation not universally accepted, despite its benefits. Believing that the vaccine will give him the disease, one man kills Waldman. The bodies of Waldman and the killer provide Frankenstein with the basis for his own work. He is delighted to be able to utilize Waldman's brain in his experiments — both before and after Waldman's death. Rather than the brain of a criminal, as in Whale's film, the Creature will have the brain of a brilliant scientist. However, the brain is never mentioned again and seemingly plays no part in the development of the Creature. Waldman's interest in scientific experimentation acts to soften Frankenstein's responsibility for his actions by showing that he is working within a tradition. Like Waldman, Frankenstein has good intentions that go awry.

Clerval provides a moral voice to counter Frankenstein's scientific inquiries. Believing that there is something unnatural and wrong with Frankenstein's obsession, Clerval states that there will be a terrible price to pay for Frankenstein's experimentation. Frankenstein enjoys the companionship of Clerval from the start of his college career. Clerval provides a contrast with Frankenstein, as he is less serious in his ambition than Frankenstein and maintains a moral path. Rather than the more-innocent self of the novel, Clerval becomes the voice of a higher morality in the film, a voice easily dismissed by Frankenstein. In contrast to Clerval, Frankenstein neglects the care and consideration of others within his immediate circle in his desire to benefit the human race. Although his behavior is not monstrous, it is not well advised either.

Frankenstein's stated goal in his experimentation in Branagh's film is to benefit all humanity — "to allow people who love each other to be together forever." There is no mention by Frankenstein of the fame and honor that might result from his experiments — a motivating force in the novel. In Branagh's film, his motivation is not selfish. But the world that Frankenstein envisions of harmony and peace becomes a world of tragedy and death because Frankenstein seeks something outside of the natural order.

Frankenstein engages in ghoulish behavior as he comes closer to finalizing his project: he hacks up cholera victims and collects amniotic fluid. Frankenstein refuses to abandon his work, as "it must come first." Branagh sought to expand, beyond the short description in the novel, the creation scene, to "enhance a modern audience's appreciation of Shelley's great story" (Branagh 9). Branagh's Frankenstein uses huge machines and even eels to provide electricity. As Frankenstein, Kenneth Branagh works with his shirt off, showing both Frankenstein's intense dedication and his own buff physique. As he sees the eyes of the creature open, Frankenstein repeats the famous line from the Whale movie, "It's alive." Removing the Creature from his birthing vat, he tries to get it to breathe and stand. As Frankenstein and the Creature roll around together in amniotic fluid (made from jello), they momentarily connect but cannot bond. Suddenly the Creature appears as a Christ-figure when Frankenstein accidentally hangs it on chains from the ceiling. Thinking the Creature is dead already, Frankenstein repeats twice, "What have I done?" Branagh's Frankenstein, like his Creature, is self-reflective but easily distracted from feeling guilt.

Like the Frankenstein of the novel, Branagh's Frankenstein attempts to escape his own creation by going to bed. In the film, Professor Krempe's voiceover intones the words, "Evil will have its revenge. God help your loved ones." His words suggest that the creature has been made from evil, and a sense of foreboding prevails. Critical of Frankenstein's behavior from the start, Krempe here provides a voice of reason and morality, as Clerval does elsewhere. By comparing the pose of the Creature to Christ on the cross and then reminding the viewer of the evil within the Creature, Branagh's film indicates the capacity for greatness and evil in everyone.

When people act as a mob, true evil emerges. Branagh seeks to understand and explain the actions of Frankenstein and the Creature, but mob action cannot be comprehended. As the Creature runs away from Frankenstein, he runs into the townspeople, who accuse him of carrying cholera — of being the personification of the disease and spreading it. Frankenstein has seen the Creature as the embodiment of disease and death, and his feelings are echoed by the townspeople. The Creature has superhuman strength and learns quickly, but he is not yet a threat to the world. He simply seeks to survive. The monstrousness displayed in this film is the action of the mob, action undertaken out of fear, without thought or reason.

The Threat of the Monster

The Creature frightens because of his looks; he appears diseased because of his looks and manner of movement. Stitches on his face, back, and chest are large and crude; but the audience is led to develop sympathy for him. The haunting eyes of the Creature are vividly depicted in Branagh's movie. The Creature has mismatched eyes, suggesting his capacity for good and evil, with much scarring around them. The Creature's eyes also reveal his longing for a family, and for love and acceptance. The camera focuses on his eyes as the Creature looks through a chink of the pig sty into the interior of the De Lacey home. Thus the eyes become a means of gaining audience sympathy and understanding for the Creature.

Branagh employs other devices in the movie that produce sympathy for the Creature by establishing his connection with Frankenstein. When the Creature rescues a woman from drowning, he is shot, and Frankenstein develops a bruise and feels the pain. There is an intimate connection between Frankenstein and the Creature. Frankenstein's relationship with the Creature is also emphasized through the image of his coat. The Creature's coat is his only clothing in the film, a coat that was originally Frankenstein's. When the Creature wears the coat, it appears as though he is taking a piece of Frankenstein with him. When first seen on Frankenstein, the coat is fashionable, but slowly it becomes tattered and loses its form until it hangs on the Creature like his skin.

Intercutting the activities of Frankenstein and the Creature further establishes their link. While Frankenstein falls ill, the creature makes his way through the woods, hungry and afraid. In an early play adapted from the novel *Frankenstein*, the Creature is tamed by playing music. The theme of the ability of music to "soothe a savage breast" is continued in this film. Hearing music, the Creature seeks its source and finds the De Lacey family. As Frankenstein awakes from his fever, he hears music and sees Elizabeth. Both Frankenstein and the Creature respond to music, creating a link between them and the existence of a musical theme for each.

The Creature has memories that are awakened by experience. Unlike the Creature in the novel, who arrives as a blank slate, and unlike the Monster in Whale's movie, who learns very little, the brain of Branagh's Creature has retained some of its earlier knowledge. Hearing music, he can play it without being taught how to do so. This super-human facet of his intelligence allows the Creature to learn to read quickly so that he can understand Frankenstein's journal, which is in the pocket of his coat.

Although the Creature implicates Justine in the murder of William Frankenstein, it is the evil of the vigilante mob that kills her. This is the real evil of the film. A mob had previously attacked the Creature, and now they hang Justine, showing the evil aroused in a group. When Frankenstein realizes that the Creature has killed William and is responsible for the death of Justine, Frankenstein says, "Oh God, Justine; forgive me," implicating himself in the murder of Justine and showing his tie to the Creature. The evil of both Frankenstein and the Creature appears when they act from selfishness. The Creature has acted selfishly in exacting revenge on Frankenstein by murdering William. Branagh's Frankenstein has been careless in not thinking through his experimentation and being neglectful of his responsibilities, but has not yet revealed his own capacity for evil. He is not guilty in the death of Justine — the mob is.

The Nature of the Evil

James Whale presents a Monster who is separate from Frankenstein, who kills not to inflict pain on Frankenstein but because he has difficulty existing in the world. He kills first a man who torments him, then a man who intends to kill him, and then a young girl by mistake. The evil comes from outside the characters, because of the Monster's reaction to a society that has no place for him. Branagh's *Mary Shelley's Frankenstein* demonstrates the deep connection between Frankenstein and the Creature. As in the novel, the Creature kills in order to hurt Frankenstein and to make him suffer as the Creature does. First they share physical pain, and then, through the murder of William, Frankenstein comes to share the Creature's emotional pain. Finally they come together to talk.

The encounter on the Sea of Ice between the Creature and Frankenstein reveals Branagh's vision of the Creature as vulnerable and human. The Creature states that he began life with feelings of kindness and benevolent intentions which have become rage and hatred. In Branagh's film, the Creature blames the murder of William on Frankenstein and believes that they share the guilt for the deaths. He interrogates Frankenstein about his own history in a way that the Creature never does in the novel. Branagh's Creature accuses Frankenstein of not teaching him, and inquires if Frankenstein ever considered the consequences of his activities. Seeking self-knowledge, he asks his creator, "Who am I?" Frankenstein cannot answer his questions. The Creature must remain in the state of uncertainty shared by all mankind. By showing the Creature's uncertainty, just as with his point of view, the viewer comes to identify with him.

Finally, the Creature asks for a friend, a companion, a female who is like him. Frankenstein seems to have been convinced by the Creature's arguments and feels he has behaved badly towards the Creature. Frankenstein agrees to make the woman, saying, "If it is possible to right this wrong ... then I will do it." Left with the conviction that it is his responsibility to improve the life of the Creature by making him happy (since he gave the Creature life), Frankenstein acknowledges his connection to the Creature and seeks to help him. The developing relationship between Frankenstein and the Creature identifies both characters as sympathetic and human.

The Creature and Elizabeth have become opposite pulls on Frankenstein's life, and Frankenstein can satisfy only one of them, not both. Branagh shows how Frankenstein is torn between the Creature and Elizabeth by crosscutting scenes of Frankenstein unpacking his equipment to make a mate for the Creature and Elizabeth packing her suitcases to leave Frankenstein. The Creature and Elizabeth are linked because unless the Creature gets his mate, Frankenstein cannot have his. Frankenstein, the Creature, and Elizabeth perform a delicate dance leading to the actual scene of her deciding between them.

The Creature brings the body of Justine to Frankenstein, almost as though the Creature and Frankenstein are working together. This, in Branagh's movie, is the moment at which Frankenstein decides he cannot build a mate. Frankenstein is deterred by his materials rather than the consequences of his actions. The Creature reminds him that Justine is only materials, but the sight of her body shocks Frankenstein. His emotional reaction decides him against continuing with the creation. When he gives up the process of making a mate for the Creature, he believes he can reclaim Elizabeth. Frankenstein's reasons for abandoning the creation of the mate are selfish, as he seeks to satisfy his own desire for a mate. Following this, the Creature seeks vengeance by preventing Frankenstein from enjoying the pleasure that he refuses the Creature. The evil of the Creature erupts as he destroys the innocents loved by Frankenstein.

Frankenstein hopes he can return to normality by marrying Elizabeth; instead, he exposes Elizabeth to the Creature. On Frankenstein and Elizabeth's wedding day, Branagh emphasizes their vows of honesty and being together till death, showing the dangerous nature of their marriage. Frankenstein has not been honest with Elizabeth, nor with anyone else in his family. For a moment

Frankenstein and Elizabeth are united by the bed of Frankenstein's father, witnessed by their friend Clerval. In the next scene the camera looks in from outside a window of the Frankenstein house under which is written the word "Godliness." Inside the room the Creature walks to the bed and shuts the eyes of Frankenstein's dead father. This intimate gesture suggests both that he has killed the father and that he has taken over Frankenstein's filial duties. The "Godliness" of Frankenstein's father has been destroyed by the Creature. The Creature has begun to devastate everything that gives Frankenstein pleasure.

Rather than take responsibility for the Creature, Frankenstein attends to his own personal life. He selfishly interprets the Creature's statement that he will be with Frankenstein on his wedding night as a threat to his own life. In his honeymoon suite, Frankenstein passionately embraces Elizabeth when he hears flute music — the theme of the creature. As Frankenstein leaves the room to find the Creature, the Creature takes Frankenstein's place, lying on top of Elizabeth. The physical position shows Frankenstein and the Creature as doubles, both wanting a mate, both entranced by the beauty of Elizabeth. As if destroying her love for Frankenstein, the Creature thrusts his hand into Elizabeth's chest and rips out her heart, which continues to beat in his hand. The Creature says, "I keep my promises." Frankenstein has not been able to keep his wedding vows because he has not kept his promise to his creation.

The Monster Destroyed

Rather than vowing to kill the Creature, Frankenstein attempts to right the wrong that the Creature has done to him when he killed Elizabeth. He seeks to make a bride for himself. Frankenstein immediately carries Elizabeth to his laboratory — a ghoulish parody of the marriage ritual of carrying the bride over the threshold. She is wrapped in a blood-red cloth, reminding the viewer of the blood from the death of Frankenstein's mother. Frankenstein uses the bodies of Elizabeth and Justine to fashion a female for himself. All pretense of experimenting for the benefit of humanity is gone, as is his promise to create a mate for the Creature. Frankenstein acts out of selfishness in order to satisfy his own desire for a mate. Clerval once again tries to stop Frankenstein, acting with reason and morality in opposition to the obsessed determination of Frankenstein.

Frankenstein claims his bride — created by fusing Elizabeth's head onto Justine's body — by putting her body back into her wedding dress and placing a wedding ring on her finger. Like the creature, she is the product of a hasty sewing job. Frankenstein attempts to awaken memories in Elizabeth, asking her to remember and to say his name. He dances with her in a mockery of the traditional dance following a wedding. As Frankenstein celebrates his success, the Creature arrives and calls Elizabeth to him, telling her that she is beautiful, and challenging Frankenstein for her possession. Although both Frankenstein and the Creature want her, Elizabeth destroys herself.[10] She cannot cope with the difference between what she was and what she is. This is a beautiful and fascinating scene, showing Frankenstein's emotional and desperate involvement in his work. Frankenstein's passion and selfishness have led him further into immorality. The terror of the scene comes from Elizabeth's reaction, her understanding of what Frankenstein has made her. As Elizabeth destroys herself, she destroys the last thing that Frankenstein holds dear, and also burns down the House of Frankenstein.

Appearing nowhere in Shelley's novel, this scene makes a powerful statement about Frankenstein's selfish obsession. He seeks to reanimate Elizabeth no matter the consequences and regardless of what she wants. The situation places Elizabeth between the two men and places the two men in direct competition with each other. They are equals, equally monstrous, vying for the love of a woman. Visually stunning, the scene is also emotionally stirring. Although Branagh has changed Shelley's vision, he has created his own statement about the motivations and passions of his characters.

Normality Restored

After the destruction of his world, Frankenstein dedicates himself to the annihilation of the Creature and pursues him ever northward. The first scene of Branagh's film traces the two indistinguishable forms of Frankenstein and the Creature as they race through the Arctic ice. Heading towards death, they have become indistinguishable. Walton and other members of the crew witness the Creature sobbing over him and saying, "He was my father." They participate in a traditional funeral for Frankenstein, with the Creature standing by himself, mourning. The Creature refuses an offer to go south with Walton and his crew; he responds, "I am done with Man" (139). After the death of Frankenstein in Branagh's film, the Creature achieves some of the recognition and respect he has sought because Walton treats him as an equal. Ultimately the Creature and Frankenstein will burn and freeze together. The screenplay for the film announces, "Father and son. Close at last. Peace at last." This ending provides a means of their uniting in death in a way never possible on Earth.

At the end of the film, Frankenstein is burned with his journal on his chest so that his knowledge will be extinguished. Frankenstein has lived out his fate as a tragic hero, destroyed by his ambition and selfishness. However, Branagh's view of the Creature as a "noble savage" rather than a monster, "the disadvantaged creature who through misfortune discovers wisdom and compassion in a way that arrogant and complacent man cannot," seems false. The Creature has acted monstrously in killing William, putting blame on Justine, and murdering Victor's father and Elizabeth in order to seek revenge on Frankenstein.

"Father and son. Close at last. Peace at last": Victor Frankenstein (Kenneth Branagh) and the Creature (Robert De Niro) in Kenneth Branagh's *Mary Shelley's Frankenstein* (1994) (Tri-Star/American Zoetrope/the Kobal Collection/David Appleby).

It is Walton who has learned "wisdom and compassion." Walton and the audience share sympathy for the Creature. In treating the Creature as a human rather than a monster, Walton has assumed a humanity that Frankenstein never does. By heading back to civilization with his crew, Captain Walton separates himself from the madness of Frankenstein. Because of Walton at sea and Clerval on land, normality can be restored. In Branagh's film, Frankenstein and the Creature are treated as equals, sharing a coat, sharing pain, and sharing the desire for a mate. The viewer begins to identify with the Creature, and he is seen as more understood and less evil. Likewise, because Frankenstein is not responsible for the murder of Justine, he is less evil as well. Both are ultimately revealed to be only men, composed of good and evil.

2

The Duality of Good and Evil

Strange Case of Dr. Jekyll and Mr. Hyde, by Robert Louis Stevenson (1886)

While Victor Frankenstein forms his Creature because of overweening ambition, Dr. Henry Jekyll, in Robert Louis Stevenson's *Strange Case of Dr. Jekyll and Mr. Hyde*, creates the monster Edward Hyde so that he can behave as he likes as Hyde while keeping his reputation as Dr. Jekyll unsullied. Jekyll's sin is that of hypocrisy, a sin that may not be considered that terrible in the modern world. But Stevenson believed it was a pervasive and corrupting influence in Victorian society. Hypocrisy keeps men silent about their world and consequently unable to change that world.

Throughout his life Robert Louis Stevenson (1850–94) was intrigued by the duality of man — man's ability to be both good and evil. He stated that the idea for his novel came to him in his dreams, including the scene of Jekyll's first involuntary transformation into Hyde. He subsequently wrote a draft of the novel in three days, but his wife objected, saying that the work was just a story and should be an allegory, a work that in saying one thing also says something else. Stevenson burned the draft and rewrote it in another three days, and then reworked the story over a period of a month or six weeks (qtd. in Stevenson 77–78). The resulting book is an allegory for the evil and good in mankind, two parts that are inextricably mixed in everyone.

Stevenson's novel encompasses other meanings as well. The split between Jekyll and Hyde can also be read as an allegory for the state of society towards the end of the Victorian era (see Linehan, Stevenson 204–13). While claiming to adhere to strict moral codes, many Victorians were flirting with the desire for more exotic tastes. Although Gabriel Utterson acts to repress his own desires (for example, in not drinking wine), many Victorians did not and began to indulge their unsocial desires. Jekyll's behavior can also be seen as an addiction, analogous to drug or alcohol addiction.[11]

Do we all have an evil double inside ourselves? Gerard Manley Hopkins (1844–89), a poet and Jesuit priest, wrote a friend that his Hyde was much worse than that envisioned by Stevenson (qtd. in Stevenson 101). In Stevenson's view the monster is within Jekyll himself, just as the possibility of a monster exists in each of us. The chemical — in his case, an unknown contaminant — brings out a side of Jekyll already within him. Because the monster stems from within, albeit bodied forth with the help of chemicals, Jekyll is somewhat responsible for his behavior.

In this chapter I will show that the real evil revealed in *Dr. Jekyll and Mr. Hyde* is within society and consequently within each person. Having contact with Mr. Hyde produces murderous impulses. Mr. Hyde is a hideous-looking monster who brings out feelings of revulsion and rage in all who meet him. The films discussed here present the monster in very different ways from the novel, and each ends with the redemption of Dr. Jekyll's soul (as shown by the corpse of Mr. Hyde turning into Dr. Jekyll). John S. Robertson's *Dr. Jekyll and Mr. Hyde* (1920) shows a large divide between Dr. Jekyll and Mr. Hyde, suggesting the monster as coming from outside of Dr. Jekyll. In Robert Mamoulian's *Dr. Jekyll and Mr. Hyde* (1931), the real evil is the sexual repression forced upon Dr. Jekyll by his future father-in-law; while Victor Fleming's *Dr. Jekyll and Mr. Hyde* (1941) reveals a Jekyll who lives in a world where most people are kept reined in by government and religion.

The films are linear, showing Jekyll determined to become someone other than himself for various reasons. *Dr. Jekyll and Mr. Hyde* is a novel of suspense, a slow uncovering of the relationship between Jekyll and Hyde until the moment when the reader realizes they are the same person. Even though it is no longer a surprise for us because of common references to "Jekyll and Hyde" in our society, this was a shock for the novel's first readers.

The World at the Start of Stevenson's Novel Dr. Jekyll and Mr. Hyde

The normal world in Stevenson's novel, the world that will be threatened by the monster, is that presented by Gabriel Utterson and Richard Enfield at the start of the novel. This is a world of routine, where middle-aged bachelors enjoy a professional and personal relationship with each other. Utterson and Enfield, cousins and friends, frequently walk together. Utterson, although austere with himself, seems to have a hidden self within: "something eminently human beaconed from his eyes; something indeed which never found its way into his talk." He drinks gin because he likes wine more and doesn't go to the theater although he enjoys it. The kind of austerity practiced by Utterson was not uncommon for the Victorians, especially Victorians of the upper class with a religious bent. Many people kept themselves under control by denying themselves opportunity for the appearance of emotion or dissipation.[12] Perhaps by denial of the flesh, they hoped to feed their spirit. "I incline to Cain's heresy" (7), Utterson likes to say, indicating that he does not interfere in the lives of other people. At the same time that Utterson keeps himself under control, he, like Cain, can say, "Am I my brother's keeper?" Although he may be curious about the situation he uncovers with Jekyll, he does not feel responsible for Jekyll's behavior, nor does he forcefully intervene in Jekyll's business. In the world of Stevenson's novel, friends do not interfere with the behavior of others.

During their weekly walk together, Enfield points out a door to Gabriel Utterson and tells him the story of a man who trampled a girl and then went into the door and emerged with a check from an eminent man for 200 pounds to mollify her family. Enfield says he cannot mention the name on the check, although he wonders if it is a case of blackmail. Enfield has not asked this man, whom he knows and whom we learn is Dr. Jekyll, about the door because, "I feel very strongly about putting questions; it partakes too much of the style of the day of judgment" (11). Like Utterson, Enfield does not sit in judgment on others or interfere in their lives. Utterson remarks that he knows the name of the man who wrote the check. But at this juncture he and Enfield make an agreement not to discuss the matter between themselves; as Enfield says, "Here is another lesson to say nothing. I am ashamed of my long tongue. Let us make a bargain never to refer to this again" (12). Enfield believes he has already said too much. It is interesting that he makes a "bargain" with Utterson rather than an agreement. It would seem that, like making a bargain with the Devil, such an act puts his soul in jeopardy. By not delving into the irregularities of their world, Utterson and Enfield desperately attempt to keep the world as it is.

The Monster Within and Without

Duality is evident in many aspects of this novel, as well as in Dr. Jekyll himself. Dr. Jekyll's home opens on one side to a respectable thoroughfare and on the other to a run-down area. While Jekyll maintains an excellent reputation, Hyde does as he likes. Jekyll is introduced to the reader with the initials following his name, "M.D., D.C.L., LL.D., F.R.S., & c.," indicating that he is a doctor and a lawyer as well as the holder of an honorary degree and a member of a highly esteemed society — and who knows what else (13, note). Because of Jekyll's reputation, his friends cannot understand his connection with Hyde. They guess that Hyde may be his son from an old affair and that Hyde is blackmailing him. They may even guess that Hyde is his homosexual lover. Although no mention of homosexuality is made in the novel, women are conspicuously absent from the lives of the men. Utterson thinks of Jekyll, "He was wild when he was young; a long while ago to be sure; but in the law of God, there is no statute of limitations. Ay, it must be that; the ghost of some old sin, the cancer of some concealed disgrace: punishment coming ... years after memory has forgotten and self-love condoned the fault" (18–19). Utterson thinks like a lawyer, using the legal term "statute of limitations" in a moral sense. He believes that any misdeeds will eventually catch up with Jekyll. If Jekyll sinned, he is now paying the price. Yet Hyde is located within Jekyll, and the possibility of a Hyde exists within each of his friends.

Utterson also considers, briefly, his own past. The point is frequently made in this novel that what happens to one of these men, could happen to any of them. They are of similar age, profession, and life style. Utterson believes that Hyde results from a sin from Jekyll's past rather than a current sin. Indeed, it is because of a sin of "self-love" that Jekyll becomes Hyde: he does not want to be identified with certain kinds of behavior, he does not want to see himself as a whole, and he refuses to acknowledge his misdeeds and even his desire for them. Jekyll is guilty of hypocrisy, and in many ways, Lanyon and Utterson are just as guilty as Jekyll.

While talking to Utterson, Enfield describes the action of Hyde as "like some damned Juggernaut." The word "Juggernaut" indicates that Hyde is a foreign, inhuman, and unstoppable monster. He describes his reaction to Hyde, although he cannot depict the man with any detail:

> He is not easy to describe. There is something wrong with his appearance; something displeasing, something downright detestable. I never saw a man I so disliked, and yet I scarce know why. He must be deformed somewhere; he gives a strong feeling of deformity, although I couldn't specify the point. He's an extraordinary looking man, and yet I really can name nothing out of the way [12].

We learn later that Hyde is younger and smaller that Dr. Jekyll, although no one is ever able to remember details of his looks. Rather, they describe how they feel in his presence. After seeking him out, Utterson reflects:

> Mr. Hyde was pale and dwarfish, he gave an impression of deformity without any nameable malformation, he had a displeasing smile, he had borne himself to the lawyer with a sort of murderous mixture of timidity and boldness, and he spoke with a husky, whispering and somewhat broken voice; all these were points against him, but not all of these together could explain the hitherto unknown disgust, loathing and fear with which Mr. Utterson regarded him [17].

Hyde is a monster masquerading as a human. He looks almost human, but he has the hybrid quality of the monster that makes everyone who comes in contact with him feel uneasy. Something, very difficult to define, just seems wrong. Utterson thinks that perhaps Hyde is harboring a deformed soul: "Is it the mere radiance of a foul soul that thus transpires through, and transfigures, its clay continent?" (17). During the course of the novel Hyde becomes larger as the evil within him grows. The world of this small band of friends in late nineteenth-century London has already been disturbed by the presence of Mr. Hyde. Hyde seems like an outsider, someone who has arrived and alarmed everyone with his activities.

But unbeknownst to Enfield, Utterson has another reason for worrying about Jekyll. Returning home from his walk with Enfield, Utterson pulls out Dr. Jekyll's will. He has been upset about the will without knowing anything about Hyde; now that he knows something, his feelings are worse. Jekyll's will is out of the ordinary: it states that if he dies or if he disappears for three months, everything will go to Hyde. A will is a person's last statement on earth, since it is read after his death. In a way it is an indication of his human accomplishments in that it indicates what he has managed to accumulate during the course of his life. This will intimates something unsavory about Jekyll. In addition to his horror of Hyde inheriting, Utterson fears that Hyde may kill Jekyll in order to hurry the inheritance. Utterson assumes Hyde is blackmailing Jekyll and thinks of blackmailing Hyde:

> This Master Hyde, if he were studied ... must have secrets of his own: black secrets, by the look of him; secrets compared to which poor Jekyll's worst would be like sunshine. Things cannot continue as they are. It turns me cold to think of this creature stealing like a thief to Harry's bedside; poor Harry, what a wakening! [19].

Judging by Hyde's looks, Utterson believes that Hyde must have done worse things than Jekyll. If he can find out what Hyde has done, he will be able to protect his client by blackmailing Hyde, the blackmailer. He therefore dedicates himself to talking with Hyde. "If he be Mr. Hyde ... I shall be Mr. Seek" (15). He phrases it like a game, and yet the results can be deadly. It also indicates Utterson's own hypocrisy, his willingness to do something illegal, such as blackmail, under certain circumstances. The reader discovers the truth of the relationship between Jekyll and Hyde along with Utterson.

Utterson undertakes his research on Jekyll by talking to Hastie Lanyon, Jekyll's former friend and colleague. Where Utterson is strict with himself but lenient with others, Lanyon is rigid with others and himself. Lanyon explains his current estrangement from Jekyll:

> But it is more than ten years since Henry Jekyll became too fanciful for me. He began to go wrong, wrong in mind; and though of course I continue to take an interest in him for old sake's sake as they say, I see and I have seen devilish little of the man. Such unscientific balderdash [14].

Lanyon's use of the word "devilish" suggests the evil in Jekyll, while "balderdash" connotes something less serious. Utterson is relieved at this answer and thinks they have only differed on "some point of science." But, of course, their difference is more than that — it is a moral point, a way of living one's life. Here we learn that Jekyll has been talking about what he wanted to do as long as ten years ago.

Like Lanyon, Utterson intervenes in Jekyll's life on a professional level rather than a personal one. When Utterson meets Hyde, Hyde wonders how he knows about him, and Utterson remarks that they have common friends, like Dr. Jekyll. Hyde says, "He never told you ... I did not think you would have lied" (17). Utterson is not exactly lying, but he is not being forthright. He is interested in Hyde because of the connection with Jekyll, because he wants to uncover the truth about the relationship between Jekyll and Hyde. When Utterson speaks to Jekyll about his will, Jekyll makes Utterson promise "that you will bear with him [Hyde] and get his rights for him" (21) if something happens to Jekyll. In trying to help Jekyll, Utterson involves himself further into what he doesn't feel comfortable with or understand. Jekyll lumps Utterson with Lanyon: "I never saw a man so distressed as you were by my will; unless it were that hide-bound pedant, Lanyon, at what he called my scientific heresies" (20). Jekyll's choice of words indicates that Lanyon may have a bit of Hyde within him also, as "hide-bound" is so much like "Hyde-bound." Both Utterson and Lanyon are more concerned with the professional aspect of Jekyll's life than the personal. Perhaps they are more comfortable on a professional level. Jekyll assures Utterson that it is a "private matter" and Utterson should "let it sleep" (20). Thus the evil is allowed to remain undisclosed within Jekyll, the relationship between Jekyll and Hyde seeming tangential to his friends.

The Threat of the Monster

In the novel, Jekyll enjoys a beautiful winter day in Regent's Park when he feels "the animal within me licking the chops of memory." He continues:

> The spiritual side a little drowsed, promising subsequent penitence, but not yet moved to begin. After all, I reflected, I was like my neighbours; and then I smiled, comparing myself with other men, comparing my active goodwill with the lazy cruelty of their neglect. And at the very moment of that vainglorious thought, a qualm came over me, a horrid nausea and the most deadly shuddering. These passed away, and left me faint; and then as in its turn the faintness subsided, I began to be aware of a change in the temper of my thoughts, a greater boldness, a contempt of danger, a solution of the bonds of obligation [58].

In this passage Jekyll contrasts his "active goodwill with the lazy cruelty of their neglect" (58), considering himself the superior of other men. Here Jekyll would seem to be lying to himself: in his account of himself, the reader never sees Jekyll indulging in "active goodwill." The closest he comes to it is when he states that he attempts to clean up the difficulties caused by the misdeeds of Hyde. Although he may think himself different, Jekyll seems very much like other men, and they are much like he. He is different in that he has actively taken steps so that he can misbehave and hide his misbehavior. The threat is that Dr. Jekyll can no longer control the appearance and activities of Mr. Hyde.

It is Jekyll's repression of Hyde while he is once again leading a "normal" life that causes Hyde to come out with singular ferocity and kill Sir Danvers Carew. Frightened by the murder of Carew, Jekyll swears never to have anything to do with Hyde again. He resolves "in my future conduct to redeem the past" (57), although Jekyll has lost the ability to be honest with himself. Yet how can one redeem a murder? Jekyll becomes once more what he terms an "ordinary secret sinner" (58) or hypocrite, and he promises subsequent penitence. He feels virtuous for leading an ordinary life, yet covers his tracks by being decep-tive with Utterson. Jekyll shows Utterson a letter from Hyde saying that he has found a means of escape so he will not be found. Jekyll asks Utterson to tell him what to do because he wants to keep his own character unexposed by this business, and "I have lost confidence in myself" (26). Utterson is suspicious enough to ask about the origin of the letter: Jekyll states that he burned the envelope, and later Utterson learns from Poole that no letters came for Jekyll. A handwriting expert points out to Utterson that the handwriting is the same as Jekyll's, but sloped in the opposite direction. Utterson comes to think that Jekyll has forged the letter for Hyde, which is in a way correct, as Jekyll has written it for Hyde while he was still Jekyll.

As he loses his moral battle of keeping Hyde at bay, Jekyll's health fails. Utterson and Enfield walk by Jekyll's house, see him in a window, and think they are doing some good by visiting Jekyll, even from the outside. They witness a look of "abject terror and despair" (32) on the face of Jekyll that frightens them. They walk away without speaking, although both feel the same — "there was an answering horror in their eyes" (32). Walking away from Jekyll, Utterson says, "God forgive us, God forgive us" (32), the repetition of the phrase indi-cating his despair. Perhaps after witnessing something evil, they feel the need to evoke the name of God. They may worry that if such an unknown but ter-rifying thing could happen to Jekyll, it could also happen to them. They know that they have been in the near presence of something frightening. Utter-son may feel the need of forgiveness for not having helped their friend, even possibly for having contributed to the circumstances that lead Jekyll into this situation. And now, both Utterson and Enfield walk away from the problem, distancing themselves physically as well as psychologically and morally from their friend.

The Nature of the Evil

One question left unresolved by the novel is: What does Jekyll do when he is Hyde? The movies show him drinking and having sadistic sex with a woman of questionable virtue, but we don't see that in the book. A previous draft of the novel has this in "Henry Jekyll's Full Statement of the Case": "From an early age, however, I became in secret the slave of certain appetites" (Veeder

34). In the novel as it was published, Hyde hurts people, and he commits murder when he has been pent up for too long.

Jekyll is aware of the transformations to his body as he becomes Hyde. Although Jekyll wants to be free of becoming Hyde involuntarily, Hyde seeks control of Jekyll's body. During Jekyll's first involuntary transformation, he goes to bed as Jekyll and awakens as Hyde. His first thoughts are that it is strange that he is not in the home of Hyde:

> I smiled to myself, and, in my psychological way, began lazily to inquire into the elements of this illusion, occasionally, even as I did so, dropping back into a comfortable morning doze. I was still so engaged when, in one of my more wakeful moments, my eye fell upon my hand. Now the hand of Henry Jekyll (as you have often remarked) was professional in shape and size; it was large, firm, white and comely. But the hand which I now saw, clearly enough, in the yellow light of a mid–London morning, lying half shut on the bed clothes, was lean, corded, knuckly, of a dusky pallor and thickly shaded with a swart growth of hair. It was the hand of Edward Hyde [54].

The style of the writing is fitting with the action, for the account begins with lengthy and languorous prose, reflecting his half-wakeful state, but ends with the jerking realization, in a short sentence, that he is Hyde. Jekyll has kept his dual life compartmentalized. He has lived in Jekyll's home as Jekyll and Hyde's home as Hyde. Here, he recognizes that he is out of place as he wakes up as Hyde in the home of Jekyll, and he becomes aware of his situation because of the change in his hands. Hyde's hand has hair, something like the hair on Dracula's palms. This contrast of the hands of Jekyll and Hyde forms the basis in the movies for the emphasis on hands; often the first hint the viewer has that Jekyll is becoming Hyde is a shot of his hand transforming.

Because he has transformed involuntarily, Hyde has become master of Jekyll. Jekyll can no longer control Hyde, nor can he use his chemicals to transform, as the causative ingredient is unknown. What began as a lark, with Hyde's murder of Sir Danvers Carew, becomes deadly serious.

After committing murder in the form of Hyde, he must transform himself back into Jekyll in order to hide from the police. However, he must arrange access to his chemicals, since he cannot enter his own home or walk the streets in the guise of Hyde. In the novel, Lanyon does as Jekyll asks him and retrieves the chemicals; but because of his fear, Lanyon arms himself with a revolver. Lanyon remarks not so much on Hyde's looks when he arrives but on the effect on him. He feels a "subjective disturbance," a "sinking of his pulse," and a "personal distaste" due to the hybrid nature of the evil. Hyde is delighted to see the box of chemicals and quickly begins mixing his potion. Hyde says to Lanyon, "Will you be wise? Will you be guided? Will you suffer me to take this glass in my hand to go forth from your house without further parley? Or has the greed of curiosity too much command of you?" (46). Hyde puts the fault with Lanyon.

Lanyon will not be wise or guided and is too greedy of curiosity — those traits that perhaps led Jekyll to become Hyde at the start. Hyde continues that if Lanyon is to stay, "Your sight shall be blasted by a prodigy to stagger the unbelief of Satan" (46). Reference to the Devil makes sense here, as Hyde has become damned. Yet he questions whether Satan will perhaps believe man a God if he sees what one man, namely Jekyll, has accomplished. Hyde reminds Lanyon of his professional vow of silence and then says, "You who have denied the virtue of transcendental medicine, you who have derided your superiors— behold!" (47). Hyde is thrilled with his success and considers himself and Jekyll superior to Lanyon. As Lanyon witnesses the transformation and reveals the unity of the characters, Lanyon screams "O God!" in shock. As Jekyll talks to him, Lanyon's "soul sickened" (47). He feels terrified, suffering under a physical oppression that slowly kills Lanyon. Lanyon now knows that Jekyll is hiding Hyde. He, in turn, is hiding his knowledge of both.

The Monster Destroyed

It is Poole, Jekyll's faithful butler, who seeks help in intervening with his master. As a servant and a member of the lower class, Poole cannot act on his own. Afraid for his master and at his wit's end, Poole comes to Utterson and asks him to come to Jekyll's home with him. Poole explains that he has heard a voice coming from the laboratory, but that it is not Jekyll's voice. They believe they are going to find that Hyde has murdered Jekyll. They hear Hyde's voice inside begging them not to come in. When they break down the door, they find no trace of Jekyll and that Hyde has committed suicide. Within the room they discover written material that Utterson examines, including Jekyll's own explanation and confession.

In the final documents of the novel there is a divergence in the ideas of Jekyll and Hyde — Jekyll is penitent, and Hyde is proud. Hyde is practical, he has assured himself of Lanyon's silence by reminding Lanyon that he cannot tell anyone what he saw because of his professional vows (46). However, Jekyll applied for Lanyon's help as a friend and not as a patient; consequently, Lanyon should not be under any obligation to keep Jekyll's secret. By doing so, Lanyon helps conceal a murderer.

According to Lanyon, Jekyll cries tears of penitence, saying that he is never going to transform again. Lanyon talks to Jekyll, but Lanyon does not seek help, he does not tell Utterson or anyone else what is going on. He takes the secret to the grave rather than reveal the truth he knows, and the truth kills him. Lanyon writes up his experience with Hyde and directs the letter to Utterson, to be opened after the death of Jekyll. In this he undoubtedly thinks he is being a good friend and abiding by his professional ethics. Yet from the experience of Jekyll he must recognize his own hypocrisy and his own desire not to get involved

Like Lanyon, and the other characters, Utterson is foremost a professional man. In accordance with the regulations of his profession, he does not open the letter he has from Lanyon before the appropriate time. He respects the "rules" of his profession. Yet earlier he borders on doing something illegal when he considers blackmailing Hyde. He wants to help Jekyll professionally in any way that he can, and yet on a personal level he does not help him. Both Lanyon and Utterson are hypocrites like Jekyll, wanting to save their own reputations and believing that what is happening to Jekyll has nothing to do with them. They are not their brother's keeper, perhaps because they are afraid of their own Hydes.

The agreement, formed in the very first chapter, not to exchange information about Jekyll or Hyde allows evil to happen or to progress uninterrupted. Utterson and Enfield do not discuss together what they know. Enfield tells his tale as an interesting story, not as something that they need do anything about. Interestingly, we never learn what Enfield was doing in such a place at such an hour. But his presence there indicates a similarity, although unstated, between himself and Hyde, just as there are similarities between Utterson and Enfield. All of these men live in a society in which they must hide their impulses in order to maintain their reputations.

In the last chapter of the novel, "Henry Jekyll's Full Statement of the Case," Jekyll presents his own story to the reader. Jekyll admits to a "profound duplicity" in his life (48). But as he tells his tale, he dismisses his own moral responsibility. He writes, "It was Hyde, after all, and Hyde alone, that was guilty" (53). He attests to the true separation of himself. He does not feel responsible for what he has created. In many ways this is very like Dr. Victor Frankenstein in Mary Shelley's novel *Frankenstein* (1818), who does not feeling responsible for any of the actions of his creation. Both Frankenstein and Jekyll acknowledge they started the process, but once the other was created, they are not responsible for it, as it is no longer part of themselves. This is a short-sighted view.

Like Frankenstein, Jekyll has released something that he cannot control and disclaims responsibility for: "It was Hyde, after all, and Hyde alone, that was guilty. Jekyll was no worse; he woke again to his good qualities seemingly unimpaired; he would even make haste, where it was possible, to undo the evil done by Hyde. And thus his conscience slumbered" (53). The problem is that Jekyll enjoys being Hyde. And then once he gets scared and wants to stop being Hyde, he can't stop and turns into Hyde without the chemicals. While Jekyll remains human, Hyde is a monster. Although he looks human, his looks are unsettling and his actions immoral.

The end of Jekyll's account of his life is poignant, as he knows, as he is writing, that he is going to turn again into Hyde and that he cannot get the correct chemical, the unknown substance, to stop the transformation. Hyde has come to hate Jekyll. He would ruin himself in order to ruin Jekyll, but feels the need for Jekyll because of his terror of the gallows—being hanged for the murder of Carew. As Jekyll finishes writing his final statement, he lays down his pen knowing he can no longer influence the fate of Hyde, and he is once again transforming involuntarily. Jekyll feels death drawing near, so he ends with a pun, a double meaning, "I bring the life of that unhappy Henry Jekyll to an end" (62), signifying that he is dying and ending his autobiographical statement simultaneously. It is a fitting end for a man encompassed by duality.

Normality Restored

In this novel, each of the members of the coterie of friends looks out for himself. No one takes an active role in helping Jekyll; no one thinks to contact the police. Although Hyde dies, and Jekyll along with him, the evil that was the monster Hyde lives on. It is an integral part of each person and cannot be separated out.

This is a novel in which life is shown to be very stable and calm, with nothing out of the ordinary happening until Mr. Hyde comes along. The best thing in these men's lives is having a quiet evening of wine or going for a walk. Suddenly they see a very different side of life, and it's literally a different side. One side of Jekyll's house is all conformity, the other is completely irregular and representative of the immoral nature of Hyde. The attempt to bring the two sides together is killing. One indication of how cut off the characters are from each other and from themselves is that they don't put their information together. Enfield has witnessed the attack by Hyde on the girl, but Utterson knows whose door Hyde enters and doesn't tell. Learning the truth about Jekyll actually kills Lanyon. Jekyll creates Hyde because he is a hypocrite. Jekyll wants to appear proper to the outside world while secretly engaging in behavior that would not be considered correct. At the end of the novel both Jekyll and Hyde are dead, but society has not been changed. The hypocrisy and lack of communication continue.

Stevenson implies that a person cannot separate the parts of his personality without dire results. Instead, people need to integrate the different parts of themselves, as well as connect on a more personal level with other people. Thus, Utterson, Enfield, and Lanyon are hypocrites like Jekyll and at fault for not attempting to come to the aid of their friend, Jekyll. We all have Hyde within us, Stevenson intimates, and we must recognize our bad as well as our good characteristics. No one is composed of all virtue or all evil. We cannot completely control ourselves, but we can try to keep the parts of ourselves integrated so that no one part gains the upper hand.

Vladimir Nabokov comments on the connection between Robert Louis Stevenson's death and *Dr. Jekyll and Mr. Hyde*:

> And there is something in Stevenson's death in 1894 on Samoa, imitating in a curious way the wine theme and the transformation theme of his fantasy.

He went down to the cellar to fetch a bottle of his favorite burgundy, uncorked it in the kitchen, and suddenly cried out to his wife: what's the matter with me, what is this strangeness, has my face changed?—and fell on the floor. A blood vessel had burst in his brain and it was all over in a couple of hours [qtd. in Stevenson 188].

In his transformation from life to death, Stevenson himself seemed to repeat the transformation of his most famous character, suggesting the Hyde within himself.

The first adaptation of Stevenson's novel, *Strange Case of Dr. Jekyll and Mr. Hyde,* was a play by Thomas Russell Sullivan written for the American actor Richard Mansfield in 1887. This play began the process of adding female characters with names to the story, a route that subsequent adaptations have continued. Robert Louis Stevenson never saw the play, but he did hear about it. He wrote in a letter to John Paul Bocock in November 1887:

The harm was in Jekyll, because he was a hypocrite—not because he was fond of women; he says so himself; but people are so filled full of folly and inverted lust, that they can think of nothing but sexuality. The Hypocrite let out the beast Hyde—who is no more sexual than another, but who is the essence of cruelty and malice, and selfishness and cowardice: and these are the diabolic in man—not this poor wish to have a woman, that they make such a cry about [qtd. in Stevenson 86].

Stevenson also denies that sexual emotion, sadistic or otherwise, drives the plot of his novel. Later adaptations not only provide a pure woman for Jekyll, but also make available a loose woman for Hyde. Among other considerations, the presence of a good woman for Jekyll and a bad woman for Hyde remains popular because it supplies roles for two leading ladies.

Many of the adaptations of Stevenson's *Dr. Jekyll and Mr. Hyde* have taken the idea of the separation of a single man into two opposing parts but kept little else from the work. Whereas the novel involves the duality of good and bad in one character, the films present Jekyll as an excellent person who is not completely to blame for the existence of Mr. Hyde. While the novel suggests that a Mr. Hyde lurks within each of us, the films make his appearance the result of an unusual set of circumstances. In the films, Dr. Jekyll is often better than we are; he is a gifted and dedicated man. When he is shown as superior, the distance between Jekyll and Hyde becomes greater, and Dr. Jekyll's fall becomes more dramatic. Jekyll moves from being morally superior to those around him to being worse as Hyde. While good and evil both exist in Jekyll, and the potion releases Hyde, there are mitigating circumstances in the films. Hyde becomes less of a monster arising from within Jekyll.

In most major adaptations, Jekyll has been transformed from a hypocrite into a sexually repressed sadist. I have chosen to talk about three different adaptations of *Dr. Jekyll and Mr. Hyde* that are particularly well acted and well directed. In all of these films Jekyll becomes less responsible for releasing his

Hyde than he is in the novel. Hyde is released through chemicals, but Jekyll takes the chemicals for reasons that are outside of himself: in the 1920 version because he is teased by his future father-in-law, in the 1931 version because he is sexually repressed, and in the 1941 version because he is attempting to do something benefiting mankind. In the adaptations that have been made since 1941, Hyde has graduated from murdering one person, as in the novel, to murdering many more. In each new adaptation, the body count grows. Perhaps because the Jack the Ripper murders happened about the same time as the first adaptation of *Dr. Jekyll and Mr. Hyde*, many adaptors conflate the two stories, leading to the murder and mutilation of prostitutes by Hyde.

Dr. Jekyll and Mr. Hyde (1920)

DIR.: John S. Robertson. PERF.: John Barrymore, Charles Lane, Brandon Hurst, Nita Naldi. Kino, 2001. DVD.

John Barrymore, the star of Robertson's version of *Dr. Jekyll and Mr. Hyde*, was a unique, notorious, and dramatic actor. Descended from a famous family of actors, he was the grandfather of the current star Drew Barrymore. Known for his handsome profile on stage and on screen, Barrymore's face is shown in profile throughout most of this movie. A mannered acting style accompanies most silent movies; arm gestures and facial expressions are exaggerated for emphasis. Because of difficulties with the speed of the film, it appears that positions are held for longer than necessary, and sometimes people seem to move too quickly. Alan Vanneman has commented on Barrymore's Shakespearean background by suggesting that Barrymore played Jekyll as Hamlet and Hyde as Richard III (Vanneman). Barrymore's Dr. Jekyll may have more in common with classical tragic heroes than with ordinary human beings like ourselves.

Tempted to sin by his future father-in-law, the spidery Mr. Hyde (John Barrymore) in John S. Robertson's *Dr. Jekyll and Mr. Hyde* (1920) (Famous Players/Lasky/the Kobal Collection).

In addition to the style of acting, the film differs from more recent black and white movies because it is not strictly black and white and shades of gray; sometimes a wash of blue represents night scenes, and other colors are used as well. A background of organ music suggests the pianist or organist who accompanied the showing of silent films in the theater. The story line of silent films is simplified more than in talkies, since ideas cannot be explained in dialogue between characters. The lip movements of the characters often do not match the words that appear on the screen. The words are usually spoken first by a character and then given on an intertitle card. The viewer must fill in the gap between the acting on the screen and the words written on the screen on cards. At times the intertitle cards give information directly to the viewer. In this movie, many cards are decorated with an appropriate picture, suggesting the words on the card. The attempt is to give a symbolic representation of the words that may aid the understanding of those who cannot read and underline the point being made for the rest of the audience.

The World at the Start of Robertson's Film
Dr. Jekyll and Mr. Hyde

"In each of us two natures are at war — the good and the evil. All our lives the fight goes on between them, and one of them must conquer. But in our own hands lies the power to choose, what we want most to be, we *are*." This statement, on the screen at the start of this movie, is not taken from the book. It indicates a belief that man can rule his own destiny, that he can choose whether to be good or evil, an idea belied by the book as well as this movie. Perhaps this idea of choice points to the opinion of a country that had just vanquished the enemy during World War I, despite great losses to all sides. Having won the war, the United States felt proud of what it had accomplished and adopted a positive feeling about its role in the world of the future. The statement is what Jekyll wants to believe, an idealized vision that will not be borne out by his experiences. Jekyll believes he can separate his parts and act as either Jekyll or Hyde as he chooses; but he cannot, for he begins to turn into Hyde involuntarily and cannot return to Jekyll as he wants.

In traditional Christian theology, morality rests on choice. What begins as a choice for Jekyll becomes involuntary. The introductory quote above intimates that Jekyll chooses to be evil. Yet in the movie, at first Jekyll wants most to be good, then he wants most to be bad, and finally he desires to be good again but cannot go back to his former innocence. He loses his ability to choose. In reality we are all somewhere in the middle, combining aspects of good and evil. As played by Barrymore, Jekyll is better than the ordinary person, while Hyde is a sadistic sensualist who is ultimately guilty of murder.

The film stresses the opposition between Dr. Jekyll and his friend and colleague, Dr. Richard Lanyon. In the first scene of the movie, Jekyll looks into a microscope. He observes, as does the audience, two different kinds of organisms that separate from each other. Across the room from him is the conservative Lanyon, formally dressed and impatiently waiting for Jekyll. Jekyll suggests to Lanyon that man is on the verge of much scientific knowledge. Although he does not want to at first, Lanyon does take time to look at what is under the microscope, but does not approve. Lanyon says, "You're tampering with the supernatural," and, "Stick to the positive sciences." On the table next to Jekyll is a skull. Here, while he is looking at life, is a suggestion of death. And, indeed, his experiments in science will lead to his death.

The normal world shown in this film is a changing world. Science is changing and coming into the modern world; the class system is becoming more open. Poole, the valet, is stated to have "inherited" Jekyll, which becomes almost an excuse for having a servant. This detail suggests the shifting nature of household help in that few people had servants at the time the movie was made. Jekyll is made into an object rather than Poole, since Jekyll has not inherited Poole. Jekyll has everything—good looks, wealth, and reputation—but his world is starting to change as well. Whereas he thinks he has a choice about what he wants to be, he soon loses the power to choose.

The Monster Within and Without

Jekyll's positive position as a philanthropist is clear when he works at his clinic. The intertitle calls the clinic maintained at Jekyll's own expense a "human repair shop," which sounds callous, but below the words there is an illustration of the good Samaritan helping a sick man by the side of the road. This gives a religious cast to the work of Jekyll. The people at this clinic overwhelm Jekyll; there seem to be more people than he could possibly treat. Jekyll is presented as a political idealist as well as a philanthropist. He comforts an older lady and touches her when he comes in, showing his willingness to deal with people of a lower class. His presence is comforting, and all gather around him. In his top hat, cape, and evening dress, Jekyll contrasts starkly with the poverty surrounding him. There is nothing evil about this Jekyll. Although Lanyon has accused him of tampering with the supernatural, Jekyll spends his time in a hands-on position helping the poor.

The idea of moral choices is brought up during an after-dinner conversation among the men at Sir George Carew's dinner party. Carew, Jekyll's future father-in-law, looking like a snaky devil, says that man has two selves, a strong and a weak one, and we must use both of them as we use both our hands. Asserting that the strong man fears nothing, and that he must face temptation in order to resist it, Carew lures Jekyll into temptation. Carew announces that a man must test himself, that the way to defeat temptation is to yield to it, and that a man should live it up in his youth so that when he is older he can have memories. Carew's desire to tempt Jekyll stems from his own immorality, as we see him flirting with a married woman, telling her that she is a paradise for the eyes and a hell for the soul, bringing up the idea with which Jekyll is obsessed — that the soul can be separated from the body. Perhaps Carew wants the assurance that all men are the same. Jekyll's innocence allows him to be bullied by Carew and overwhelmed by the world.

Jekyll is contrasted with the men-of-the-world surrounding Sir George Carew. Because of his reputation for goodness, Jekyll is referred to by Enfield as London's Saint Anthony, the Patriarch of Monks, who gave away his property and lived a monastic life. St. Anthony resisted the temptations of the Devil, who wanted to corrupt him, much as Carew wants to corrupt Jekyll. Even Enfield relates that he lost a wager on him, suggesting that he has tried to tempt Jekyll in the past. Whereas Jekyll in the novel has acted on his own and in secrecy, in this movie Jekyll is led towards temptation by Carew, much like Dorian Gray is corrupted by Lord Henry Wotton in Oscar Wilde's novel *The Picture of Dorian Gray* (1890).

To complete the temptation of Jekyll, the group of men attend a Music Hall where Miss Gina, "who faced her world alone," dances. She is an outcast because she is a professional performer, much as Jekyll is an outsider because of his virtue. Gina does not have the advantage of a rich and protective father, like Jekyll's fiancée, Millicent. Although Dr. Jekyll does not want to enter, he is teased into doing so because the men accuse him of being "afraid of temptation." Outside the music hall the men pass by an older, frumpy woman, an indication of what Gina will become. The older woman provides a symbolic reminder that youth and beauty are transitory. Miss Gina comes to the table and embraces the handsome young doctor, who then leaves, but the card tells us, "Jekyll had wakened to a sense of his baser nature."

Jekyll has within him the capacity for both good and evil that all men have. He admits to Lanyon that he would like "to yield to every evil impulse and leave the soul untouched." But it is through the influence of Carew that Jekyll is seduced into releasing his inner monster. As Jekyll concocts the potion that will transform him into Hyde, he experiences a moment of doubt. The image of Carew is superimposed on the screen, and Jekyll remembers Carew taunting him. This highlights Carew's guilt in Jekyll's reason for going ahead with the transformation. Although the evil is inside Jekyll, it has been brought out because of the urgings of his future father-in-law.

The Threat of the Monster

By turning into Hyde, Jekyll first threatens his own well being. As Barrymore transforms into Hyde, his body contorts, and his chin and eyes develop completely different looks. At the end, the transformation of Jekyll into Hyde is shown most clearly in his hands and nails, which are artificial. His nails are long, heavy and split — quite fantastic; while his fingers are long and bony with the addition of another joint. As he continues to transform, Hyde develops a pointed head. His look is less than human, like a monstrous, spiny spider. John Barrymore's Hyde becomes more grotesque the more he transforms.

After his initial transformation, Jekyll has a mirror placed in his laboratory. The mirror is a doubling of the self and an indication of an inability to see one's self directly. Jekyll has wanted to see himself as Hyde, but he cannot see his full self; he can only see himself as Jekyll or as Hyde, but not both simultaneously. By looking in the mirror he recognizes the split within himself. On the screen, Barrymore must convey the pain followed by the excitement of the completed transformation without words. His contorted body expresses the pain. After taking the antidote, he experiences a moment of triumph as he looks in the mirror and sees that he is back to his normal Jekyll state. For the time being he has control of himself as both Jekyll and Hyde.

But Hyde threatens much more than just Jekyll himself. Hyde is an unknown threat who could be capable of anything because he acts on instinct without the guidance of conscience. As Hyde ventures out into London, he acts on the repressed desires of Jekyll.

The Nature of the Evil

In addition to what he looks like, those making a movie have to decide how Hyde behaves. What behavior does Hyde indulge in that Jekyll would never do? In the movie, Hyde, equipped with a shillelagh (an Irish walking stick and weapon), rents a room and "sets forth on a sea of license," as the intertitle card states. He kisses the hand of Gina in the music hall, just as Jekyll kissed Millicent's at the dinner party. While kissing her hand, he notices her ring and yanks it off her finger. The story of the poison ring and the Italian dancer, as told on the screen, is completely unclear, having been partially removed from the film. The scene ends with a juggler throwing balls in the air. Although the symbol seems out of place, it may represent Jekyll now attempting to balance the different aspects of his life.

There are several "victims of his depravity," as Hyde tramples over a young boy who rides a hobby horse across the street. Society intervenes, as the police encourage him to get a check signed by Dr. Jekyll. The scene is presented as a means of showing Hyde as an uncaring person whose life is going to affect Jekyll in ways that he has not anticipated. After throwing the dancer, Gina, out of his apartment, Hyde enters an opium den, which conveys how Hyde spends his time — in a place where people dream their lives away. Hyde has the opportunity to further disrupt the life of Miss Gina. Hyde flirts with a young woman at a

Mr. Hyde (John Barrymore) attacks the sophisticated Sir George Carew (Brandon Hurst) in his art- and book-filled study in John S. Robertson's *Dr. Jekyll and Mr. Hyde* (1920) (Famous Players/Lasky/the Kobal Collection).

bar and then sees Miss Gina, who has fallen lower since Hyde dismissed her. Hyde humiliates Miss Gina by holding her up to a mirror so that she must see herself next to a "fresher" young woman. The scene ends with Hyde kissing this young woman — like a vampire. Hyde spreads his degeneracy over other people, causing them misery.

Eventually Jekyll cannot keep the two parts of his life separate. An intertitle card announces, "The shadow extends to Millicent," who is depressed at the disappearance of Jekyll from her life. When her father comes to investigate what has happened to Jekyll, Jekyll tells Carew that it was his cynicism that made him ashamed of his goodness. Jekyll's agitation causes him to turn into Hyde who then kills Carew. The murder appears completely out of place in Jekyll's art- and book-filled study, as murder should be the act of a primitive being, not a modern, sophisticated man.

Jekyll's dissipation as Hyde takes over his life, as the monster within him comes out in the dark of the night. An intertitle card sets the scene: "And now in his hours off guard, outraged nature took her hideous revenge and out of the black abyss of torment sent upon him the creeping horror that was his other self." Jekyll sleeps in a four-poster bed in a beautiful, tidy room. On the wall there is a picture of a mother and child. There is something very innocent about the scene. Robertson has chosen a third state, neither Jekyll nor Hyde, to convey the essence of what Jekyll has become and the evil that is inside of him. While sleeping, a monster spider comes out of Hyde—it is actually the same actor who plays both Jekyll and Hyde, John Barrymore, in a spider suit, looking like something out of a nightmare. This is a lesser form of life and something elemental and hideous, but with his human face. It's like a subconscious presence being made conscious. Jekyll then tries to go back to sleep and wakes up as Hyde; he scratches himself and then realizes he has transformed. In the bottom right hand corner of the screen we clearly see the poison ring, the symbol of his inability to keep the parts of his life separate.

The scene graphically sets out Jekyll's lack of control and the growing of the elemental beast within him. As Jekyll wakes up and gets out of bed, wearing a white sleeping gown, he dramatically holds one hand to his forehead while stretching out his other hand as if to stop the creature from coming back into him. He then faints. This scene can be read as a symbol of Jekyll's situation. He has become someone else in order to indulge in temptation. Because that other self is within him, the demarcations between Jekyll and Hyde are no longer clear. He cannot control his selves and turns involuntarily, without any potion, from Jekyll into Hyde. His two selves are no longer clearly separated. In addition, this creature seems to have a connection with the psychological belief in the subconscious becoming popularized during the time the movie was made. The works of Sigmund Freud have made it a commonplace conceptualization that man is not always responsible for his own actions. Jekyll's lack of control increases as he runs out of the drugs that will "secure his identity." Finally he has none left, and, locked in his laboratory, Jekyll starts to transform. He drops to his knees to pray, crosses himself, and lifts his arms to heaven. In the novel, religion is kept to the background. The last thing that Hyde does in the novel is to call on Utterson, rather than God, to have mercy and not break down his door (38). But in the movie, religion becomes a serious part of Jekyll's life, and God has the ability to save, or at least redeem, Jekyll.

Jekyll "gave a hostage to his soul" by proposing to Millicent and kissing her passionately. He hopes that she will be able to help him save himself. Involving someone else with his life and promising to quit his double life, Jekyll renounces his indulgences until Hyde bursts forth once more.

The Monster Destroyed

Jekyll must sacrifice himself to save the woman he loves. As Lanyon and Millicent arrive at his home, summoned by Jekyll's staff to help him, Jekyll starts to transform. Knowing that he cannot control his behavior as Hyde, Jekyll takes the poison in the ring he took from Miss Gina in order to save Millicent from being raped by Hyde. The intertitle card states that Jekyll has "taken his own life in atonement." Rather than a suicide that would damn his soul, this suicide saves Jekyll as well as Millicent. The goodness remaining in Jekyll overcomes his Hyde, indicating the possibility of human salvation. The dead body of Hyde turns back to Jekyll — Jekyll has beaten Hyde at last for possession of his immortal soul. Lanyon announces, "Hyde has killed Dr. Jekyll." Jekyll's motive in this film is not selfish, but an unselfish attempt to protect the woman he loves.

Normality Restored

At the end of this film a new future is imagined for Millicent. This movie posits that while Miss Gina may be lost in an underground warren of sin, Millicent will make a suitable wife for a promising professional man, even if that man is not Jekyll. In the movie, Utterson has proposed to Millicent and has been refused even before Jekyll has a chance to make his intentions known. Utterson has never lost interest in her and will be an available suitor for her after Jekyll's death. Even though she will not be able to marry Jekyll, she will be able to have what would have been considered a proper and satisfying life.

When Jekyll dies, Millicent holds his hand as she kneels by his side. She has not seen the transformation and is not aware of the whole story — that Jekyll and Hyde are the same person. Nor is she told anything negative about Jekyll. By saying nothing, all of the men protect Millicent's innocence. She will be able to revere both the memory of her father and of Dr. Jekyll, and to blame the murder of both on Hyde. This film subscribes to the belief that women are not equipped to understand the truth — they need the softer, kinder deception of a lie.

This is just the kind of hypocrisy that Stevenson's book railed against. In his story of a man who cannot bear for society to think him immoral, Stevenson attacks a society that wanted the appearance of virtue, whatever the reality underneath. One of the virtues the Victorians supported was the belief in the sanctity of women. Carew is praised by his friends for having raised his daughter "as only a man of the world could." It was good for a man to be experienced, but not for a woman. Jekyll, however, certainly proves this theory wrong. Millicent herself is innocent and unaware of the reality of the world around her. Of course, the addition of women to the movie suggests that part of what Jekyll wanted was sexual satisfaction, which he found with both Miss Gina and the fresher young woman at the opium den. Then, women also expand the parameters of this tale beyond the small group of men who knew Jekyll in the novel. This movie also includes the corrupting influence of Carew, who becomes a kind of devil, leading Jekyll into trouble. Jekyll is less to blame for his own downfall than in the novel.

Jekyll has no predilection for evil at the start of the film. Although dabbling in the supernatural, this part of his life has not influenced the good he does. The evil that becomes Hyde comes in part from without, from the man of the world, Carew, who challenges Jekyll to give in to temptation. Although this does not absolve Jekyll of guilt, it diminishes his responsibility. Some of the monstrousness of Hyde comes from the wrongs of men like Carew, who enjoy corrupting the innocent. This evil comes from outside of Jekyll. Jekyll regulates himself during his last moments on earth, dying to protect the woman he loves. God, the ultimate judge, deems his soul worthy of salvation.

Dr. Jekyll and Mr. Hyde (1931)

DIR. Rouben Mamoulian. PERF. Fredric March, Miriam Hopkins, Rose Hobart, Holmes Herbert. Dr. Jekyll and Mr. Hyde Double Feature, Warner Home Video, 2004. DVD.

Rouben Mamoulian's version of *Dr. Jekyll and Mr. Hyde* diverges sharply from Stevenson's novel in terms of themes and characterization. Whereas Stevenson explored the good and evil in the Victorian professional man, Mamoulian shows the distinction between the spiritual and the animal in man. Believing that viewers would identify more with his Dr. Jekyll than Stevenson's, Mamoulian said, "I thought that a more interesting dilemma would be not that of good versus evil or moral versus immoral but that of the spiritual versus the animalistic which are present in all of us" (notes by Greg Mank on DVD; qtd. in Geduld 176). Stevenson's Jekyll is guilty of hypocrisy; Mamoulian's Jekyll is guilty of sexual desire, leading to a Hyde who envies Jekyll his relationship with women. But in this movie neither Jekyll nor Hyde can find satisfaction with a relationship. The attempt to secure love leads to murder and death. In order to accomplish his objective, Mamoulian heightens Jekyll's spiritual standing and brings out the animal side of Hyde. In

Motivated by sexual frustration, the Neanderthal Mr. Hyde (Fredric March) in Rouben Mamoulian's *Dr. Jekyll and Mr. Hyde* (1931) (Paramount/the Kobal Collection).

this film the protagonist's name is pronounced "gee-kill," emphasizing the French pronoun "I" and the word "kill," marking Jekyll from the start as a killer.

Fredric March won an Oscar for his performance as Jekyll and Hyde in this movie, and it was the first time someone in a "horror film" won an Oscar for best actor. Before this movie, March was known for his performances in romantic comedies. Indeed, he is young and handsome in the role, and his looks are reminiscent of John Barrymore in the silent version. As in the silent film, we are a long way from the middle-aged bachelor of the novel. By making Jekyll young, Mamoulian can emphasize the establishment of his life, of his career and marriage, rather than the steady continuation of routines that Jekyll dreads in the novel. When Rouben Mamoulian set himself to find an actor to play in *Dr. Jekyll and Mr. Hyde*, he believed that anyone could play Hyde — what was difficult was to find someone who made a believable Jekyll. Fredric March certainly accomplishes this by showing how a talented, brilliant man who seemingly has everything could jeopardize his reputation and more in a chemical experiment. March also portrays Hyde so energetically and enthusiastically that the viewer can understand why Jekyll would be drawn to return to his transformed state again and again.

The World at the Start of Mamoulian's Film Dr. Jekyll and Mr. Hyde

Mamoulian's movie begins with what the director termed a "subjective camera approach," in which we see the world from Dr. Jekyll's point of view. This forces the viewer to see with Jekyll's eyes and consequently to see him sympathetically. Jekyll walks through his apartment, then plays the classical music of Bach on an organ. But all the audience sees are his hands on the piano keys as he talks to Poole, his servant. The highbrow music introduces Jekyll as an educated intellectual, a judgment born out by his beautiful home, filled with paintings, sculpture, candles, and flowers. The emphasis on Jekyll's hands corresponds to the later emphasis on his hands when Jekyll transforms into Hyde. We anticipate seeing Jekyll's face during the first few minutes of the film. We don't do so until he puts on his hat and cape and looks in a mirror; then we see him as he observes himself. Although in this case the mirror shows Jekyll to the audience, mirrors play an important role in this film of showing a character to himself. Via the "subjective camera," the audience identifies with Jekyll as they see the world through his eyes.

Showing Jekyll's world from his point of view at the beginning of the movie is an innovative technique. Mamoulian incorporates other innovative camera work that underscores the themes that he accentuates. For example, he frequently uses a split screen to show the simultaneous action of two different characters. This technique underscores the doubling theme by showing the contrast of two characters or two activities, as well as the basic division in all men between their dual natures (and, of course, between Jekyll and Hyde).

In Mamoulian's film, Jekyll's character is shown to advantage in his interchanges with his servant, Poole. Jekyll has a flippant attitude with Poole, as he blames Poole for his own appointments. Jekyll says to him, "Your sense of duty is as impregnable as Gibraltar." As in Oscar Wilde's play *The Importance of Being Earnest* (1894), the servants are expected to set an example for the upper classes. His relationship with his servant establishes Jekyll as a man who likes to joke and who takes the time to interact with people, even people of a different social class. We immediately witness the respect with which others, including the faithful Poole, treat him. Made during the Great Depression in the United States, a time when class barriers were being questioned, Mamoulian's Jekyll has the material objects of his class but not the superior attitude.

The Monster Within and Without

The presence of something unstable within Jekyll is hinted at from the start of the film. Jekyll has within his personality something excitable that allows him to feel passionately about his work and his life. This makes him sympathetic both to his viewers and his students. In the movie there is more emphasis on the professional life of Jekyll than there is in the novel. Here, in Mamoulian's film, Jekyll functions as a chemist, a general practitioner, a surgeon, and a lecturer. As Jekyll leaves his house, we continue to see from his point of view as he rides up to the university and is greeted by some students there. As he starts to lecture, the point of view shifts, and we now see him from the point of view of his audience, which is made up of younger, worshipping students and older, doubting colleagues. He mentions London's pervasive fog, which he uses as a metaphor for not being able to see. According to Jekyll, we are all fog-bound (just as he calls Dr. Lanyon a "hide-bound pedant" in the novel); yet it is Jekyll's innovative thinking that leads to his destruction and death. Jekyll lectures on the soul of man, stating that man is truly two, "one part of man tries for nobility; the other ties himself to some dim animal relationship from his past." If these two were separate, he believes, the "good would soar while the evil would fulfill itself and trouble us no more." He confides that he has done experiments on this subject. As Jekyll lectures, he throws a shadow on the wall behind him, separating the space into light and dark, underlining both his subject and the change that will soon envelop him, and suggesting the theme of doubles.

Jekyll holds his medical practice above his social life. His closest professional colleague, Lanyon, is disturbed that Jekyll will not treat an aristocratic woman with him. Clearly, Jekyll is not in the practice of medicine to make money. At the free clinic Jekyll encourages a young girl to give up her crutches and walk on her own. She does this and feels that it is a miracle. As Greg Mank states in his commentary on the DVD, this establishes Jekyll as a Christ figure who can cure the crippled. Indeed, he also brings out the girl's self-confidence, which parallels, in an inverse way, how Hyde will destroy Ivy Pearson's self-confidence. Jekyll behaves differently from the people around him from the start of the film; he is in opposition to his colleagues. He is both more altruistic and more reckless. His difference is played out against his associate Dr. Lanyon and also the father of his fiancée, Brigadier-General Carew, a slight but imposing military man. Carew's military bearing marks him as someone used to giving orders and being obeyed. Jekyll upsets both Lanyon and Carew by spending the evening at a free ward hospital rather than attending a dinner at the latter's home.

Jekyll also spends a great amount of time in his laboratory. The emphasis on science is greater here than in the novel, as evidenced by the rows of equipment and bottles in his laboratory. Science had become more important to the world by the time this movie was made. The Victorian gentleman dabbled in science, but by 1931, science was a serious profession. Here Jekyll works through the night, with his pipe in his mouth, which definitely seems dangerous. Jekyll's last thought of the outside world before his transformation to Hyde is to write to Muriel — not a love letter, but an avowal of his dedication to science: "If I die it is in the cause of science."

Jekyll is definitely in love with his fiancée; indeed, he is in love with life. He dedicates himself to the moment and neglects the world around him. His flaws, which might be virtues in a different society, are suggested by his lateness and his impatience in love. He wants to get married immediately. When he kisses his fiancée, they are interrupted by the shadow of the butler, who calls them in to the guests. As in the lecture hall, the shadow anticipates the destruction of an ideal, of something literally "casting a shadow" across their happiness. But the real shadow will arrive in the form of Hyde. Carew doesn't want to move up the wedding date because "It isn't done" and "It's not decent." He wants Jekyll to be married on his own wedding date, to do things the way he does them. Carew brags that he has never been late for dinner; Jekyll, on the other hand, is never on time. Carew objects to the excitability of Jekyll's personality. Jekyll explains during the movie that he isn't marrying to be sober, but to be drunk. Jekyll wants to be spontaneous and excitable and not sensible. These traits of Jekyll's are charmingly presented, yet they lead Jekyll to become vulnerable to other influences.

Muriel Carew is the ideal Victorian woman, the Angel of the House, to whom Jekyll looks to make him a better man. She encourages his spiritual side rather than his physical side. Muriel combines virtue and patience as she tries desperately to please both her father and her fiancé. She continues to believe in Jekyll and the importance of his work despite his neglect of her. Like the earlier movie directed by Robertson, this film boasts both a good and a bad woman. Jekyll's secret life begins as he returns from the party at the Carew home with

Lanyon (Herbert Holmes) disapproves of the kiss between Ivy Pierson (Miriam Hopkins) and the good Dr. Jekyll (Fredric March) in Rouben Mamoulian's *Dr. Jekyll and Mr. Hyde* (1931) (Paramount/the Kobal Collection).

his friend Lanyon. He stops to help a woman who is being hit by a man. Jekyll carries this woman to her room, and she seeks to prolong the situation. The woman, Ivy Pierson, played by the beautiful Miriam Hopkins, carefully undresses while coquettishly throwing her garters and stockings towards Jekyll in a strip tease, and showing him her legs and body as a way of flirting with him. Jekyll appreciates her beauty and accepts a kiss after assuring her that her bruises are not debilitating. The kiss is interrupted by the shocked Lanyon. Jekyll accuses Lanyon of hypocrisy, indicating that he thinks there is nothing indecent about the incident. Ivy says to Jekyll, "Come back soon." The words are repeated over the image of her beautiful and exposed leg swinging from the bed while Lanyon and Jekyll walk down the stairs.

The image of Ivy's swinging leg remains in Jekyll's head and on the screen (and undoubtedly longer than that) while Lanyon tells Jekyll to control his impulses. Ivy may be of easy virtue, but she is not "bad." She is independent but longs for someone to take care of her. Ivy Pearson has sex appeal, and she attempts to attract Jekyll with her physicality. She seeks pleasure and realistically tries to find it by the means closest at hand. Jekyll is not someone who would ordinarily appear in her life, and she attempts to make the most of the opportunity that she has been given of attracting a handsome, concerned, wealthy, professional man.[13] Jekyll has helped Ivy, but he has to use self-control in order to get away from her. She is part of the reason he becomes Hyde, and he will seek her again as soon as he makes the transformation.

Jekyll transforms into Hyde because he is bored, lonely, and sexually repressed, and he wants Ivy. When he transforms to Hyde, he immediately finds her. In this movie Jekyll becomes Hyde because the father of his fiancée keeps putting off the wedding. He pleads with Muriel, but Muriel and her father go out of town for a month. Jekyll says that he will wait, and Jekyll is still waiting when a letter arrives from Muriel saying they will be away for another month. In the back of Jekyll's mind is Ivy's swinging leg, with her waiting for him to come back. Jekyll's willingness to take the potion stems from the conflict of Jekyll's personality with society. There is a lightness to his personality in the movie which represents a love for life, but also a tendency towards the risky and unstable. For example, he takes a kiss, and enjoys it, from Ivy. Such tendencies, including his chronic lateness (resulting from his becoming absorbed in his work), show that he may not be as stable as he believes.

Jekyll is a saint (as in the 1920 movie) or an angel (according to Ivy) and clearly wants other people to think well of him. Poole suggests Jekyll amuse himself, that London "offers many amusements for a gentleman like you." Poole intimates that Jekyll might take up with a young woman of "easy virtue," like Ivy. Jekyll replies that it is because he is a gentleman and must protect his reputation that he has to be careful about what he does and says. It is the ungentlemanly Hyde that will seek out Ivy to find the sexual satisfaction denied to Jekyll.

In Jekyll's lab the pot on the flame in his laboratory boils over, indicating Jekyll's overwrought brain and out-of-control emotions. Outside we see rain; inside we see the dreariness of Jekyll's attitude and hear the repetition of Carew saying the word "wait." The camera focuses on the pot boiling over, showing the need for Jekyll to find an outlet. Mamoulian explains, "I occasionally use the image of a boiling pot surrounded with flames — the turmoil within a human being, within a man like Jekyll. Yet the flame is a pure thing, a clean thing.... His experiment failed, but his aim was noble" (qtd. in Geduld 177). Despite Mamoulian's claim that Jekyll's goal is noble, it is definitely mixed. Jekyll's original intention in his transformation is to make himself pure and leave his lesser self behind, but when he becomes Hyde he enjoys the sensation. He wants to have the pleasure of being both Jekyll and Hyde. Although he wishes to better the situation of mankind at the start of his experimentation, his continued transformations confirm his selfishness. Despite the pull of Ivy and his transformed self, Jekyll asks Muriel to marry him. It is as though Jekyll looks to Muriel to save him from his other life. He still hopes that by a suitable marriage he will be sexually fulfilled and will have no need of being Hyde.

Jekyll's lightness of manner and his desire for a sexual relationship mark him as a man out of sync with the times. The forced restrictions of his father-in-law move him towards the dramatic maneuver of attempting to rid himself of temptation. This plan backfires and he becomes Hyde, who gives in to all temptations. Others within his society, like Lanyon, play by the rules, but Jekyll cannot. Throughout the film the difference between Jekyll and his friends has been stressed. Jekyll's monstrousness is within him, and he cannot keep it repressed; it is ultimately brought out because of the forced sexual repression of his future father-in-law. Mamoulian shows that the evil is under the surface, like the pot of water, just waiting to boil over.

The Threat of the Monster

In Mamoulian's film, Hyde is given a simian look and movements. Karl Struss, the cameraman on the movie, described the process of filming Jekyll's transformation to Hyde:

> When you photograph someone and change them into something else without cuts or dissolves (as with [Fredric] March from Jekyll to Hyde), you have to put red makeup on the actor's face. Then, when you put a red filter on the camera, it doesn't show the red makeup at all. The lips of course remain the same, so they are painted a neutral grey. You move the filter up or down very slowly, and as it moves, you see the makeup emerge. I worked it out for Mamoulian. I thought they made a very bad mistake; the change from Jekyll should have been largely a psychological one, with subtle changes only in the makeup. But they foolishly changed the hair and put false teeth in, and made him look like a monkey. That was terrible [qtd. in Prawer 95].

Some critics think the enactment is racist, as Jekyll appears more Negroid. De-evolution was a common thought following the acceptance of Darwin's theory of evolution, and one which fits in with Jekyll's statement about evil in his lecture. During the Victorian era many people believed that humans were getting better and better through the civilizing centuries. Here, the man, the Victorian gentleman, has become something outside of his experience, a throwback to an earlier type of man, a Neanderthal. Mamoulian stated in an interview:

> I didn't take a monster but our common ancestor, Neanderthal man. Mr. Hyde is a replica of the Neanderthal man. He is not a monster or animal of another species but primeval man, closest to the earth, the soil. When the first transformation takes place, Jekyll turns into Hyde who is the animal in him. Not the evil but the animal [qtd. in Rose 140].

His body hair and his sharp teeth (his teeth stick out forward and are uneven) are emphasized. His nostrils are darker and enlarged; his hair is darker and frizzier. Hyde's simian aspect represents de-evolution, as he becomes a more primitive form of the human. We see this in his looks, hair, noises, and faster physical movements. He is also more like an animal in terms of his showing emotion, his anger, and even his breathing. He has no inhibition and speaks as he pleases. As Hyde, he runs and jumps quickly, and thus escapes from his pursuers. In a movie, a decision has to be made as to how to show Hyde. The change in this film is not at all subtle, as it will be in the Spencer Tracy (1941) version directed by Victor Fleming, wherein Tracy uses very little makeup as Hyde.

Jekyll's first transformation takes place in front of a skeleton — like the skeleton head in the silent movie — evocative of the death that awaits Jekyll. Next to him there is also a statue of a dark Oriental warrior, linking Hyde to the foreign and ferocious. The film slowly builds up to the transformation of Jekyll into Hyde. Jekyll adjusts the chemicals, stops to write the note, and locks the doors. The curiosity of the audience builds with each step. As in the first scenes when we anticipated the face of Jekyll, we now wait with bated breath for the appearance of Hyde. Jekyll drinks in front of a mirror, as curious about the transformation as his audience. As the transformation begins, memories come back to him of Lanyon and Carew's disapproval, and of Ivy's inviting leg. When he drinks, the room spins around, and when it stops, the room is the same but he is different. Hyde first hides, almost as though he is scared of himself, and then stretches and says with great satisfaction, "Free, free at last. Ah." His Hyde feels free from the moral restraints incumbent upon a proper Victorian gentleman.

The Nature of the Evil

Hyde enjoys every moment he spends as Hyde, but his behavior is destructive. He indicates his love of life by opening his mouth in the rain, letting himself be drenched, and drinking life in — what has been referred to as a "baptism by rain" (Mank). His pleasure is palpable. It is a primitive enjoyment of the natural amid his sophisticated evening wear and strange, simian looks. Hyde finds Ivy in a music hall where she sings, "Champagne Ivy is my name; good for any game in town." She will sing this song a second time in the movie, sadistically forced to do so by Hyde. Hyde introduces himself to Ivy in a non-threatening manner by asking her to share champagne with him. His movements are sudden and quick. Although his looks put her off, he woos her with both money and abuse. By suggesting that she is afraid of him, he psychologically forces her to pretend not to be afraid and do as he wants. We can see how frightened she is underneath her cool exterior and how quickly she is caught in his trap. He offers her a place to live befitting her looks, as well as appropriate clothes and jewelry. By saying that he is not a gentleman ("Gentlemen are hypocrites"), he anticipates Ivy's objection to him and displays his own distaste for Jekyll. He refers directly to Jekyll as he speaks disparagingly of those "who talk about your garter while looking at your leg." The abusive nature of the relationship is immediately obvious, as Hyde says to Ivy that he hurts her because he loves her. Hyde is not to be denied. "You'll come with me," he states with mesmerizing eyes. Hyde has an attitude of "what I want, I get." His approach is also flattering; he calls her "My bright little bird," identifying her as something pretty and vulnerable, and anticipating the use of bird imagery later in the movie.

Briefly, Jekyll attempts to balance the two parts of his life. Hyde has made life in his "love" nest a living hell for Ivy through beatings and psychological torture. Hyde demands that Ivy show the obedience and self-control that Jekyll lacks. After a wild night during which he whips Ivy, Jekyll attempts to regain his own identity for the return of Muriel. Jekyll asks Muriel for help, telling her that he has been ill in soul. He goes to her — the human angel who can intervene between God and himself. She can help him save his soul, and can do so by pleading with her father and arranging an earlier marriage to assure his physical satisfaction. Back in his home, Jekyll shares his happiness over his impending marriage with Poole, looks at the letters from Muriel that he has neglected (indicating the amount of time he has been away), and throws away the key to his back door so that he cannot exit and enter the establishment as Hyde.

Jekyll assuages the guilt he feels towards Hyde's treatment of Ivy by sending Poole to give Ivy 50 pounds. This act of kindness and expiation of sin through money brings Ivy to see him and starts her on the road to death. Ivy Pearson arrives and interrupts Jekyll's happiness, saying she needs help. She says that Hyde is not human, he's a beast. Telling Jekyll, "You're an angel," she pleads with Jekyll protect her and make her part of his life: "I will slave for you." Jekyll promises her that Hyde will not return. He is determined to control himself, but fails to understanding that he *cannot* control himself. Finally, although he is still drawn to her, he prevents himself from kissing her again, seeming to get a hold on his impetuous behavior. But his guilt cannot be cleansed through money, just as her wounds cannot be healed with salve.

Jekyll's first involuntary change in the film occurs as he happily walks through the park on his way to his engagement party, and stops to listen to a bird, surveying the scene with pleasure. He quotes John Keats' poem, "Ode to a Nightingale" (1819): "Thou wast not born for death, immortal bird." Suddenly he sees a black cat in the tree, suggesting the fate of the bird. Jekyll transforms into Hyde and says, "But it is death." Although Jekyll has seemed to be full of life, his experimentation leads him towards death as well. The relationship between the cat and the bird is reminiscent of Alfred Tennyson's description of nature in his poem "In Memoriam" (1850) as "red in tooth and claw." The law of the jungle exists right in the center of London. The natural scene brings out the natural and primitive in Jekyll, which is Hyde. There follow two split screens in a row: the guests and Muriel waiting for Jekyll at the party, and

Hyde walking out of the park; then Muriel waiting while Ivy is celebrating her belief (since she believes all that Jekyll says) that Hyde will not return by drinking champagne. The split screen technique effectively shows the pulls on Jekyll, of Muriel and Ivy, and suggests the division between Jekyll and Hyde.

Like the split-screen camera technique, mirrors provide an unusual way of seeing things in this movie. Ivy raises a toast to Jekyll ("Here's to you, my angel") in the hope that "Jekyll will think of Ivy once in a while"—just before she observes in her mirror Hyde entering the apartment. She drops her glass. In some ways the scene suggests a double image, an indirect way of seeing, of not seeing clearly. Thus, in the first scene Jekyll looks at himself in the mirror, thinking that all is well with his life. Hyde relies on the mirror to make sure of his transformation (in both the novel and the movie). And here Ivy cannot believe her eyes when Hyde returns after Jekyll has told her that she will not see him again.

Hyde kills Ivy because he becomes jealous of the way Ivy feels about Jekyll. He calls Ivy, "my little bird, my little starling," reminiscent of the scene of the cat killing the bird in the park. He tells her, "I will tell you something but then I will have to kill you." Hyde says he hates Jekyll, and also, "I am the angel Dr. Jekyll." Equating love with murder, he asks, "Isn't Hyde a lover after your own heart?" There is an emphasis in their apartment on the art collection which is composed of modernist pictures of nude women and the Canova statue of Eros and Psyche, "The Kiss." Hyde murders Ivy in the strange re-enactment of a love scene suggested by this statue, a mythological scene of a woman who is not allowed to look at her lover. When she does look at him, she loses him. She looks at him because she fears he is hideously ugly. Instead, he is supremely handsome, but he can no longer be with her once she has seen him. So Ivy can no longer be with Jekyll once she learns that he is also Hyde.

Lanyon is used as a contrast to Jekyll and Hyde throughout the film. Hyde is all shaking and tics, like a drug addict seeking his fix when he visits Lanyon to get his chemicals so that he can return to being Jekyll. "You will be blasted by a sight that would stagger the Devil himself," Hyde states, enjoying his superior knowledge. In the film he gives the same speech as in the novel, reminding Lanyon of his vows, and stating that Lanyon has "derided [his] superiors." The camera cross-cuts to both faces. The audience sees both Hyde becoming Jekyll and the horror and fear on the startled face of Lanyon. Jekyll walks towards Lanyon and holds out his arms as though he doesn't know what to do. His fate is in Lanyon's hands. A burning candle marks the passage of time and makes the form of a cross on the desk. Jekyll sits in front of the desk, asking for help; Lanyon stays behind the desk, like a doctor, and on a higher level, above them both, reigns Queen Victoria in a portrait. Justice will pass from her to Lanyon to Jekyll. Lanyon expresses his belief that Jekyll has damned his soul, while Jekyll believes there is still hope for himself. Jekyll swears he will not take the drug again and will fight Hyde's influence. In the end Jekyll vows to give up Muriel, and Lanyon agrees to keep his secret. The Lanyon of the movie sits in judgment on Jekyll as the representative of Victorian society, seeming appointed by Queen Victoria herself. His knowledge will not kill him, but will enable Lanyon after the death of Carew to point the finger of guilt at Jekyll and then be available as a substitute for Jekyll with Muriel. Lanyon triumphs.

In the next scene, back in his own home, Jekyll reads about the murder of Ivy in the newspaper and prays to God, saying that he has trespassed on his domain. If Stevenson condemns everyone in the novel and Victorian society itself, Mamoulian clearly distinguishes between the guilty and the non-guilty. Only Hyde is guilty, for Jekyll's soul can be saved.

The Monster Destroyed

Muriel suffers from Jekyll's treatment of her. She distractedly thumps down on the piano keys, playing poorly, expressing her emotions in an acceptable manner and thinking of something else. She still believes in Jekyll and stands up to her father about seeing him. For the first time, she is dressed in black like a widow rather than in white like a virgin. "I am damned," Jekyll tells her, and tries to give her up and set her free. He states that he is beyond help and in hell. He believes that by sacrificing the love of Muriel he will somehow square things with God. While Jekyll and Muriel speak, a musical accompaniment, a waltz from their former happy time together, plays in the background, marking a contrast once more between Jekyll in the past and the present Jekyll who has had the knowledge of Hyde. Looking back after he has left, Jekyll sees Muriel alone, weeping for him. He prays, and we don't see his face. Then he lets himself in and comes up behind Muriel. We look from her point of view. At first, thinking it is Jekyll who has returned to her, she turns with excitement and happiness until she sees Hyde, who is about to rape her, and screams. He fights off her father and servant, ultimately killing her father with his cane. Hyde may be jealous of the love that Muriel has for Jekyll just as he was jealous of Ivy's love for Jekyll.

Lanyon, immediately on the scene, leads the police to Jekyll's house where Hyde has transformed himself into Jekyll. In the novel, Lanyon waited until after Jekyll's (and his own) death to reveal the truth. He didn't want to interfere in the situation. In the movie, Hyde is shot by the police during his attempted escape after Lanyon has pointed him out as the killer. This may suggest scenes of racism — the black man hunted down and killed by police for his sin of murder of a white woman and attempted rape of another. But it indicates that society is intervening, that matters cannot be settled privately among upper class gentlemen as they were in the novel. Having Hyde shot by the police rather than committing suicide shows society's ability to regulate its inhabitants rather than their being responsible for themselves. Hyde's body goes back to being Jekyll when he dies, suggesting, as in the silent movie, that his soul has been redeemed. In the last scene we hear Poole crying, and the pot boils over again in the lab. Jekyll may be dead, but men's brains are still teeming with ideas. Within each man the ideal and the primitive exist together.

Normality Restored

Although in the film Carew is basically a negative figure, Lanyon becomes a positive representation of order. He is the liaison between Queen Victoria and the police who carry out her orders. In addition, Lanyon has shown some interest in Muriel throughout the movie, and Lanyon himself is available at the end to step in, so Muriel will be well taken care of. She will not become a single or redundant woman, but will take a proper place in society with a man who has her father's approval.

However impossible in reality, the characters of Jekyll and Hyde are believable as presented in this film. The emphasis on women and sex rather than hypocrisy reflects a time in society when the sexuality of women was becoming more acceptable. More women, like Ivy, were independent, while others still clung to the Victorian ideal, like Muriel. Whereas the message of the novel was against hypocrisy and suggested the need for the integration of the positive and negative impulses in every person, the movie presents a more positive view of Jekyll — a man of impulse, but nonetheless a man with great strengths, and who is drawn to religion and Ivy, saving himself by appealing to God and his religious renunciation of Muriel.

Ultimately Jekyll can only be saved in death. He is unable to continue living on earth because his separation of himself has been complete. One person cannot divide himself; rather, each person must learn to integrate the different parts of himself. In Robertson's and Mamoulian's films, the behavior of Jekyll is an anomaly; he is different from everyone around him. His purity in Robertson's movie allows him to be corrupted, and in Mamoulian's picture he is seduced because he is sexually repressed. In Mamoulian's film society rights the wrong created by Jekyll's actions, although the boiling pot in his laboratory points to the notion that it could happen again. After death, God's judgment saves Jekyll's soul.

The monstrousness is both inside Jekyll, brought out by his sexual repression, and part of the society represented by Carew. Mamoulian condemns a society which forces the repression of the self. By arbitrarily setting a marriage date for his daughter and Jekyll, Carew makes the situation impossible for Jekyll. This repressive aspect of society is made a negative in the film. Jekyll's tendency towards self-absorption would no doubt be cured by the stability of marriage.

Dr. Jekyll and Mr. Hyde (1941)

DIR.: Victor Fleming. PERF.: Spencer Tracy, Ingrid Bergman, Lana
Turner, Donald Crisp. Dr. Jekyll and Mr. Hyde Double Feature,
Warner Home Video, 2004. DVD.

After the critical and popular success of *Gone with the Wind* and *The Wizard
of Oz* in 1939, Victor Fleming directed *Dr. Jekyll and Mr. Hyde* in 1941. This was
a remake, or adaptation, of Mamoulian's 1931 film version (itself an adaptation
of a play made from the novel) rather than an adaptation of the novel. Nominated
for three Academy Awards— Best Black and White Cinematography, Best Film
Editing, and Best Scoring of a Dramatic Picture — the movie won an Oscar for
Film Editing and was popular with audiences. However, the film is more sim-
plistic than Mamoulian's in its approach to the monstrous. Made after World
War II had begun in Europe, but before American involvement in the war, the

Although he looks almost normal even at his worst, Mr. Hyde (Spencer Tracy) is a
sadistic monster in Victor Fleming's *Dr. Jekyll and Mr. Hyde* (1941) (MGM/the Kobal
Collection)

picture shows a strong, religious homefront capable of routing evil in a manner parallel to that of the time when the film was made.

When Jekyll first becomes Hyde in Fleming's film, his looks do not change very much. Little makeup was used during the transformation of Spencer Tracy from Jekyll to Hyde; rather, Tracy relied on a difference in hair style and eyebrows, a wild look in his eyes, and a strange set to his teeth and chin. Hyde, as played by Tracy, is the most human-looking of the Hydes. Spencer Tracy is well cast in this role, as he often played ordinary, intelligent, and decent characters who find themselves overwhelmed by circumstances around them. Whereas Robertson's Hyde looked more like a spider, and Mamoulian's had a simian aspect, the face of Hyde in Fleming's version is more human, more like us (Rose 105).[14]

However, the view of evil presented in this film is more simplified that in the previous adaptations. Fleming's movie sees evil as an aberration within a well-intentioned society. Although everyone may have evil within him, most individuals have no difficulty keeping it tamped down. As shown in the film, evil can be easily identified and removed by religion, government, and good citizens who step forward.

The World at the Start of Fleming's Film Dr. Jekyll and Mr. Hyde

The state of normality suggested by the start of Fleming's film is one of religion and order. Surface ruffles are quickly smoothed over in this view of Victorian London in the year of what a minister refers to as Queen Victoria's golden jubilee — 1887. As the credits roll, a heavenly-sounding choir can be heard singing "The Lord's Prayer." On the screen a church steeple represents man's striving towards God. Within the church the minister proclaims the goodness of Queen Victoria as a model for all people. He explains that because of the virtue emanating from the Queen, England is becoming better and better, and that the forces of good are in victory over evil. The film posits the possibility of the perfectibility of mankind through the trickling down of virtue from above. Goodness comes from on high — from God through the Queen to ordinary citizens. Dr. Jekyll, in church with his fiancée and her father, squirms a bit in his seat — just as the viewer does.

Life could never be as perfect as the minister describes it to be, and the calm does not last long. His moralizing sermon is interrupted by a man who claims to be familiar with evil and who laughs at the thought that it will ever be wiped out. Sam Higgins' wife has brought him to church in the hope that it might provide solace for his mind, which has been disturbed following a recent accident. His impulsive behavior is caused by damage to his brain. Higgins somehow recognizes an affinity with Jekyll and speaks to the doctor, calling him a "full-blooded young man" who knows "what is what." Ushers within the church, and the police, arrive to take Higgins away. Jekyll requests that he be brought to his hospital, and the police, recognizing Jekyll's name, oblige him. Jekyll's desire to cure Higgins brings Jekyll into the chemical research on altered states of mind that leads him to the creation of Hyde. And Hyde manifests a much more destructive form of evil than Higgins.

The Monster Within and Without

According to the minister, goodness comes from above, from outside, to serve as a model for the individual. Where does evil come from? Higgins revealed no capacity for evil behavior until he suffered some kind of brain damage that changed his personality. The disruption of his normal personality came upon him because of an outside force, an accident, and his resulting behavior is not acceptable to society. Society, according to the minister, is intolerant of evil. While Higgins has become obsessed with evil because of an accident, Jekyll will dwell with evil because of his own desires. Although the capacity for evil is within all men, it is brought out by a force from without.

From the start, Jekyll behaves in an erratic manner. He sits uncomfortably at church, he loses himself in his work, and he neglects his fiancée. Having developed a formula and tested it on animals, Jekyll tells his colleagues that there are no bad effects of his potion, and yet one of his test animals lies dead in its cage. He deliberate ignores what he doesn't want to see. Jekyll's research involves an untried approach, and he obscures the truth for his own ends, revealing his belief that his is the only correct approach. In his determination to try his formula despite the risks, Jekyll shows a complete disregard for regulations. Jekyll believes himself above the dictates of society.

On the other hand, Jekyll reveals a charming impulsivity with his fiancée by teasing her about her hat, chewing on her knuckles, and bestowing a kiss on her in public. His affectionate ways with his fiancée, Beatrix, are not a threat to society, although they annoy her father, Sir Charles Emery. More importantly, Sir Charles disapproves of Jekyll's willingness to speak openly of his unconventional beliefs. He is particularly disturbed by Jekyll's proclamation at a dinner party that every man is composed of both a good and an evil side, and that he hopes to be able to separate them. The minister, a guest at the table, responds that such matters should be left to God. Jekyll seeks to upset the *status quo*, stating that society does not want change because of the profits from established institutions. Yet this hint that the problem exists within society is taken no further by the film. Sir Charles fears the impression that Jekyll makes on his friends and neighbors—that Jekyll wants to act like God. Jekyll lacks the desire to conform to society and believes himself above the dictates of others.

Jekyll's friend, John Lanyon, is disturbed by another aspect of Jekyll. After they rescue Ivy Peterson from an abusive boyfriend, Jekyll accompanies her home and kisses this beautiful working-class woman. In explaining his actions, Jekyll agrees with Lanyon that what he calls "his evil side" got the upper hand for a moment. But Jekyll obviously does not believe that explanation and treats the moment lightly. Ivy does not. To Jekyll, kissing Ivy is not an expression of his evil side but a suggestion of his own inner desires. For Ivy, the kiss gives her dreams of a different kind of life than the one she has been living as a bartender in a music hall. Jekyll unfairly raises her expectations through the attraction of a man of a higher class. By doing so Jekyll may prepare her to accept Hyde's offer of a better life. The incident shows again Jekyll's willingness to obscure the truth in order to gain his desires. Although not an indication of evil, this prevarication shows an unattractive side to Jekyll. He is unwilling to look at the consequences of his actions.

By developing a serum which acts to separate aspects of the soul, Jekyll deems himself acting for the betterment of mankind. Jekyll believes that the laws which protect citizens from unsafe medical practices hamper his ability to cure Higgins. When he is prohibited from treating Higgins with his formula, he determines to use himself as a guinea pig. Ironically, Jekyll, who attempts to improve society, ends up becoming a threat to society himself.

The Threat of the Monster

Jekyll's descent into evil comes about because of his mad-scientist behavior, from his taking on the role of God for himself. Although he desires to help others, his dedication to medicine, combined with his own human weaknesses, lead him into evil. In Stevenson's novel Jekyll creates the potion so that he can do as he wants and have no conscience regarding his activities. Fleming's film, on the other hand, shows Jekyll as eager to help others—but outside of the established protocol of the medical community.

The potion plays on duality. When Jekyll gives the formula to a docile animal, the rabbit attacks him; when he gives it to a ferocious animal, the animal becomes calm. Thus, because Jekyll is basically good, taking the formula makes him evil. He asks himself when he first takes the formula, "Can this be evil?" He does not believe that something that makes him feel joyful can actually be evil. Jekyll fails to recognize the danger of his own behavior, nor does he desire to control himself—until he can no longer do so. Because Jekyll is a good person, the potion makes him a monster.

Three factors indicate that the evil is outside of Jekyll: (1) like Frankenstein, Jekyll has a callous disregard for the opinion of others; (2) he is unconnected with other people, except for Higgins who recognizes a similarity with him; and (3) the serum he creates transforms him into the opposite of what he is.

Although everyone may have evil inside them, they are able to keep this evil down. All of society aids this repression.

Once Jekyll discovers the freedom of having no conscience, he cannot give up taking the potion, despite its having no scientific value. The film suggests that once he tastes the sadistic pleasures of being Mr. Hyde, Jekyll's continued transformations are fed by his sexual frustration. He wants to be married to Beatrix, but her father will not allow them to marry quickly. Fearing Jekyll's ideas and behavior, Sir Charles takes his daughter away to the Continent on an extended trip. The movie does suggest, in a similar manner to the film directed by Rouben Mamoulian, that if Jekyll and Beatrix had married, Jekyll would not have continued to take the potion and might have remained a happily married man, with his potential for evil under control.

Because of her love for Jekyll, Beatrix lies to her father. However, this is not indicative of a Mr. Hyde lurking within her. Beatrix lies to her father because she doesn't want to tell him that during their long trip, she hadn't heard from Jekyll. Because of what Beatrix tells him, Sir Charles believes that Jekyll has developed a new attitude, a care for the poor and unhoused. Returning from the Continent in the belief that Jekyll has changed for the better, Sir Charles decides to let the couple wed early and encourages them to kiss in a museum. The reason for his change of heart is never made clear, but he is definitely less bothered by what society will think. Beatrix forgives Jekyll everything, even though he has betrayed her and himself. When Beatrix questions Jekyll about their relationship, he replies that everything is all right because they love each other. Yet love is not enough. Near the end of the film, when Jekyll can no longer control his transformations, they still love each other but cannot be together.

The Nature of the Evil

Jekyll is basically good, and thus the formula he takes transforms him into the evil Hyde. Fleming's film does not postulate that a Hyde lurks within any other citizen. Although the possibility may exist within all men, no other character in the movie exhibits the potential for evil. In Fleming's film, Jekyll appears to be unique in his capacity for evil. Jekyll believes that he is an extraordinary person who is above the law. He does not take the opinion of others into consideration as he forges ahead with his experimentation and his career. Jekyll's lying and his disregard for the rules of society are anti-social but not evil, as they do not hurt anyone else. His real evil is his behavior when he is Hyde.

As Hyde, he blames his actions on someone else. He lies and feels no compulsion to tell the truth. Although this tendency exists in Jekyll as well, in Hyde it is compounded. Hyde says that someone else caused the fight at the music hall, and then he uses the fight as an excuse to get Ivy fired so that she will be dependent on him. Lying is not the root of the problem, however; lying is evidence of problematic behavior, but not evil. Hyde's evil is evident in his relationship with Ivy. When he is with Ivy he takes over her life while pretending to help her. He takes no responsibility for his actions.

Hyde is sexually sadistic and ultimately murderous. As Jekyll turns into Hyde for the first time, he has an image of himself driving two horses with a whip, and then the two horses become the two women, Beatrix and Ivy. This image indicates his desire for control over both women, his using them for his own purposes. Just before transforming for the second time, Jekyll notices Ivy's garter. He pictures himself uncorking a bottle, and the cork is Ivy. Beatrix appears but looks disapproving. The screen explodes into a sea of bubbles. The bubbles, like the catchy tune that she sings, "See Me Dance the Polka," suggest the effervescent Ivy. Hyde immediately seeks her out. He takes advantage of the confusion he causes in Ivy to trap her with the suggestion that she deserves something better than what she has, and which he can provide for her. And yet he gives her much worse. Jekyll saves Ivy from being abused by one man, but she is then abused by Hyde, a man that Jekyll cannot rescue her from.

Jekyll's relationship with Beatrix contrasts with Hyde's relationship with Ivy. Beatrix has the power of a close psychic connection with Jekyll. When Jekyll drinks the potion, Beatrix wakes up in the middle of the night, fearing that something bad has happened to him. On the other hand, Ivy fears Hyde because she believes that Hyde can read her thoughts. Ivy doesn't love Hyde, and Hyde is incapable of love. His behavior is abusive physically and psychologically. Ivy desires to escape from the relationship but feels unable to do so. Yet Ivy has a momentary insight that Beatrix never can attain because Beatrix is blinded by love. Ivy alone sees a connection between Jekyll and Hyde. After Ivy seeks out Jekyll's help for her problem with Hyde, she crosses the room to leave, turns, and starts to ask a question. The suggestion is made, and later verbalized by Hyde, that she sees some of Hyde in Jekyll.

The relationship between Ivy and Hyde is a sort of dark mirror image of the relationship between Beatrix and Jekyll. Although Hyde's horse fantasy connects Beatrix and Ivy, the two women are from different classes, and this influences how Jekyll and Hyde treat them. When Jekyll is with Beatrix, he goes to church, to dinner parties, and to a museum. Hyde discovers Ivy in a music hall. While Hyde and Ivy are together, he behaves like an uncultured slob, sloshing his tea willy-nilly and spitting grape seeds on the floor. But worse, his torture of Ivy is psychological as well as physical. When Ivy wants to go out for an evening with Hyde, he makes fun of her by pointing out her limitations as a companion. He plays classical music on the piano and suggests they go to the Albert Hall for a symphony, an inappropriate place for Ivy. He then proposes she might read to him from Milton's *Paradise Lost*, something that would be beyond Ivy's comprehension. Finally he makes her sing to him and forces her to act as though she were having a good time, ultimately humiliating her by mashing grapes into

Dr. Jekyll (Spencer Tracy) cannot rescue Ivy Peterson (Ingrid Bergman) from the murderous Mr. Hyde in Victor Fleming's *Dr. Jekyll and Mr. Hyde* (1941) (MGM/the Kobal Collection).

her face. Her shame resulting from Hyde's abuse, and her fear of his behavior, keeps Ivy off balance and prevents her from seeking help.

Although Jekyll is determined not to become Hyde again, he can no longer control his transformations. On his way to his engagement party, Jekyll happily walks across a park. He begins to whistle the tune of "See Me Dance the Polka." Becoming aware of what he is whistling, he tries to whistle something else. Ivy's tune remains dominant. Jekyll's first involuntary transformation is hinted at through the song he whistles, indicative of the switch in his thoughts from Beatrix to Ivy.

Jekyll's good intentions are for naught. When Jekyll assured Ivy she will never see Hyde again, he does not anticipate his inability to control his changes. Ivy celebrates her belief that Hyde is gone, wishing that Hyde will burn forever while drinking a champagne toast to her "angel," Jekyll. She views the two men as a duality of good and evil, forgetting the earlier similarity she saw between them. At the moment when she hopes that Jekyll thinks of her, Hyde appears.

Hyde tells Ivy that Jekyll is a "smug hypocritical coward," and, as Hyde claims, he knows Jekyll intimately. Deciding to murder Ivy, Hyde tells her that he is going to rescue her from her confusion. He suggests that he is helping her when actually he ends her life. Hyde manipulates Ivy and the truth for his own nefarious desires.

Hyde looks like a normal human being, but Ivy states that Hyde is not human. He is "a beast" according to her, meaning that he treats her without human consideration; whereas Jekyll is a "fine, kind gentleman." Hyde is not quite human because he was created in an unnatural manner, out of Jekyll. His volatile and sadistic nature makes him impossible to be around. Because of his interstitial position between human and bestial, he makes those who have dealings with him uncomfortable. Within the film, Hyde alone behaves in an unconscionable manner. Evil appears to be under control in everyone else (except for the unfortunate victims of accidents, like Higgins). Jekyll's is a singular case which is not representative of the ills of society or the times. Evil disrupts society through the actions of such an individual as Hyde, but individual members of society can act to staunch its spread.

The Monster Destroyed

Jekyll's friend and colleague, Lanyon, acts as the opinion and agent of society. After seeing Hyde transform into Jekyll, Lanyon states, "You've gone beyond." He believes that Jekyll has crossed a line and behaved like God, something sinful for a man. He condemns Jekyll on the basis of his having created Hyde, without even knowing that Hyde has committed murder. Although Lanyon wants to protect Beatrix, he leaves it for Jekyll to break off their relationship. Lanyon is a gentleman and assumes he is dealing with Jekyll alone. When Jekyll finally tells Beatrix that he cannot see her any more, she is devastated and upset that he cannot tell her why. As Jekyll leaves her home, he hears Beatrix sobbing behind him. The viewer sees from her point of view, where she has fallen on the floor in despair, that Jekyll starts to walk back towards her. Beatrix grabs onto his leg, and slowly the camera pans up to reveal his face — the face of Hyde. When Sir Charles responds to the screams of his daughter, Hyde deliberately kills him with his walking stick.

Hyde is no longer a place for Jekyll to hide, nor is Jekyll a place for Hyde to hide. Pointing at Jekyll, Lanyon proclaims to the police, "There is your man" and "Heaven help him." Lanyon sees that redemption on earth is impossible for Jekyll, his hope of salvation is with God. Jekyll refuses to cooperate and repeats that his name is Dr. Henry Jekyll, and that he has done nothing wrong, even as he transforms into Hyde. Jekyll's sense of morality continues to be compromised, as it has been since the start of the film.

Lanyon, and not the police force, brings an end to the evil. Ultimately, as Hyde takes a knife and confronts his attackers, Lanyon shoots him. The continuation of society depends on the goodness of ordinary humans to intervene with those who think themselves superior. As America moved towards war in 1941, the ordinary but good man keeps control within society, whether on the homefront or on the front lines.

Normality Restored

As in the two previously-discussed films, in his death Hyde turns into Jekyll, suggesting that his soul has been saved. There is hope for even the greatest sinner. Poole drops to his knees beside the body and recites "The Lord's Prayer" as a heavenly chorus sings in the background, reminiscent of the first scene of the movie. The film ends with the church bells ringing, alluding to the believers in an orderly universe, the good on earth. Any evil that does appear within society can be rectified by religion, government, and good citizens who step forward. Society, rid of the evil Hyde, remains healthy. Hyde was a unique threat to the community, and following his death, normality can return.

Stevenson believed that all men were composed of good and evil, and that these elements could not be separated. He illustrates that every man has the potential to become Hyde by making Jekyll very similar to the other members of his society. In Fleming's film, Jekyll's habits of nonconformity lead him to defy religion and the rules of the medical profession by acting like God. Attempting to help those with mental illness, Jekyll becomes Hyde when he takes his own concoction. Through the grace of God and the presence of upright men like Lanyon, Hyde can be dispatched and all men can live virtuous lives. The society of Fleming's film is one that believes evil can be wiped out and seems to have accomplished that with the death of Hyde.

3

Beauty and Eternal Life

She by H. Rider Haggard (1887)

Although Frankenstein's Creature and Mr. Hyde are repulsive monsters, Ayesha, or She-who-must-be-obeyed, is the most unusual of monsters because she is the most beautiful woman in the world. She was once an attractive woman who immersed herself in a flame which gave her eternal life, unearthly beauty, and wisdom. The dreams of everyone who longs to exceed man's limited span on earth echo Ayesha's monstrousness. The novel *She* fascinated Sigmund Freud and Carl Jung, and Ayesha continues to intrigue readers today because of her archetypal significance.

Ideas of reincarnation and the interconnection of life and death appear throughout the novel. Symbolic reincarnation results from the comparison of Ayesha with such mythological figures as Diana, Venus, Eve, Satan, Circe, and a Sybil. In addition, the heroes of the novel are also connected with figures of Greek mythology, "Beauty and the Beast," and animals. All of these repetitions indicate the larger-than-life qualities of the characters — that they are types who have existed before and will exist again — and reinforce the mythic dimensions of the novel.

The pattern of repetition is heightened by the traditions of the Vincey family, whose members have passed along the Sherd of Amenartas, a large section of an amphora, from generation to generation.[15] Through the generations, the descendants have added to the writing on the Sherd, which reveals the family's beginning in ancient Egypt and then records their migration, through Greece, to Rome, to Europe and then to England. Starting with inscriptions in Greek and an indistinct map, and continuing with various signatures and notes from many generations, the Sherd details the connection between the Vincey family and a mystery in Africa involving a mighty white Queen who has the secret of eternal life.

The original story involved Ayesha, who loved Kallikrates, a Grecian who had been an Egyptian priest of Isis. Kallikrates left the priesthood and married

Amenartas. Ayesha was so jealous when Kallikrates hugged Amenartas in front of her that Ayesha killed Kallikrates. After the death of Kallikrates, his widow, Amenartas, returned to Egypt where she bore their son and originated the Sherd by writing on it the request that her son, or any of his descendants, kill Ayesha in revenge. Although several members of the family have attempted the voyage to Africa, none has been successful in finding Ayesha. In the interim, Ayesha has waited two thousand years for Kallikrates to return to her. The Sherd began as Amenartas' quest for vengeance on Ayesha, but for Leo Vincey it initiates a quest to answer the riddles it proposes and to seek immortality.

The monstrousness of Ayesha continues through the devotion of those who love her, who indeed come to believe that her evil is part of her charm. Rather than uniting to destroy Ayesha, the heroes of *She* become enthralled with her beauty and seek to join her retinue. Ultimately they dedicate their lives to waiting for her, as she spent her life waiting for the reincarnation of her love, Kallikrates.

H. Rider Haggar's *She* shows the monster springing from our greatest desire, the wish for immortality. All who come in contact with Ayesha are altered by the experience. In the film *She* (1935), directed by Lansing C. Holden and Irving Pichel, the monster is unconnected with ordinary mortals, and the hero falls victim only briefly to his desire for immortality. Ultimately he rejects the idea of eternal love for the reality of "ordinary" love. Robert Day's *She* (1965) presents the monster as a temptress who entices the man she loves to join her in eternity, only for him to find himself immortal as she dies. Because Ayesha corrupts the protagonist, he becomes the monster. The adaptations present Ayesha as a monster from without rather than a monster from within, as she is in the novel.

The World at the Start of Haggard's Novel She

The main narrative of *She*, the story of Leo Vincey and Ludwig Horace Holly, is introduced by an unnamed editor who explains how the tale came into his hands. Holly has sent him three things: a letter, a manuscript, and the Sherd of Amenartas. Holly's letter explains that he and Leo are leaving for Central Asia, and they would like him to publish Holly's manuscript if the editor sees fit to do so. Holly claims his story is more fantastic than any adventure published by the editor and completely true. The testament to the truth of the events of the manuscript belies the history of the Sherd and the extraordinary subject of Ayesha. But writers of horror novels, such as Mary Shelley and Bram Stoker, frequently attest to the truth of their work. If the work is true, the story has increased relevance for the reader, who then must expand his or her own notion of the normal on earth to include created life, vampires, or immortality. The monsters become a threat not only to the characters in the novel but to the reader as well.

The editor notes that every woman who meets Leo falls in love with him, while Holly has never had a satisfying relationship with a woman. Immediately a contrast is established between Leo and Holly. Leo is handsome in face and strong in body; and because of his golden hair, with curls close to the scalp, and his build, he resembles a statue of Apollo. While Leo is commonly referred to on campus as a Greek God, Holly is shorter, older, and ugly, reminding the editor of a gorilla; his campus nickname is "Charon," the ferryman in Greek mythology who rows the dead across the river that divides the living from the dead. Holly, by virtue of being the writer of the tale, has charge of it and, indeed, ferries the reader into a land of mystery and nightmare. Eventually these opposites will vie for the love of the most beautiful woman in the world, Ayesha.

Holly seems unsuited for a relationship with a female. In his manuscript, Holly explains that "Women hated the sight of me. Only a week before I had heard one call me a 'monster' when she thought I was out of hearing, and say that I had converted her to the monkey theory" (17), indicating that he is proof of Darwin's theory of evolution that man is descended from primates. Another woman pretended to care for Holly and one day held a mirror up to their two faces, saying, "If I am Beauty, who are you?" (17). Holly would have to be Beast and someone from a different realm than the woman.

These references to mythology, like Apollo and Charon, connect Holly and Leo with a long tradition and suggest that they inhabit a world larger than their life spans. The mythological references to Holly and Leo reveal their archetypal significance. Other references to Beast and Beauty, and, later in Africa, Baboon and Lion (while Job, their manservant, is Pig), perform a kind of doubling by making them greater than themselves. They are not just individuals but representatives of different classification systems and different ideas about humans and relationships. In a way, they are reincarnations of how mankind has been seen within other belief systems, even alternatives of human archetypes. This presents a different kind of reincarnation or immortality to both the Sherd and the eternal life of Ayesha herself. These archetypes, like our children and the words and memories of ourselves we leave behind, are the only kind of immortality we can know.

The published manuscript of Holly introduces Leo Vincey, who will grow up to fulfill the Vincey quest for the flames, and who became the ward and adopted son of Ludwig Horace Holly when Leo's father killed himself. Leo was brought up in an all-male community, at Cambridge University, where the two were attended by the faithful Job. Holly and Leo led a somewhat monastic, intellectual existence until Leo's twenty-fifth birthday when they opened the trunk that Leo's father had entrusted to Holly containing the Sherd and his knowledge of the family history. Leo decides to undertake the search for Ayesha and the flames, continuing the legacy of the Vincey family; Holly declares that he goes to keep his eye on Leo and do some game hunting, while Job declares that he will go to take care of Holly and Leo. Holly, however, will become as dedicated to Ayesha as Leo.

Leo's father brings up the question of whether the quest is a worthy undertaking. His letter to his son states, "He who would tamper with the vast and secret forces that animate the world may well fall a victim to them. And if the end were attained, if at last you emerged from the trial ever beautiful and ever young, defying time and evil, and lifted above the natural decay of flesh and intellect, who shall say that the awesome change would prove a happy one?" (35). Leo's father expresses the idea that tampering with secret forces may lead to disaster and the implication that even if eternal life were secured, it might not bring happiness. As Leo's father imagines, Leo, Holly, and Job encounter disaster seeking the "secret forces." Job dies from exposure to shock, while Leo and Holly are forever changed by their experience. As alluring as immortality sounds, the unnaturalness of it within this temporal world leads to unhappiness and the spread of evil.

The Monster Within and Without

Frequently the characters in this novel reveal their inner souls through their faces. When meeting the People of the Rocks or the Amahagger who are ruled by Ayesha, Holly remarks, "Notwithstanding their beauty, it struck me that, on the whole I had never seen a more evil-looking set of faces. There was an aspect of cold and sullen cruelty stamped upon them that revolted me, and which in some cases was almost uncanny in its intensity" (75). He perceives a look of evil behind the beauty of the tribe, and he proves to be correct. After providing an initial kind reception, the Amahagger frequently subject their guests to acts of cannibalism. They have a tradition of heating pots and then putting the hot pots over the heads of their victims, thereby cooking their brains so they can eat them. Even before knowing their intentions, Holly finds that, although he did not know why, "their appearance filled me with a sick fear of which I felt ashamed" (76). The tribe makes Job uncomfortable as well, as he feels something is not right, not natural. Holly, attempting to be a good guest, feels ashamed of his discomfort. But his instincts prove correct.

In his portrayal of the Amahagger tribe, Haggard envisions a society where women have a great deal of power.[16] The women of the tribe have equality with the men and can announce their desire to marry by kissing a man. He can accept a woman by kissing back. The tribe also has a means of keeping the women in check — every other generation the men kill off the older women to show the young ones how to behave. Despite the characters' fright at aspects of this tribe, Leo returns the kiss of Ustane and consequently marries her. Job, however, runs from one woman who is eager to marry him, and it is her revenge that begins the attack on the Englishmen. The woman scorned by Job encourages the tribe to attack and hot pot the men.

The Amahagger are ruled by Ayesha, and their evil is akin to hers. The evil in *She* comes from exceeding natural limits, like the length of the life span.

Ayesha has ruled her land for 2000 years. What Holly learns of Ayesha defies everything he has learned at Cambridge University. Ayesha has magical powers — the power to produce a picture in water of things which have occurred and also to "blast" someone as punishment, whether it be to stop someone in his tracks or to kill him. When Ayesha reveals to Holly, within a pool of water, a picture of something happening at the same time but in a different place, he is "disturbed at this most uncommon sight" (141). That which is not within the normal course of knowledge and events disturbs and hints at the unnatural and evil. Yet by the time Holly and Leo observe the monstrousness within Ayesha, they have fallen in love with her. Like Ayesha, they begin to lose their moral sense.

The evil within Ayesha stems from the desire for immortality. The only person able to resist this temptation was a religious man who kept the flame from others until Ayesha learned his secret. Every other person who knows of the flame seeks to partake of its magic. This desire is not limited to the characters in the novel — it's a human desire to want more than the term of life we have been allotted. This desire, common to mankind, is the monstrousness in man when it is not under control. This is a general evil that can lead to the monstrousness of everyone because the capacity for evil is within us all.

The Threat of the Monster

The monster of the story, Ayesha herself, has seemingly-eternal life, unearthly beauty, and the intelligence and knowledge of two thousand years of history. Ayesha is the most beautiful woman in the world, and her beauty is graced by her voice and ability to enchant men. She appears to have perfection of both body and mind, but Ayesha is a monster and can be perceived as one because such perfection on earth is unnatural. Before meeting Ayesha, Holly has a dream in which:

> a veiled form was always hovering, which, from time to time, seemed to draw the coverings from its body, revealing now the perfect shape of a lovely blooming woman, and now again the white bones of a grinning skeleton, and which, as it veiled and unveiled, uttered the mysterious and apparently meaningless sentence: — "*That which is alive hath known death, and that which is dead yet can never die, for in the Circle of the Spirit life is naught and death is naught. Yea, all things live for ever, though at times they sleep and are forgotten*" [102–103].

Holly's dream reveals the truth of Ayesha. He envisions a veiled form that is both a beautiful woman and a skeleton. She is both alive and dead, and, as the mysterious sentence indicates, in a world of reincarnation, everyone is both alive and dead. Holly, even before meeting Ayesha, has begun to have prophetic dreams, much like Ustane and Ayesha herself. He is already alive to this world of mystery and possibility.

In this mysterious world the gulf between life and death is diminished through the use of mythology, reincarnation, and other ways as well. Leo's father had written to his son, "I stretch out my hand to you across the gulf of death, and my voice speaks to you from the unutterable silence of the grave. Though I am dead, and no memory of me remains in your mind, yet am I with you in this hour that you read" (33). The suggestion of the presence of the dead among the living becomes stronger through the novel. It is more than the religious belief that the dead in heaven look down on and perhaps look after the living. Ayesha explains how she killed Kallikrates—"In the Place of Life *I* gave thee death" (212), suggesting the irony of the situation. The dead are not always permanently dead. In an uncanny moment, Ayesha brings Leo face to face with the preserved body of Kallikrates; his body is in perfect shape, like many of the dead within the dead city of Kôr. Ayesha destroys the dead body, saying, "Kallikrates is dead, and is born again!" (213), confounding the difference between life and death. Looking at the sculptured pictures on the cave wall in Kôr, Holly reflects on the possibilities of reincarnation, "Perhaps I was you and you are I," and then laughs, "and the sound of my laughter rang dismally along the vaulted roof, as though the ghost of the warrior had uttered the ghost of a laugh" (147). The laugh seems to echo through the centuries. Hearing the echo of his laugh accords with the idea of reincarnation. Ayesha believes that Leo is the reincarnation of Kallikrates, and Leo and Holly, at the end of the novel, seek a reincarnation of Ayesha. Like Ayesha, they have come to believe in reincarnation and accept that Leo is the reincarnation of Kallikrates.

The city of Kôr has been the home of an earlier civilization, consequently, the living sleep in the burial chambers of the dead. The dead also have a place and a function among the living. The bodies of the dead, having been mummified in a mysterious process, are lit and burned to provide light, like giant candles. Touring the remains of Kôr, Holly sees those who have achieved in death what they have not found in life. Among the dead are a man and a woman who never enjoyed happiness with each other during life, but who are together in death. This seems another way of expanding the possibility of life on earth. The whole city where Ayesha lives is a catacomb of the dead. The city of Kôr is a lost city, reminiscent of archeological dreams and also of the cycles of civilizations, many of which Ayesha has outlasted.

Within the city of the dead, Ayesha has waited two thousand years for the return of her murdered true love, Kallikrates, who died at her own hand. The triangle of Leo and Ustane and Ayesha reflects the original triangle of Kallikrates and his wife and Ayesha. Two thousand years before, Ayesha killed Kallikrates because she was jealous of his love for his wife. This time she tries to do things differently. Ayesha is jealous of the relationship between Leo and Ustane. Believing that Leo is the reincarnation of Kallikrates, Ayesha wants him for herself.

Ayesha first banishes Ustane and then kills her when Ustane refuses to leave her husband. When Ayesha brings Leo back to life from near death, her first words to him, explaining the fate of Ustane, are a lie. Consequently, according to Holly's Christian tradition, no good can come of the relationship which has started on an untruthful footing. Indeed, the love of both Leo and Holly for Ayesha will lead them towards evil. Both Leo and Holly give themselves to her monstrousness, and although they cannot become like her, they will do anything they can to be with her.

The Nature of the Evil

Beauty cannot be seen as an external indication of Ayesha's inner soul. In this novel, as with the Creature of *Frankenstein*, Ayesha's appearance is no indication of her moral worth. Like the Creature and Mr. Hyde, Ayesha is not quite human, as she was created by extraordinary means. Although something of her monstrousness seeps through her wrappings and her beauty, men ignore this when bewitched by Ayesha. When Holly first sees Ayesha, she is veiled: "I felt more frightened than ever at this ghost-like apparition, and my hair began to rise upon my head as the feeling crept over me that I was in the presence of something that was not canny" (132). Holly feels her unnaturalness and wants to look on her face. He feels her beauty will have no influence on him, as he has "put my heart away from such vanity as woman's loveliness, that passes like a flower" (142). Of course, her beauty does last longer. But she knows that any man who sees her cannot get her out of his mind. Looking at Ayesha, Holly reads her looks as saying, "Evil have I done, and with sorrow have I made acquaintance from age to age, and from age to age evil I shall do, and sorrow shall I know till my redemption comes" (144). Thinking of her, Holly is simultaneously horrified and attracted by her *diablerie* (146).

Holly sees something unnatural in Ayesha's looks: "This beauty, with all its awful loveliness and purity, was *evil*— at least, at the time, it struck me as evil" (143). Her beauty is stamped with experience, the sublimity was a dark one, the "shadow of sin and sorrow" (143). Holly will find his feelings about Ayesha change, and he comes to accept and even love her evil. He gives a hint of the change that will take place within him when he states that her looks "at *the time* ... struck me as evil" (143, emphasis added). Holly has fallen in love with her, "this white sorceress" (147), thinking of her awfulness and loveliness (148). Watching Ayesha, Holly realizes he is held not by the power of her beauty "but by the power of fascinated terror" (150). Holly is enchanted with her because he has no choice, and that attracts him. He cannot control his feelings for Ayesha, and she must act to counter her power over Holly: "Reaching out her hand, she held it over my head, and it seemed to me that something flowed from it that chilled me back to common sense, and a knowledge of propriety and the domestic virtues" (173). Thus Ayesha can both charm him to have eyes only for herself and recall him to the world "of propriety and domestic virtues."

Leo and Holly's servant, Job, who never observes Ayesha without her coverings, sees Ayesha most clearly. He never becomes mesmerized by the sight of her. Job fears the coverings she wears, as they remind him of death. They are like a shroud, hiding her from view. He compares Ayesha to the Devil, saying, "*Ayesha* is the old gentleman himself, or perhaps his wife" (217). Job shrinks from things that are "above Nature" (217). While seemingly immune to the temptations of women, Job feels and articulates what is unnatural in Ayesha.

Ayesha is presented as both a version of the seductive woman and as the Devil. She is frequently associated with snake imagery, reminiscent of the Devil, who assumed the guise of the snake in the Garden of Eden. Ayesha moves in snake-like ways. Holly describes Ayesha as she shook her white wrappings, "and came forth shining and splendid like some glittering snake" (171), and frequently mentions her serpent-like grace (143). Like the snake in the Garden of Eden, her voice and words are entrancing. In addition, she wears a gold double-headed snake around her waist. Because Ayesha's appearance is unnatural, as it has been enhanced by the flames of immortality, her beauty suggests evil.

Ruling through bewitchment and fear, Ayesha uses her power for evil purposes. Ayesha has developed a philosophy based on strict control and moral relativism to justify her behavior. She believes that good can come out of evil, and evil can come out of good: "My life has perchance been evil, I know not — for who can say what is evil and what good?" (139). Holly witnesses Ayesha's judging of the Amahagger people who attempted to hotpot them, and requests that the offenders not be punished so harshly. But the men are put to death by Ayesha. Her power shines like "the flow from some unseen light" (159), like a halo — but not from saintliness. The aura around Ayesha is derived from the unnatural source of her power.

Despite their knowledge of the ruthless evil of her nature, neither Leo nor Holly can resist Ayesha. Holly describes Ayesha's power: "The temptress who drew him into evil was more than human, and her beauty was greater than the loveliness of the daughters of men" (205). Holly even states that he would give his immortal soul to marry her (172), although he knows that Ayesha "had confounded and almost destroyed my moral sense." Within the Christian religion, sexual relations with an unnatural being is a sin. In order to follow Ayesha, Holly leaves Christianity behind. Although Leo hates Ayesha at first for the murder of Ustane, he soon comes to love her. Similarly to Holly, Leo loses his moral sense in the presence of Ayesha — he quickly forgets about Ustane. Ayesha lies to get what she wants, keeps her people ignorant, and spends her time waiting for the return of her love after she is the one who killed him. A similar self-absorbed desire for personal happiness and power arises briefly in Holly when he becomes jealous of Ayesha's love for Leo. Although Holly feels the full arousal of jealousy, he never allows himself to succumb to its force.

Ayesha kills Ustane despite the warning delivered by Holly on the repercussions of murder: "It would be a wicked crime; and from a crime naught comes but what is evil. For thine own sake do not this deed" (183). Ayesha does not distinguish between right and wrong, as she believes herself above the law: "Therefore doth it not become us to say this thing is evil and this good, or the dark is hateful and the light lovely; for to other eyes than ours the evil may be the good and the darkness more beautiful than the day, or all alike be fair" (184). Holly comments that she is outside of human law, "absolutely unshackled by a moral sense of right and wrong" (184). Holly includes a footnote in his story, indicating his thought on these events at some remove from them: "It is perfectly true that Ayesha committed a murder, but I shrewdly suspect that, were we endowed with the same absolute power, and if we had the same tremendous interest as stake, we should be very apt to do likewise under parallel circumstances" (215). Thus, according to Holly, the evil within Ayesha is no different from other human evil; absolute power allows it to come forth. Because of her unusual position, Ayesha has not been exposed to the tenets of Christianity. The belief of Holly and Leo may give them a moral edge. Holly does not commit murder because of jealousy as Ayesha did. Yet the more they are enamored of Ayesha, the more they forget their religious heritage.

Although she believes that the consummation of her love will make her a better person, Ayesha plans to go to England with Leo and set him up on the throne in order to improve the world. She asserts that together they can use their knowledge for the good of all mankind. Holly voices his opinion: "Though I was sure that she would speedily make ours the most glorious and prosperous empire that the world has ever seen, it would be at the cost of a terrible sacrifice of life" (226). Despite their seeing the price of this conquest, neither Holly nor Leo objects to Ayesha's plan. They have become corrupted by Ayesha's evil.

While Frankenstein's Creature acted out of revenge, and Mr. Hyde from a love of freedom and impulsiveness, Ayesha acts from a desire for immortality and then from her desire for Kallikrates. Despite the fact that he did not want to be with her, Ayesha has waited for Kallikrates for two thousand years. While the Creature and Mr. Hyde die and their evil dies with them, Ayesha dies, but Leo and Holly's desire for Ayesha becomes even greater after her death.

The Monster Destroyed

Leo is torn by the sense of the awfulness of all that has happened and his desire for Ayesha: "I am sold into bondage, old fellow, and she will take my soul as the price of herself!" (214). Although Leo sees his situation clearly, he cannot defend himself against Ayesha. Both Leo and Holly are addicted to her beauty. However, Holly believes that any marriage can be fatal. He says of Leo, "True, in uniting himself to this dread woman [Ayesha], he would place his life under the influence of a mysterious creature of evil tendencies, but then that would be likely enough to happen to him in any ordinary marriage" (213). Any woman then might lead a man to evil, but not any woman has Ayesha's capacity to do evil. Yet it is through love that Ayesha hopes to be led to the good. Ayesha believes that her past "is compounded of evil and of good — more of evil than of good" (247). After exposing themselves to the flames, Ayesha plans to marry Leo. In the traditional manner of a Christian wife, she promises to obey and be guided by her husband.

As Leo, Holly and Ayesha near the presence of the eternal flame, bathing in which will bring them extended life, Ayesha declares, "We go down into the presence of Death, for Life and Death are very near together" (247). So it happens that stepping into the eternal flames of life, she finds her death. Ayesha intends to find redemption from love: "Thy love, oh Kallikrates, shall be the gate of my redemption, even as aforetime my passion was the path down which I ran to evil" (248). Ayesha swears that in the future, united with her lost love, "I will abandon Evil and cherish Good" (249).

When they reach the area near the flame, they are all moved by the effluvium, the outer reaches of the flames. Like Ayesha's aura, the influence of the flame can be felt by those who are nearby. Although Holly has stated that he does not want eternal life, when they reach the flame Holly changes his mind and decides to accept prolonged life with Ayesha and Leo. Ayesha prepares for the flame as though for death (254). As she leads the way into the flame, Holly records, "How sweet she looked — and yet how divine" (255); he sees her both as vulnerable and immortal, more like a mother than a tyrant. But once Ayesha is in the fire, something goes horribly wrong and she begins to grow old rapidly. Ayesha looks as though she is turning into a monkey, a baboon. Attempting to become even more beautiful by entering the flames again, Ayesha instead quickly ages and dies. Seeing Ayesha's final remains, Holly reminds himself, "It was the *same* woman!" (257). Holly does not understand what went wrong with the flame, but states, "Thus she opposed herself against the eternal Law, and, strong though she was, by it was swept back to nothingness — swept back with shame and hideous mockery" (258). When she bathed in the flames the first time, Ayesha was given increased beauty and extended life, both beyond the natural human limit. In the flames for the second time, her immortality is taken away, and Ayesha's body goes through a speeded up process of dying and turning to dust.

Normality Restored

With the death of Ayesha, Holly thinks, "That little heap had been for two thousand years the wisest, loveliest, proudest creature — I can hardly call her woman — in the whole universe. Ayesha had been wicked, too, in her way; but alas! Such is the frailty of the human heart, her wickedness had not detracted from her charm" (261). He recognizes the evil of Ayesha but dismisses its seriousness as he views her with his frail and "human heart." Both Holly and Leo have been changed by their exposure to Ayesha. After her death, they vow to remain faithful to her, and, as recorded in the introduction, they ultimately travel to the East to seek her elsewhere. Their belief in reincarnation has become absolute. Although they have not completely succumbed to the evil of Ayesha, their lives have taken a strange turn. They may not be the complete monsters that Ayesha was, as they lack immortality, but neither are they fulfilling their potential on earth. They have lost interest in the normal world.

Ustane serves as an alternative to Ayesha in this novel. She has some magical power to foresee the future, but less than Ayesha. Likewise, she is beautiful, but not as beautiful as Ayesha. Her powers and physical attraction are natural and consequently limited. Her response to fears of the future is to enjoy the present. Kallikrates had chosen a woman like her over Ayesha and was killed for his choice. Even after Ayesha has killed Ustane, Leo chooses to spend his life with Ayesha and ultimately seeks her reincarnation. Rather than enjoying the present and improving the world for the span of his life, he will live in the hope of pleasure in the future as Ayesha did.

Holly writes near the end of his manuscript, "And that is the end of this history so far as it concerns science and the outside world" (275). But it's not the absolute end for Leo and Holly, as they have dedicated their lives to Ayesha. Indeed, Haggard subsequently wrote of their further adventures. The men will continue to look for her, wait for her, and seek signs of her presence. While Ayesha waited two thousand years for Kallikrates to come back, their lives are much more limited. However, they are dedicated to Ayesha in her death just as they had been during her life. Ayesha was able to forcibly recall Holly to the world "of propriety and domestic virtues." After her death, Holly has no interest in the normal, ordinary world at all.

That Ayesha continues to be a presence even after her death is shown by the fact that her cloak, which was blown off of her in the caves, comes back and covers Leo during the dark night — as though Ayesha were protecting him. At the beginning of the novel Holly and Leo shared Christian belief, as well as a strong cultural tradition through the writings on the Sherd and in their linkage to mythological beings. Now they will seek the purpose of their lives in an unnatural way, much as Ayesha had done. Rather than create a future for themselves, they will wait for the return of the past. The cloak is like the mantle passed from Elijah to Elisha; Holly and Leo will assume Ayesha's role of awaiting the one they love.

The evil of the world that Ayesha represents, the desire for immortality and immortal love, still exists. Her evil lives on both in the frantic searches of Holly and Leo and in the dreams of all mortals. We can only hope that we don't become so addicted to the idea as to spend our lives looking for immortality.

The only kind of immortality we can hope to find is through the words and generations that live after us. Like Mary Shelley's "hideous progeny," and the details of Dr. Jekyll's "Strange Case," Haggard's novel continues to live on, resonating with readers.

Many film adaptations of Haggard's novel *She* have been made. The 1935 *She*, directed by Lansing C. Holden and Irving Pichel, and the 1965 *She*, directed by Robert Day, stand out because they take such opposite approaches to the idea of immortality. The 1935 film ends with Leo Vincey finding true love, mortal love, while in the 1965 film Leo succumbs to the temptations of immortality and is doomed to live forever without his love. The differences in the films suggest the times during which the movies were created. The 1960s were a time of change for young people who sought freedom for alternative life styles and romantic possibilities. By contrast, in 1935 the western world suffered from a major depression, leading people to dream that the possibilities of life elsewhere were more exciting than their own lives. Many movies made during this time emphasize that happiness could be found at home and that the only important thing in the world is love. One of the most popular proponents of this point of view was *The Wizard of Oz*, released in 1939.

The mood of the 1935 film *She* is enhanced by the sets and the music. Made just after the monstrously popular hit *King Kong* (1933) at the same studio, RKO Radio Pictures, and with the same producer, Merian C. Cooper, and same special effects team, *She* was advertised as "from the creator of King Kong." In *She,* as in *Kong,* a small band finds a lost tribe who make human sacrifices to a monster. Whereas in *King Kong,* the monster falls in love with one of the women, in *She* the monster is a beautiful woman rather than an enormous gorilla, and has already been in love with one of the men for centuries.

She (1935)

DIR.: Lansing C. Holden and Irving Pichel. PERF.: Helen Gahagan, Randolph Scott, Helen Mack, Nigel Bruce. Commentary on DVD by Ray Harryhausen and Mark Cotta Vaz. Legend Films and Kino International, 2007. DVD.

The exotic world of *She* is captured during the opening credits: two huge pots of fire, on either side of a platform, give rise to flames, while smoke erases the words on the screen and allows the next screen to be shown. The picture, at once familiar and exotic, gives a sense of waiting for the scene to be populated, for something to happen. The dramatic music of Max Steiner adds to the atmosphere during the entire film. The set designers created the land of fantasy with miniatures and paintings that were filmed to make them seem real. Sulfur was used on the set to make volcanic areas glow. The locale is brought to life with such exotic elements as a saber tooth tiger and native dancing in the Hall of Kings, which is populated by huge statues.

Haggard's novel took place in a lost city in Africa. In this film the action is moved to the northern reaches of the earth. The frozen expanse of ice brought new visual images to the movies, including a beautiful spectacle of an ice wall breaking up which was incorporated into later films. The heroes find that beyond the ice is a volcanic area where a primitive tribe worships their beautiful queen in a lush, tropical paradise. Just as the cold gives way to the warm, they learn early on that things are not always as they first appear.

In the novel *She*, an implicit comparison is made between Queen Ayesha and Ustane, an Amahagger woman who chooses Leo Vincey to be her husband. Ayesha is beautiful, powerful, and immortal, while Ustane is lovely but human. Leo never is forced to choose between them, as Ayesha murders her rival. In this film, Leo must choose between the human Tanya, with whom he could enjoy "ordinary" love, and the immortal Queen, with whom he could know eternal life and love. The theme is reminiscent of the traditional Hollywood

She (Helen Gahagan) believes Leo Vincey (Randolph Scott) is the reincarnation of her beloved Kallikrates in *She*, directed by Lansing C. Holden and Irving Pichel (1935) (RKO/the Kobal Collection).

story of the man torn between the good girl and the bad girl. The bad girl in this film is the beautiful and powerful Queen who hides her evil from Leo, carefully shielding him from the fact that she achieves her goals with inhuman cruelty. Leo cannot recognize the Queen's evil, and he must learn to see clearly in order to choose a human life span of love over an eternity of his fantasized desires.

Helen Gahagan (later Douglas) plays She, here officially known as Queen Hash-a-Mo-Tep of Kor. Douglas was a Broadway actress with regal bearing, and this was her first and only movie. Although Randolph Scott is rather wooden in his role of Leo Vincey, this serves him well, as he represents everyman, caught in a wild dream of immortality. Even with all eternity stretched before her, the Queen becomes greedy and jealous and will stop at nothing to secure the love of Leo Vincey. The Queen manifests an evil found to a lesser extent in another character and that she temporarily brings out in Leo Vincey. But evil does not triumph.

The characterizations differ from the book so that Holly plays a less important role and the mortal woman, Tanya in this film, has a larger role. Tanya and She provide a contrast between earthly time and eternity, and the right and wrong way to live. Tanya would make the perfect wife for Leo, as she is not of native blood (as Ustane was in the novel). Like Leo, Tanya has white skin. During the 1930s, most people were adamantly opposed to mixed marriages. Tanya is loyal and domestic and is able to see through the Queen to the monster beneath her skin.

In this film, the monster, selfishness and the desire for eternal life is less a problem for ordinary mortals. This alteration is made through one major change in the film from the novel: the fact that Tanya can be a real love interest for Leo Vincey. Because he can marry her, the kind of love she represents becomes a real alternative to that offered by Ayesha. The monstrous desire for immortality becomes a manageable force that is defeated by true, but temporal, love and the presence of God on the side of the righteous.

The World at the Start of Holden and Pichel's Film She

The normal world shown in this movie is a temporal world, where life is short, which is basically life as we know it. On the screen appears the swinging pendulum of a grandfather clock, ticking away the minutes. The first words of the film are John Vincey saying, "Holly, Holly, what time is it now?" This effectively announces a major theme of the film — human time contrasted with the eternity of She. John Vincey is particularly interested in time because he is dying and has something to impart to his nephew before he dies. Horace Holly and John Vincey have cabled John's nephew, Leo, ordering him to come home from America (which accounts for the actor's

American accent) and mentioning intriguingly, "Greatest mystery in the world." That mystery turns out to be man's quest for immortality, which can free him from time.

John Vincey and Holly have spent their lives attempting to discover the source of immortality. John is dying of radium poisoning contracted from his work in their laboratory to find the element which will bring eternal life. According to them, their experiments prove such an element exists, but that it cannot be artificially produced — thus the Hollywood pseudo-science indicates that they must find the element in nature since they cannot create it. In this manner the extraordinary is made to seem ordinary and possible. Radium, known to be radioactive and the cause of death for many workers exposed to it (including its discoverer, Marie Curie), was the focus of much scientific investigation at the time. The research of John and Holly has not brought immortality; rather, it has brought death to John Vincey through radium poisoning.

Their interest in finding the source of immortality arose through the adventures of an earlier relative, also John Vincey. As the fire burns in the fireplace, indicative of the centrality of the domestic hearth for warmth and comfort, the two Vinceys and Holly talk about the resemblance between Leo and the portrait on the wall — the John Vincey who lived in the fifteenth century. The discussion leads John Vincey and Holly to explain to Leo that they have spent their lives seeking a way around man's enemy, time. They believe that their forefather John Vincey discovered a means of "overcoming man's enemy, the enemy of all living things, time which brings death, relentless, death." They explain to Leo that 500 years ago John Vincey's widow wrote a letter to her family explaining that John Vincey was killed because he refused to abandon her. John Vincey understood the importance of the traditional love between a man and a woman. In her letter she mentions the eternal flame, and she included a gold icon of a woman surrounded by flames, reading "Here burns the flame of life."

Rather than 2000 years, as in the novel, the tradition of the Vincey family only goes back 500 years, and in the film this tradition is European rather than Egyptian and Greek. But the tradition does show a pattern of repeated names and similarity of physical appearance that will account for the connection between Leo Vincey and his relative. The legend handed down is a form of immortality — of what lasts. Leo will learn the advantage of mortality and morality over immortality.

The Monster Within and Without

Traits like greed and selfishness are evident throughout the film, and are opposed to goodness and loyalty. While traveling north, Leo and Holly are accompanied by Dugmore and his beautiful daughter, Tanya, who have contrasting personalities and interests. Tanya can immediately be identified as nurturing and kind, as she first appears carrying a puppy in her arms. Tanya talks to Leo and looks in his eyes, falling in love at first sight. In contrast to Tanya's love of a man, her father is transfixed by the look of the gold icon they have of a woman bathed in fire. Dugmore is greedy and seeks to get as much as he can for himself out of the expedition, while Tanya cares for others.

Tanya tells a native legend about a white woman who long ago came out of the Shugal barrier, beyond which no inhabitants are known to exist. The woman escaped from a strange place, and if a man finds his way there, he will never die. However, natives are afraid to go beyond the barrier because no one who ever went over ever came back. In Mrs. Vincey's original letter she mentions that a man, carrying quantities of gold, was killed by a saber tooth tiger. The group comes upon this man, dead next to the tiger, so they know they are on the right path. But as Dugmore, overcome with greed, attempts to take a gold chain he sees around this man's neck, he causes an avalanche that kills everyone but Leo, Holly, and Tanya. There is an immediate retribution to be paid for Dugmore's greediness.

But greediness is not the true evil in this film; there are different levels of evil. Greed is but a small part of the ruthlessness and selfishness exemplified by the Queen. Indeed, her evil, which infests others but never defines them, is much greater than that of the other characters. The Queen and her selfishness are contrasted with Tanya, who is motivated by love and devotion. Within the film, the enemy appears at first to be time and death, but during the course of the film the real monster is revealed to be selfishness, greed, and the desire for immortality. While everyone may fear growing old and dying, that fear must be controlled. Because mankind, at least as exemplified in this film, can overcome this selfishness, the evil is shown to be centered in the Queen. As evil is disseminated from the Queen, so goodness comes from God. The Queen acts as a force from without who temporarily corrupts Leo. But God ultimately punishes her as he has punished Dugmore. Thus both evil and salvation are sources from without that can be reflected in the hearts of the characters.

The Threat of the Monster

The contrast between two ways of life emerges as Holly lights a pipe and Billali, the High Priest, asks if Holly worships smoke and fire, indicating that *he* certainly does. Holly assures him he does, but his is the worship of the domestic form of fire. Billali worships the eternal flames that She has bathed in. Holly does not fall for She as Leo does. Because he is not under her spell, Holly sees the Queen as she really is.

At their first sight of her, the Queen is wrapped in mystery, covered with smoke and gauzy clothes. "Who are you?" asks Holly, and she responds, "I am yesterday and today and tomorrow. I am sorrow and hope." Her words are baffling and suggest that she is time itself. There is pain in her voice as she complains about those who disobey her. She feels sorry for herself, for her fate of immortality, and also for the lack of absolute obedience she receives from her subjects. As a Queen, she has not sought to enlighten her subjects, and she rules by keeping them in fear of her.

The Queen enters into a contest with Tanya for the love of Leo. Having arranged for Leo to be brought to her forbidden room, She catches Tanya in her room as well. Tanya clings protectively to his left forearm, while She maintains that Leo does not need Tanya. Tanya asks why She hates her. She replies honestly that Tanya is nothing, but "long ago a woman like you destroyed my happiness. The same thing shall not happen again." She blames the woman who John Vincey loved for his loving her, which hardly seems fair, and yet the Queen killed him rather than her. When Leo awakes, he explains to the Queen that Tanya is nothing to him. Being around the Queen leads Leo to deny his feelings for Tanya; the evil of the Queen seeps even into Leo. But his basic morality is shown by the fact that he feels guilty.

Her wickedness comes to the fore as She condemns the prisoners who hurt Leo. In her Hall of Kings she looks just like the wicked queen in *Snow White* (1937, distributed by RKO), while Tanya has the innocence and natural beauty of Snow White. Tanya and then Leo beg for the lives of the men who attacked them. She is deceptive: although she appears to have saved the lives of the condemned men at the request of Leo, She gives orders to kill all prisoners, to "make an end." "Would I could kill my fears so easily," She says to herself, alarmed over Leo's relationship with Tanya. Fear makes She act monstrously.

The Nature of the Evil

Tanya is the only one who intuits something evil about She, who feels her unnaturalness. Tanya senses that She is wicked but cannot convince Leo; Leo has come under She's influence. He believes She is "strange — and wonderful," and exhorts Tanya not to be "too hard on her." Leo thinks that She can be influenced to do good, as he believes that she didn't go through with the killings of the natives; however, the viewer knows that she has already executed them. Leo remains blinded by his own desire for immortality.

The Queen hopes that she can make Leo remember their past together by showing him the perfectly preserved body of the first John Vincey. As in the novel, she killed him for jealousy, but She has hoped his "love of life would be stronger than death" and so has waited for his return for 500 years. Because she has the original with her again, She eradicates the body of John Vincey easily with a vial of liquid that she pours over the corpse. The scene shows the ephemeral nature of even a long-preserved body. She explains that immortality

The wicked Queen (Helen Gahagan) and Leo Vincey (Randolph Scott) are made of "different clay" in *She*, directed by Lansing C. Holden and Irving Pichel (1935) (RKO/the Kobal Collection).

has been a burden that she has shouldered in the hope of love. They cannot kiss, however, due to the nature of her hybridity — "because," she explains to Leo, "we are made of different clay."

Leo reveals his own selfishness when he tells Holly that he is going to learn the secret of the flame but is not going to share it with Holly. Leo exposes his shame at his own behavior by avoiding looking directly at Holly and Tanya. Leo has become infected with greed. But he justifies his feelings to Tanya by explaining, "What man would say no — be fair." Who could resist immortality?

Tanya offers Leo a different kind of love from She, mortal love. Attempting to change Leo's mind about She, Tanya asks, "What's the point of living a thousand years if you go on being cruel and selfish?" Tanya does not want the kind of love that She offers, "never knowing age nor grief, living in this tomb." Tanya wants "to share little things, laugh, grieve, grow old together and when one is gone, to hope to be together again after death. That isn't much to offer compared to kingdoms and power and glory that will never change." Just for the moment, Leo seems to choose Tanya, as he takes her in his arms. However, they are interrupted by the arrival of Billali to take Leo and Holly to a ceremony to celebrate the flame that keeps She young. Billali enters, saying, "Hail Vincey," in a foretaste of the power Leo will have in the future.

Having gotten nowhere with Leo, Tanya goes to She and asks to be allowed to leave with Leo and Holly to go back to their own country. The Queen asks if Tanya is mad, telling Tanya that Leo is realizing a dream, and she is not going to send him back to you "and your little model love." Tanya then says, "If you won't send him back, will you let me stay here where I can see him sometimes." As the Queen turns to leave, Tanya asks why She is afraid of her, answering her own question with the words, "Because I am human and you are not, because I am young and you know love belongs to the young. Your magic makes you seem young, but in your heart you are old, old ... too late for love forever. He will never love you." Tanya plays on She's fears, reveals the contrast between them, and shows She as old despite her apparent youth.

The Queen explains to Leo that the girl being brought into the Hall of Kings for the gods is given in gratitude for the gift of enduring life. "Is this a human sacrifice?" asks Leo. She responds, "It is the immemorial practice of the people of Kor," slyly intimating that anything done traditionally is all right. Leo objects when he sees that it is Tanya who is about to be sacrificed, and then he fights to save her life. He shoots his way out of the Hall and then tips over a big container of flame to keep everyone back. Pursued by soldiers, Holly, Leo, and Tanya run and leap onto a stone over a chasm. They find they have arrived through the back way at the chamber of the eternal flame, and there they find She and Billali.

Leo has finally come to his senses about She and broken the spell she has held over him. He says to She, "I want no power you have to give, I want nothing you have to give," and hugs Tanya. In a condescending effort to be accommodating, the Queen offers to wait out Tanya by keeping Tanya around until she is old and ugly and Leo is no longer attracted to her. When Leo doesn't budge, She threatens that if Leo refuses to go into the flame, the girl will die. He says he will always love Tanya and addresses her with the words, "Trust me, believe in my love." These feelings of love and trust are very different from the power and control shown by the Queen. In order to prove that the flames are not a trick, and that he will not be harmed, She enters the flame alone. In this film Leo has first been motivated by the desire for immortality, then has been fascinated with She, and finally will be forced by her into immortality in order to protect Tanya's normal life span. Leo acts as the Queen demands because of his love for Tanya.

After trying to have Tanya murdered, the Queen attempts to use Tanya as a hostage in order to force Leo to be with her. The Queen's desperation has led her into an evil for which there is no solution. The evil within She is hers alone, but it is evident to a lesser degree in Billali. Dugmore exhibited greed, and Leo briefly turned on Tanya and Holly in his desire for immortality, but when the truth of the Queen's actions come out, She is a monster. Her wicked heart deserves, according to Tanya, to be punished by God.

The Monster Destroyed

Tanya says to She, "You will not be unpunished forever. Somewhere there is a power that won't let such wickedness and cruelty go on." God is that power, and just as God punishes Dugmore for his greed, God punishes She. She enters the flame, describing how she will remain beautiful forever while harping on Tanya's mortality. She says to Tanya, "Your eyes will lose their brightness." As the Queen says this she starts to age. She continues to address Tanya, "Your cheeks will wrinkle ... while I defy the years and laugh at time"—except now She is an old woman. She realizes her eyes are not strong, her voice doesn't sound right, and that she is dying.

There is a wonderful irony in the way that She dies, lording her beauty and immortality over Tanya. Her selfishness and greed have aroused the avenging hand of God, and She pays for her evil. Rather than the natural passage of time, her aging, death, and deterioration become sudden and hideous.

As they leave the area of the flames, Holly says, "The greatest secret in the world and we are turning our backs on it." Leo and Holly have come to believe that Tanya was correct when she said, "What's the point of living a thousand years if you go on being cruel and selfish?" There is something better than immortality—a life lived with love. As in the films of Dr. Jekyll and Mr. Hyde, Hollywood demands that the end of a movie allow for the love interest to marry and regenerate in the proper fashion, to live on and achieve the continuance of her life through her offspring.

Normality Restored

In the novel, Leo and Holly first seek eternal life, but after the death of Ayesha their focus switches to her, and eventually they await her reincarnation. Haggard's novel shows that Leo and Holly have been corrupted by the basic human desire for immortality. In this film, however, the evil is no longer within Leo and Holly; they disassociate themselves from the evil of She. They come to be grateful for the comforts of home. The film presents on the screen first the aurora of the eternal flame, which then dissolves into the fireplace at Holly's home, showing the shift in their interest. Holly has recorded their story in a manuscript and is reading the story to Leo and Tanya who sit in comfortable chairs in front of the fireplace. He sums up by saying that She died speaking of eternal life, and that her gold symbol gave them safe passage through the native area on their way back to civilization. Leo says, "It seems as though it couldn't have happened," underscoring their present comfort and happiness, and the unreality of their earlier adventure and the thought of eternal life.

Holly tries to explain She's end by providing two possible explanations: perhaps bathing in the flame a second time was too much of an exposure to the unknown element; or such inhuman immortality was never meant to be, and some greater power than She reached out and destroyed her. He posits both a scientific explanation and a religious explanation for She's destruction. Because Tanya has previously mentioned the retribution of God, that seems more likely. Tanya is the moral center of the film, and was also correct about her initial feeling that She was evil. When Leo says maybe there is no real flame of life, Tanya reveals that she thinks there is—"right here, in this fireplace the flame in any fireplace in any home, where two people live and love each other and in their hearts." The fantastical thought of immortality has become a metaphor for earthly love stemming from the hearth and home. Her statement is much like that of Dorothy at the end of *The Wizard of Oz*, "There is no place like home."

Home is the proper environment for real love. This film contrasts love with someone you can grow old with and eternal love. Leo Vincey had been torn between the two women, Tanya and Ayesha. While searching for the eternal flame, he comes to believe in fulfillment from human love. Finally, at the end, real love is found to exist in the home: "the flame of life exists here, in any fireplace in any home where two people live and love each other." The monster, based on selfishness and dreams of eternity, has been defeated, at least temporarily.

Ray Harryhausen, who worked on the film when he was a young man and recently colorized the movie, states in an interview on the DVD that although in his youth he was convinced by the sentimentality of Tanya as to the superiority of human love, as he has gotten older, he now would eagerly enter the eternal flames with She.

She (1965)

DIR.: Robert Day. PERF.: Ursula Andress, Peter Cushing, Bernard Cribbins, John Richardson. Optimum, 2001. DVD.

The 1965 film *She*, directed by Robert Day, lacks the clear structure and excitement of the novel and the earlier film. Enhanced with color, elaborate sets, and flashback explanations, the 1965 film seems overblown and wooden. By making subtle changes in the character of Leo, the story itself has been changed from H. Rider Haggard's 1887 novel. Leo Vincey is remade as a product of the 1960s, a man who is unsure of the future of the world, of his own future, and is most interested in temporal pleasure. In this way Day alters the meaning of *She* for a new generation by changing Leo's behavior and consequently how the film ends.

Other factors in the film also reflect the era in which it was made. By the 1960s a butler was something of an anomaly, and in Day's film the butler acts throughout as comic relief. As in the novel, there is concern over the role of women and the discomfort engendered by a powerful woman. Whereas the novel was written at the start of the New Woman's movement, this film was made at the start of the Woman's Movement of the 1960s—both times when women were questioning their place within society. Whatever their opinion of women in positions of political power, the men in this film are comfortable socializing with women. Appropriately to the 1960's, dance is an important means of social intercourse and entertainment. The film opens with a scene of the British characters dancing with Arab women in a bar. Later the Oo-Bla-Da Dancers perform African-style dances. The easy attitude towards relationships between the sexes and between the races is evident. Leo, who is not prone to monogamy, is quick to have a physical relationship with both Ustane and Ayesha, and seems to have no difficulty sustaining the relationships simultaneously.

By the 1960s relationships between members of different races were fairly widely accepted. In the novel *She*, Leo Vincey cannot find happiness with Ustane, the native woman he marries, because a mixed-race relationship would not be accepted back in Victorian England. Since Leo could not bring her home to be his wife, Ustane must die in Africa. In the 1965 version of *She* the relationship between Leo and Ustane poses no problems on the basis of their racial difference.

At the end of the novel *She*, Leo and Holly become tainted by Ayesha and change their lives so that they await the return of Ayesha. The monster, the desire for eternal life, has become part of them. In the 1935 film Leo starts to be tarnished by Ayesha, but ultimately he is saved by choosing the love of a mortal woman over that of Ayesha. Leo defeats the desire for immortality, and the viewer is expected to applaud his choice. In the 1965 film the character of Leo becomes corrupted through his desire for immortality and sexual love. Leo eventually replaces Ayesha as a monster. Whereas in the novel the evil is widespread and evident in all of humanity, in the 1965 adaptation the evil is remote from the rest of humanity. The monstrous is presented as being an outside force, evident in only a few individuals, rather than a chord that runs through all mankind.

The World at the Start of Day's Film She

At the start of the 1965 version of *She*, the world is not normal because the world has just endured the devastation of World War I. Holly, Leo, and their servant Job are in Palestine in 1918, having finished their military service. The exotic locale is made invitingly intriguing by sexy dancing girls, immoderate drinking, and even a barroom brawl. But then again, the men behave as they would in a pub in Piccadilly — they waste time. They know they don't want to go back to their old life (Holly taught at the university, and Leo was a student). Leo is young and unformed, unsure of what to do with his life other than live in the moment. However, since they are running out of money, Holly and Leo will need to make a decision soon as to their future. By using such phrases as "when we return to our own land," they underline the foreign nature of their current existence. In the meantime, they spend their time drinking and flirting with attractive women.

Leo and Holly differ not in looks but in temperament. The contrast in the looks of Leo and Holly as Beauty and Beast, so well developed in the novel, does not exist here. Both Leo and Holly are handsome men in the 1965 film. Holly is darker, more distinguished looking, and older, while Leo is young and fair. However, Holly acts with intelligence and kindness, while Leo reveals his character flaws from the start. Holly and the valet Job seek to help Leo, the youngest of the group, to go with him and to protect him. Leo's character is selfish.

All three men are interested in the beautiful and exotic woman Ustane when they see her in a bar. Leo immediately tells the other two to sit down while he pursues her, despite the danger signs of the Arab men who watch Leo intently. After leaving the bar with her, Leo stops on the street to kiss Ustane, showing his willingness to do anything involving a beautiful woman. Taking advantage of his distracted state, Ustane's accomplices hit Leo over the head, render him unconscious, and take him to Ayesha. (Undoubtedly Leo would have gone willingly to Ayesha had he been shown a snapshot of her.)

The actress Ursula Andress certainly looks beautiful as Ayesha. Having previously played the quintessential Bond girl, she has become what every man desires. She is more accessible and less austere than Helen Gahagan in the 1935

Like a phoenix seeking rebirth, She (Ursula Andress) in Robert Day's *She* (1965) (Hammer/the Kobal Collection).

film. While in the earlier movie She resembles an icy, wicked queen, here Ayesha rules as a gilded raven, a living version of the Maltese falcon, "the stuff that dreams are made of."

Ayesha has come to find Leo instead of waiting for Leo to find her. She herself becomes the reason that Leo will journey across Africa. Ayesha speaks to him of their past, but Leo has no recollection at this point in the film. She opens her arms to him, saying that there will be a long and dangerous journey, and then "everything you desire will be yours." He asks, "Even you?" and the answer is clearly in the affirmative. They kiss to seal the deal. This Ayesha is not made of "other clay," and they will be able to consummate their relationship eventually. This phrase, "everything you desire will be yours," spoken by the beautiful Ayesha as she beckons to him, is repeated through the film in Leo's visions and dreams. Rather than immortality, something immaterial, Leo seeks the very real Ayesha.

Leo is never completely honest with Holly and Job. He follows the trail to Ayesha not to seek adventure, as in the novel, but because of his carnal desire for Ayesha herself. Leo interests Holly in accompanying him by talking about the lost city of Kumar that Holly is keen to discover. Leo reveals his selfishness in taking advantage of his friends, in getting them to accompany him on the journey to Ayesha. Ayesha gives Leo a ring and map to guide him to the area of Africa where she rules over a tribe of natives, but does nothing else to help him as Leo, Holly, and Job cross the desert to find her. Indeed, things become more difficult for Leo when men slice their water bags, steal their camels, and then attack and shoot Leo.

Although Leo is infatuated with Ayesha, she is not in love with Leo. She does not want him, but the man she knew two thousand years before, Kallikrates. When informed that Leo may not recover from the gunshot wound, Ayesha replies that if he does not survive, he is not Kallikrates. The journey itself is a test; if Leo is successful in reaching Ayesha, then she will know he is the reincarnation of Kallikrates.

The Monster Within and Without

The passivity of Leo, clearly perceptible in the novel, becomes the center of this film, along with a selfishness often associated with the 1960s. Leo becomes a pawn in the hands of a beautiful woman after he has been corrupted by the idea of immortal love. The evil has its source in the selfishness of Ayesha, but it finds a willing mate in Leo.

Having been the bait that first attracts Leo, Ustane subsequently has a change of heart. She feels responsible for Leo, but she is too late in changing her mind to prevent his being kidnapped by Ayesha. She can only mutter, "Keep safe, my Leo," revealing her own kindness and consideration for someone else. Ustane later overtakes Leo in the desert to help him on the journey. Ustane seems, like the Ustane of the novel, to know that she will be discarded, and yet she continues with Leo as long as she can. Love of Leo and her desire to protect him has made Ustane a better person. Unfortunately, love or the desire for love does not increase Leo's morality.

The evil shown in this film stems from the misuse of power, and the power stems from Ayesha. Ayesha keeps the Amahagger people enslaved in a primitive culture, dominated by fear. When the British men are captured by the Amahagger people, the natives intend to sacrifice Leo because of their fear of his face. Ayesha had used Leo's face as a symbol of her power. The Amahagger devise a ceremony during which a false Ayesha, a young woman with long, fake-blonde hair, rubs herself against Leo in preparation for his sacrifice. In this pantomime of sexuality and attempted murder, Leo should be warned of his future. But nothing will stop him from his pursuit, even after being rescued by Billali and brought to Ayesha's Great Hall to witness Ayesha's administration of "justice." Ayesha punishes representatives of the tribesmen who attempted to harm Leo by chaining them together and then pushing them one by one into an open volcano.

Ayesha is aided and abetted by Billali's counsel. Billali advises her not to get rid of Ustane herself, but to deprive Leo of "soul and conscience": "To be rid of her would be simple, but unwise. If you are to prevail, it is the fair one [Leo] who must banish her, who must turn him against her. He is a man of soul and conscience. These you must destroy." Ayesha intends to destroy the center of Leo's morality, to make him like herself. Consequently, she must find a situation in which Leo can turn on Ustane.

Two thousand years before, Ayesha's jealousy caused her to kill Kallikrates. This time she is determined to behave differently in order to get the results she wants. Yet Ayesha is immediately jealous of Leo's love for Ustane, just as she was in his previous incarnation. Maintaining her power and control through ruthless behavior, Ayesha takes Ustane captive and suspends her in a cage over a bottomless pit of fire. Ayesha forces Leo to make the decision: he must either kill Ayesha or let Ayesha kill Ustane. Only the death of Ayesha, stabbed with the dagger that she used to kill Kallikates, will save Ustane's life. Faced with the choice of killing Ayesha or letting Ustane be murdered, Leo crumbles at Ayesha's feet. She robs him of his manhood but declares that he will be a man again. Rather than Ayesha killing Ustane, as in the novel, Leo allows Ustane to be killed by his passivity. Ayesha believes, because she listens to Billali, that she can change the way that things work out by making Leo responsible for the death of Ustane. Yet she remains the source of the evil in this film, an evil that has tapped into a likeness in Leo.

Leo passively allows Ustane to be murdered because of his desire for immortality and his love of Ayesha. His dreams appear to come true as they go to her room together. Through the murder of Ustane, the monstrous can be seen to have taken over Leo's heart; the evil that is within Ayesha spreads to Leo. Aside from some basic human frailty and ignorance evident in others, the evil resides with Ayesha and Leo and is not part of the community.[17]

The Threat of the Monster

Ayesha's threat is her selfishness; she is capable of hurting others to advance her own desires. She reigns as a ruthless queen, demanding obedience from her subjects through the use of force. They obey her because they fear her. "Is your world so much better?" she asks provocatively. The world depicted in the 1965 film *She* is the world of 1918 that has been through a brutal world war, destroying the lives of millions; but the war was fought in order to make the world safe for democracy, as Woodrow Wilson said. At least many people believed they were acting for the benefit of other people.

Holly responds that Ayesha "is not the first to dream of such power," indicating that she is not unusual in her evil. Ayesha seeks power for her own personal enrichment. She believes her world will begin again, and not end, when she is united with Kallikrates, and at that time she intends to found her new world on love. However, by attempting to unite with Leo, Ayesha leads him to evil. Deception and murder cannot be the basis for a world of love.

Leo believes that anyone would make the choices he makes. He asks Holly, "Have you ever been in love?" suggesting that love can be an excuse for any outrageous behavior. Wanting Ayesha, Leo loses his moral judgment. Leo says to Ayesha, "Is there anything I will not forgive you for?" He forgives Ayesha for making him choose between the women and allowing Ustane to die. Leo has lost his soul and conscience. He shows no concern for what their future will be, how they will rule. Leo only cares that he will be together with Ayesha forever.

Because Holly is not in love with Ayesha, as he is in the novel, he becomes the voice of reason. When Leo speaks of the flame that brings immortality, Holly brings a match to his pipe and thus contrasts eternity with the brief and ephemeral light of the match. Holly believes that love wasn't meant to last forever, at least the physical aspect, and warns Leo against seeking immortality: "If you accept I only hope you don't live to regret it."

The Nature of the Evil

Although she is beautiful, Ayesha is also deadly. Ayesha combines a human look with eternal life, something which is unnatural and consequently monstrous.

Dressed alike and about to suffer the same fate, She (Ursula Andress) and Leo Vincey (John Richardson) in Robert Day's *She* (1965) (Hammer/the Kobal Collection).

By seeking to share this with her, Leo exposes himself to the mysterious flames which are the source of Ayesha's beauty, power, and immortality. Two thousand years ago Ayesha bathed in the flames and received immortality. She plans to return to the flames with Leo so that they may share their power together.

Early in the film Leo sought a good time with any attractive woman. After meeting Ayesha, Leo seeks love and immortality, although, as Holly warns, sexual love is not intended to last forever. In wanting more than man's allotment, Leo forgets that immortality is unnatural. The desire for immortality leads to every other evil.

The Monster Destroyed

As in the previous versions, Ayesha goes into the flames for a second time. Ayesha believes the flames will refresh her beauty and immortality. In the 1965 film, Ayesha and Leo enter the flames at the same time. For a moment they embrace triumphantly. But when a person goes into the flames for a second time, the flames take back their power. Ayesha starts to age, and Leo, fearful of what he sees, leaves the circle of flames in a panic. Shriveled to an unrecognizable form, Ayesha crawls out of the flames and attempts to reach Leo. Being in the flames a second time has erased the effect of her first exposure so that her body deteriorates as it would have naturally over two thousand years, but in just a few minutes' time. Under the prodding of Holly and Job, who return to help Leo, Leo tries to go back into the flame to reverse the effects, so that he will no longer be immortal — but he cannot do so, as the flame disappears.

Leo has been punished for his desires. He will have eternal life but will have to spend it without Ayesha. Holly clearly blames Leo's fate on Leo himself, saying, "You wanted immortality." Leo's youth and love of sexual pleasure cause him selfishly to seek immortal love. In choosing Ayesha over Ustane, he has revealed his own character flaws, which lead him towards evil. Another monster is created, and thus there can be no end to the evil.

Normality Restored

Unlike the novel and the earlier movie, this 1965 version shows decisively that Leo is the reincarnation of Kallikrates. Leo has memories of his former life. Indeed, he says that he was never more at peace than when he was in the desert fighting, indicating his connection with the desert from another life. The route across the desert to Ayesha feels familiar to Leo, perhaps "an inherited memory," he reflects. Because reincarnation exists in the world of *She,* order exists in the universe. Things happen for a reason, and the story repeats itself forever, without the possibility of ever having a happy ending. The evil that was in Ayesha is now within Leo, and their fate will be the same, which is to suffer and to wait. He has become a monster.

Day's version of *She* points to the self-absorption of the 1960s. The desire for sexual encounters brings Leo first to Ustane and then to Ayesha. In seeking the ultimate sexual experience, however, Leo allows Ustane to be murdered. His selfishness cannot lead to good government or to personal happiness.

While Leo was left in a similar position to Ayesha at the end of the novel, here he is in the exact position of Ayesha. There is no indication of how he will spend his life. The last words of the film are spoken by Leo, "When it comes back, it will find me waiting." Thinking of himself, he awaits the return of the flame rather than Ayesha. Evil is definitely not destroyed, and the monstrousness will live on. Because Leo's flaws have been revealed throughout the film, the viewer is prepared for him becoming a monster. We don't know about his actions. What will happen in another two thousand years? Such an ending leads to the Hollywood perennial — the sequel!

4

Man and Animal

The Island of Dr. Moreau, by H. G. Wells (1896)

H. G. Wells' *The Island of Dr. Moreau* was originally subtitled "A Satire or a Satirical Grotesque" (Smith 23). The purpose of a satire is to expose the follies of mankind, and in this novel Wells examines man's belief in his superiority to other animals. In an introduction to the novel written for his collected works, Wells wrote, "[T]his story was the response of an imaginative mind to the reminder that humanity is but animal, rough-hewn to a reasonable shape and in perpetual internal conflict between instinct and injunction" (qtd. in Smith 25). Man is constantly in conflict between his instincts and how he has been told to behave by his government and his religion. Similarly to how Victor Frankenstein created his Creature, Dr. Moreau has taken animals and transformed them into Beast Men, strange hybrid monsters. In the story, Wells suggests the struggles of man through the antics of the Beast Men and satirizes man's view of himself. In this way the monstrous is shown to be within mankind, as reflected in the behavior of Wells' monsters as well as within Dr. Moreau himself.

Taking advantage of the latest scientific techniques available at the end of the nineteenth century, Dr. Moreau has used vivisection (a controversial Victorian practice of operating on awake animals), grafting, blood transfusions, and behavior modification to make beasts into men. In creating these men, Dr. Moreau becomes their god. But they are a race of monsters, hybrids between man and beast that constantly revert to their original form. Like mankind, they are in conflict between what Wells termed "instinct and injunction." Their instincts tell them to hunt and kill like animals, while their injunctions or laws require them to live passively and worship Moreau.

T. H. Huxley, known as "Darwin's bulldog" for the ferocity with which he supported Charles Darwin's *On the Origin of Species* (1859), "derided the popular notion held by many in the late nineteenth century that humanity represented the pinnacle of evolutionary development. Instead, Huxley argued, there was no guarantee that humanity would either remain as it was or continue as the dominant species on the planet" (Wells x). Many Victorians believed that man was the apex of creation and that other animals had been placed on the earth to be used by man as he wants. H. G. Wells was a student of Huxley's, as is his protagonist in *The Island of Dr. Moreau*, Edward Prendick. Despite his experiences, Prendick retains an exaggeratedly idealist view of mankind and never understands the meaning of what he undergoes. At the end of the novel, the reader must go beyond Prendick's ideas to comprehend Wells' satirical portrayal of man's behavior. Mankind goes to great lengths to avoid confronting the truth of his existence as an animal and, like Prendick, resists this knowledge. In *The Island of Dr. Moreau*, Wells presents a satire of human belief in his superiority to the animals and his relationship with god and society.

As I will discuss later, the monster in H. G. Wells' *The Island of Dr. Moreau* is within each of us. However, when Erle C. Kenton directed the adaptation *Island of Lost Souls* (1932) he portrayed Dr. Moreau as a mad scientist, a monster from without who endangers the lives of those around him. Getting out of reach of Dr. Moreau meant freedom and safety for the Prendick character, as the monster is unconnected with the other characters. In Don Taylor's *The Island of Dr. Moreau* (1977) Dr. Moreau seeks to turn the hero into an animal, revealing himself as an even madder scientist than Kenton's Moreau and another monster from without, whose evil is not seen in any of the other characters or ourselves. In John Frankenheimer's *The Island of Dr. Moreau* (1996) the Beast Men are both worse than mankind and better than mankind. Although we may be connected in some ways with the monstrous in this film, the message in the movie never hits home with the same force that it does in Wells' novel.

The World at the Start of Wells' Novel
The Island of Dr. Moreau

This novel begins with an Introduction by Charles Edward Prendick, nephew of the narrator of the rest of the novel, who quite matter-of-factly sets forth what he knows about his uncle's experiences. As in the introductions to *She* and *Dracula*, the narrator, in this case Charles Prendick, attests to the truth of the manuscript he presents, along with what facts he has gathered that corroborate the story. His approach is scientific: he suggests that the island his uncle inhabited, known as the island of Dr. Moreau, must have been Noble's Isle, an ironic name, for the island has been put to very ignoble use by the scientist Moreau. The tone of the Introduction suggests an orderly world and provides a solid base for the tale of Edward Prendick, which is both grotesque and fabulous, with its shipwrecks, cannibalism, unknown islands, and hair-breadth escapes.

In the world of the narrator, Edward Prendick, life is horrific. The reader, like Prendick, has been thrown into this world without warning. Prendick recounts his situation with two other men on a lifeboat, with no supplies, after the loss of the ship *Lady Vain*.[18] Eventually the two other men convince Prendick that they must cannibalize someone by lots.[19] The two other men fight and fall out of the boat, which leads the narrator to laugh, "The laugh caught me suddenly like a thing from without" (3). Both of the men fighting to live, die — an ironic and lucky turn of events for Prendick. Such a non-sympathetic response from Prendick as a laugh does not feel as though it originates with him because it doesn't feel human. The laugh uncovers the fact that Prendick does not have complete control of himself. Humans believe they control their emotions and their fates, but they cannot. Prendick views mankind, and even himself, as more civilized than he reveals himself to be in his extreme situation. Yet conditions do not improve for Prendick. He is exposed to fewer and fewer of the civilized aspects of mankind. The need for self-preservation exists on a lifeboat, on Moreau's island, and in London as well.

There can be no normal world because the monstrous world created in this novel is a satiric version of our normal world. Prendick is thrown into a world from which he has no recourses, no way to remove himself. Like Prendick, and like the Beast Men as well, we see ourselves as more evolved than other animals, and seek to control our instincts and keep our animal nature at bay while struggling to adhere to the rules of our society. Although we may think we act for the benefit of society, we constantly interact with others who have selfish motivations.

The Monster Within and Without

The monstrous surrounds Prendick, but it is within him as well. Prendick is well-intentioned and cannot understand the results of peeling away the veneer of civilization. Like Prendick, man is always fragile, threatened, and unable to control his environment or himself. A pattern of precipitous escapes develops: saved from the wreck of the *Lady Vain*, Prendick is endangered on a lifeboat; saved by Montgomery's doctoring, he is set adrift once again by the captain of the *Ipecacuanha*; rescued once more by Montgomery, Prendick finds himself at the mercy of Dr. Moreau and the beasts who inhabit his island. Prendick cannot discover the meaning of what happens around him because he does not recognize the monstrous within each man.

Prendick finds himself surrounded by confusion and secrets. On board the *Ipecacuanha*, Prendick first sees a mysterious figure with aspects of the human and the animal. His black face combines coarse hair, bloodshot eyes, and big teeth. Prendick reflects, "I had never beheld such a repulsive and extraordinary face before" (9), but at the same time, the face feels familiar to him. One of Moreau's Beast Men, this creature combines aspects of the human with the animal. Like all mankind, the creature is a hybrid, combining some of man's civilizing exterior with the instincts of an animal. In *The Island of Dr.*

Moreau, the evil resides in all of mankind. The novel works to point out man's vanities and follies, in particular his sense of superiority. As Prendick thinks when things are at their worst, "An animal may be ferocious and cunning enough, but it takes a real man to tell a lie" (121). Man, unlike other animals, has the ability to deceive others as well as himself.

The Threat of the Monster

As manifested in *Frankenstein, Dr. Jekyll and Mr. Hyde, She,* and *Dracula,* the sense of the unnatural, diabolical, and monstrous is caused by hybridity, the existence of a creature which falls into no single category. Seeing the black-faced man while on Dr. Moreau's island, Prendick thinks, "He's unnatural... There's something about him ... it gives me a nasty little sensation ... it's a touch ... of the diabolical" (33). Prendick describes a group of similar creatures as "human beings with the strangest air about them of some familiar animal ... some now irresistible suggestion of a hog, a swinish taint, the unmistakable mark of the beast" (38). The "mark of the beast" is the sign of Satan mentioned in the Bible. The Beast Men have been created by Moreau, who acts like god in turning beasts into men. As God made man in his own image, so Moreau has made the Beast Men in his image in that he has left his own mark on them, the mark of Satan. The Beast Men appear monstrous but play no part in their own creation; the real monster is Moreau.

Fearing that he could be the subject of an experiment (as he believes that Moreau is turning men into animals), Prendick escapes from Moreau and Montgomery and discovers where the Beast Men live. There Prendick witnesses a satire of the Ten Commandments. Having run after Prendick, Dr. Moreau explains that he has used moral education to turn "suppressed sexuality into religious emotion" (70). The Beast Men begin by reading the list of prohibitions:

> Not to go on all Fours; *that* is the Law. Are we not Men?
> Not to suck up Drink; *that* is the Law. Are we not Men?
> Not to eat Flesh nor Fish; *that* is the Law. Are we not Men? [56].

Dr. Moreau has attempted to wean his Beast Men from the taste of flesh so that they will not seek to hunt each other or to kill him. Although the Beast Men believe they are living as men, most men do eat a varied diet of fish and meat. Dr. Moreau has established an arbitrary system of rules for his own benefit. This system is a satire of the Christian religion, the laws governing the behavior of most men in Great Britain during the nineteenth century.

The Beast Men then refer to the power of Moreau, parodying man's belief in God:

> *His* is the House of Pain.
> *His* is the Hand that makes.

His is the Hand that wounds.
His is the Hand that heals [56].

"None escape" is repeated many times, ostensibly concerning any transgression by the Beast Men, but also bringing Prendick's future into question and suggesting man's fate. Prendick finds himself unsure whether to put his trust with the Beast Men or with Moreau and Montgomery. When he returns to the compound, Prendick learns that the Beast Men are hybrids and "triumphs of vivisection" (68) that have been created by Moreau.

Moreau believes that pain "is such a little thing. A mind truly open to what science has to teach must see that it is a little thing. It may be that, save in this little planet, this speck of cosmic dust, invisible long before the nearest star could be attained — it may be, I say that nowhere else does this thing called pain occur" (71). Such an astrological view of pain reduces it to nothing. Moreau continues, "This store men and women set on pleasure and pain, Prendick, is the mark of the beast upon them, the mark of the beast from which they came" (72). Moreau attempts to force the animal out of his creatures and make them human through inflicting pain. He sees the human longing for pleasure and avoidance of pain to be the mark of the beast, of Satan. But man is a beast and, like all animals, seeks to avoid pain. Moreau alone claims to be beyond pain. Once he has finished with his experiments, Moreau releases the Beast Men onto the island. He has no practical use for them. In his dedication to pain for its own sake, and his experimentation without anesthetics and without purpose, Moreau anticipates the horrors of Dr. Josef Mengele at Auschwitz.

As he gets used to them, Prendick comes to see the Beast Men as people: "I would meet the Fox-Bear Woman's vulpine, shifty face, strangely human in its speculative cunning, and even imagine I had met it before in some city byway" (82). It seems like he has met them before, as Prendick, "trying hard to recall, how he differed from some really human yokel" (82). Prendick believes that the creatures had been happy as animals, but "now they stumbled in the shackles of humanity, lived in a fear that never died, fretted by a law they could not understand; their mock-human existence began in an agony, was one long internal struggle, one long dread of Moreau — and for what? It was the wantonness that stirred me" (95). What Prendick describes is the fate of all men in a universe without a benevolent god to oversee them.

The Nature of the Evil

Dr. Moreau is the real evil of the novel. The Beast Men have been created by Dr. Moreau, as Frankenstein's Creature was created by Dr. Frankenstein. Both Dr. Moreau and Dr. Frankenstein disavow responsibility for their creations, although Moreau attempts to give them rules to live by. Frankenstein's creature becomes evil, as he chooses how to live his life. The Beast Men never become responsible for themselves, as they are controlled by Dr. Moreau's medical skills and then by his system of law and religion. Their animal instincts are held in check by rules. Dr. Moreau keeps order with a whip and the fear the Beast Men have of returning to the House of Pain. As they age they revert to their animal selves, but as animals they are not responsible for their actions because they are governed not by choice or logic, as man would like to think he is governed, but by instinct.

Montgomery, the second in command, has gotten used to the experiments and believes that Prendick will as well. Montgomery is on the island because of an unnamed crime whereby he had to leave London and cannot return to England. Montgomery states, "I lost my head for ten minutes on a foggy night" (16).[20] Hating the experiments on the island, Montgomery has drowned his doubts in alcohol. He lives a twilight existence, not looking clearly at what is going on and preferring to close his eyes to the evil around him, as so many people do.

Dr. Moreau chooses to be a malevolent god to the Beast Men. He is not crazy, but scientifically logical and responsible for his own decisions. Prendick fantasizes about the goodness and civility of human nature because he fails to see the resemblance between Moreau's island and the rest of the world. Longing to get back "to the sweet and wholesome intercourse of men" (96), Prendick continues to differentiate man from beast rather than seeing man as an animal who is controlled by the civilizing effect of society. Yet the evil within Moreau is also within each man, and soon Prendick will lie to the Beast Men to save his own life.

The Monster Destroyed

Moreau's downfall on his island begins when the puma he is working on escapes from the enclosure, wrapped in its bandages. This parallels an incident in the novel remembered by Prendick where a dog escaped from Moreau's research in England. Whereas the escape of the dog caused public outcry against him and forced him to leave England, this incident leads to general excitement and disobedience among the Beast Men. Eventually the puma and Moreau kill each other. Learning that Moreau is dead, the creatures wonder if there is still law. Prendick attempts to keep order by saying that Moreau has changed his shape but is not dead. In this way Prendick parodies the divinity and resurrection of Jesus, becoming the third in the unholy trinity begun by Moreau and Montgomery. Like Moreau, Prendick lies to create an unnatural order on the island, but he does it to avoid pain and save his own life.

While Prendick tries to think how to get off the island, Montgomery doesn't feel it is any use. When Montgomery decides to share his alcohol supply with one of the Beast Men that he has trained as a servant, Prendick says to Montgomery, "You've made a beast of yourself. To the beasts you may go" (107). In Prendick's view, Montgomery has not behaved as a man but as "half akin to these Beast Folk, unfitted for human kindred" (109). Prendick plans to take his chances in the lifeboat again, but Montgomery destroys the boat. Montgomery is then killed by the Beast Men. Despite his experiences on Moreau's island, Prendick continues to revere man over beast; he does not see the link between man and the animals. Mankind, as an animal, developed alongside other animals and, despite the workings of civilization, frequently reverts to his animal origins.

Rather than become the ruler of the Beast Men like Moreau, Prendick, "sank to the position of a mere leader among my fellows" (118). Instead of taking over Moreau's role, he becomes one of them. Prendick goes to the huts of the Beast People and eats with and sleeps near them for ten months. During this time Prendick is particularly annoyed by the Ape Man, who repeats what he has said but uses the words wrongly. The Ape Man distinguishes between "big thinks," which he can't understand but admires, and "little thinks," or everyday thoughts. Rather than see this as an aping of man's search for meaning, the Ape Man's statements grate on Prendick because they are so human — they interfere with his idea of the gulf between the animal and the human. As time goes on he sees a change in the Beast Men, a growing reluctance to talk as they revert to their original animal beings. At last a dinghy comes into the bay, and Prendick escapes the island. Although Prendick has seen Moreau as a monster and Montgomery as an alcoholic escapist, Prendick cannot see the monstrous in himself and in every man. Prendick continues to make a distinction between the instincts of animals, which he views as evil, and what he sees as the civilization of mankind.

Normality Restored

When Prendick is picked up by a ship, his story is not believed, so he continues to lie, telling people that he remembers nothing for the year since he was on the *Lady Vain*. In returning to England, Prendick anticipates being shown "confidence and sympathy" by other men (131). Instead, he feels "a strange enhancement of the uncertainty and dread I had experienced during my stay upon the island.... I was almost as queer to men as I had been to the Beast People" (131). He finds that men lack the very qualities of understanding that he expected from them. His reason becomes separated from his feelings, so that although he knows that the people around him are "reasonable creatures" (131), he still shrinks from them. His mistake is thinking people are reasonable after he has seen Moreau dedicated to an *idée fixe*, Montgomery and the captain of the *Ipecacuanha* brought down by alcohol, and the original survivors of the

Lady Vain killing each other while trying to stay alive. Man lacks the positive qualities that the Prendicks of this world hope to find in society.

Prendick has a belief in the sanctity of humanity while he is on the island. When he returns to England, he is repulsed by people. Starting to see the animalistic within mankind, Prendick perceives this as a nightmare rather than a truth about mankind: "I could not persuade myself that the men and women I met were not also another, still passably human, Beast People, animals half-wrought into the outward image of human souls, and that they would presently begin to revert, to show first this bestial mark and then that" (131). The minister in a chapel seems like the Ape Man reciting the law; commuters on trains "seemed no more my fellow-creatures than dead bodies would be" (132). His feelings of himself change as well: "And even it seemed that I, too, was not a reasonable creature, but only an animal tormented with some strange disorder in the brain, that sent it to wander alone, like a sheep stricken with the gid" (132). Although he recognizes the beast in men, he fails to recognize that man is a beast. Like a sheep with the "gid," a disease, he needs help as well, and receives some help from "a mental specialist."

Like Gulliver retuned from life among the Houyhnhnm in *Gulliver's Travels* (1726, 1736), Prendick's tolerance for humanity has changed into disgust. All creatures, whether man or beast, have the capacity for evil. Some, like Moreau, give in to the evil and try to be a god. Some hide from reality like Montgomery. Becoming human does not make creatures moral; to be themselves is not evil, for they are what they are. The beasts see no difference in Prendick and themselves. Prendick continues to assert a belief in the distinction between men and animals in a manner that rejects his experiences on Moreau's island.

Prendick's story ends in what he sees as hope and solitude. He studies chemistry by day and astronomy by night "in the vast and eternal laws of matter, and not in the daily cares and sins and troubles of men, that whatever is more than animal within us must find its solace and its hope" (133). Like Moreau, he is comforted by a cold, distant view of mankind. Prendick cannot stand association with the human, as he sees the veneer of civilization as fragile and the animal constantly struggling to assert itself within each man. He continues to claim that men and women are "perfectly reasonable creatures, full of human desires and tender solicitude, emancipated from instinct and the slaves of no fantastic Law" (131). But, of course, they are not. Prendick has not accepted that man is an animal and subject to the same instincts whereby the natural constantly struggles to assert itself despite the influence of civilization and religion. He continues to believe in the lofty nature of man despite what he experienced on the island of Dr. Moreau. The reader must see beyond Prendick's statements to understand Wells' satire and to identify the true source of the monstrous as within each man.

Three major films have been made from H. G. Wells' novel: Erle Kenton's 1933 *Island of Lost Souls*, Don Taylor's 1977 *Island of Dr. Moreau*, and John

Frankenheimer's film of 1996. Because of their visual nature, all of the films emphasize the strangeness of the looks and behavior of the Beast Men. Consequently, the films become more like action films, and the satire of Wells' novel is downplayed. Two other major changes have been made from the novel. First, women are given a prominent place in the films. Women create a highly-charged sexual atmosphere by increasing the tension in the Prendick character's position on the island, as well as awakening the sexuality of the Beast Men. This background concern of the novel, evident only with the name of the ship, the Lady Vain, and the presence of a few female Beast Men, becomes central to the plot of the films. In all three movies the Prendick character falls in love with a woman he meets on the island. The other major change occurs in the earlier two of the films: Dr. Moreau is shown to be insane. Because he is not in control of himself, the evil he represents comes from outside. Although it is inside Dr. Moreau, that evil is unconnected with any of the other characters. Dr. Moreau is only a threat when Prendick is on the island; Prendick is able to return to a normal life at the end of the earlier two movies. Things become more complicated in Frankenheimer's film, as will be discussed.

Island of Lost Souls (1933)

DIR.: Erle C. Kenton. PERF.: Charles Laughton, Richard Arlen, Leila Hyams, Bela Lugosi. Universal, 1997. VHS.

The title change from *The Island of Dr. Moreau* to the *Island of Lost Souls* resonates throughout the film. Moreau and Montgomery work to change the nature of animals and have consequently become lost souls; and having been altered by them, the resulting beast men have lost their souls as well. Other name changes are less important and make little difference to the viewer. For example, Edward Prendick's name has been changed to Parker in this film, and the name of the ship that rescues Parker has been changed.

Erle Kenton's *Island of Lost Souls* was filmed during the heyday of horror films, a year later than *Frankenstein* (1931) and *Dracula* (1931). As in the earlier films, visual motifs are used throughout the movie to heighten drama. Images of doorways and windows constantly suggest imprisonment and concealment. The sense of imprisonment is compounded by the manner in which light comes through openings, illuminating boxes and causing the contrast of black and white stripes to form bars, suggesting that the humans are the caged animals while the Beast Men run free. Fog abounds at sea, while the atmosphere on the island is exotic: the characters walk through a lava cave to reach the interior of the island, and they inhabit an area lush with tropical flora, including Dr. Moreau's huge growths from his experiments in horticultural evolution. The

The evil of Dr. Moreau (Charles Laughton) spreads to Ouran (Hans Steinke) in Erle C. Kenton's *Island of Lost Souls* (1933) (Paramount/the Kobal Collection).

Beast Men themselves are a hirsute and frightening lot. In addition, the characters hide, spy on each other, and cast menacing shadows. Everywhere the island is filled with threats to safety.

The performance of Charles Laughton as Dr. Moreau is delightfully threatening. This was Laughton's first starring role in an American film, and his appearance registers with the viewer as unusual from the moment he comes onto the screen. He, like Montgomery, wears a splendid white suit and pith helmet — the uniform of the British in a tropical climate. His body, face, and voice are soft and almost feminine, bringing out the possibility that he is homosexual. His diabolical laughter indicates the evil within him. While his manner is indolent and reserved, his short hair, trimmed beard, and moustache reveal his love of control. All of his movements and statements are deliberate. Much about Moreau and his background remain a mystery. For example, as he cracks his whip to control the Beast Men, he explains that it is a hobby he picked up as a child in Australia. But his back story is never explained.

According to historian Don Smith, H. G. Wells objected to this film because of the portrayal of Moreau. Smith explains that in Wells' novel, "[Moreau] is a brilliant man who has become as ruthless as nature in an effort to guide and shape nature. He inflicts pain not for his own pleasure but for the sake of progress.... He is not a paranoid; he desires vindication, not so much because he believes in himself but because he believes in his ideas. He is not suffering from a god complex; he is not hungry for power" (28). Laughton, however, portrays Dr. Moreau as a megalomaniac who has become insane. He has become a monster who threatens the safety of the inhabitants of his island.

The World at the Start of Kenton's Film
The Island of Lost Souls

The first shot of this film, an establishing shot, shows the shore of Dr. Moreau's island. Waves crash against the sand on which the credits of the film are written, and the names are washed away and replaced by others, suggesting the inexorable quality of the sea in its ability to sweep away the names of the cast members, as well as anything that happens on Moreau's island. The action of the film begins with fog surrounding the shipwrecked Parker in a lifeboat being picked up by Montgomery, who is onboard the *Covena* with his cargo of animals. Montgomery takes the human and animal cargo to Moreau's island.

The viewer is immersed in mystery along with Parker. The camera rests on Parker as his face reflects the nightmarish aspects of his ordeal of exposure in the lifeboat. He looks insane; his face is covered with sweat, and he attempts to scream. But this threat is not a reality, as Parker soon wakes from his nightmare and realizes he has been rescued. Parker's feeling of dis-ease begins again, however, when Parker thanks Montgomery for taking care of him, and then asks if he is a doctor; Montgomery replies that at least he was "once upon a time." As Montgomery opens the door, Parker hears the sounds of dogs barking and wild animals howling — noises that are out of place onboard a ship. The drunken captain identifies the destination of their animal cargo as Moreau's island and adds that it stinks all over the South Pacific. Even the humans seem strange: Parker notices that the ears of Montgomery's servant M'ling are hairy and pointed, like animal ears.

From aboard the *Covena*, Parker cables his fiancée, Ruth Thomas, in Apia, Samoa, that he had been picked up from the lifeboat. But the captain sends Parker ashore on Moreau's island rather than taking him to Samoa with the ship. The film cuts back and forth between Parker's movements from the *Covena* to Moreau's island, and his fiancée's search for Parker once the *Covena* arrives in Samoa without him. The world that Ruth inhabits provides a sense of the normal world in this film. Although Samoa sounds like the other side of the world, Ruth brings her no-nonsense approach to finding and retrieving Parker. She talks to the captain of the *Covena* when he arrives, reports him to the American Counsel, and hires Captain Donohue to help her search for Parker. She travels in Captain Donohue's ship to rescue Parker from Moreau's island and bring him back to society. Like Frankenstein's fiancée in the 1931 film, Ruth is an active woman who involves herself in looking out for her man.

The Monster Within and Without

Early in the film Moreau is stated to be evil and unlike anyone else. Aboard the *Covena,* Montgomery defends the doctor, stating that Moreau is a brilliant scientist. The captain replies that he is a "blackmailing, grave-robbing ghoul." The captain thinks that Moreau is a traditional kind of monster; instead, Moreau is a new kind of monster. Moreau receives wild animals by whatever means he has arranged, and for all we know it may involve blackmail, but he is not a "grave-robbing ghoul." He is a brilliant scientist, as Montgomery claims, but he is also insane. His work involves the speeding up of evolution, as he believes that all forms of animal evolution tend towards the human. But this involves a great deal of physical pain and eventually intense psychic pain for the creatures involved. As in the novel, his research serves no benefit for mankind. Moreau is ultimately alone as a creative scientist and monster.

Once Parker lands on Moreau's Island, Moreau immediately makes him part of a psychological experiment, unbeknownst to Parker. Instead of allowing Parker to leave the island, Moreau invites him to his house so that the doctor can observe a female's reaction to him. Moreau wants to see if his female panther creation, Lota, will react as a human female to a young man, and whether she is capable of having children. Lota is exotic and sexy looking, with heavily made-up eyes and a skimpy, tropical outfit. Her movements are feline, and she keeps her hands curled, hiding the claws at the ends of her fingers. Parker is human in the film; he is driven to kiss Lota and also tell her that he is in love with someone else. As Lota and Parker talk, they sit by a pool filled with water which shows their reflections. The image in the pool is a metaphor for their relationship. Although they apparently conduct a straightforward flirtation between a man and a woman, the truth is only a reflection of that reality, and all is not as it seems.

Moreau appears merely strange at first, but there is a definite menace beneath his calm surface. While Parker talks with Lota, Moreau is hidden, listening to their conversation. Explaining his work to Parker, Moreau reveals that it took infinite patience to make the Beast People talk. He remarks, "One day I will create a woman and it will be easier," insinuating that he has not created a female Beast Person. He enjoys his own joke at the expense of women and laughs. His joke pokes fun at the thought that women talk too much, but also has a more sinister meaning, as he misleads Parker as to Lota's origins. Moreau wants to keep Parker on the island in order to continue his experiment involving Parker and Lota. While telling Parker that he can depart at any time,

Dr. Moreau (Charles Laughton) attempts to discover why Lota, the Panther Woman (Kathleen Burke), cannot sustain her human appearance in Erle C. Kenton's *Island of Lost Souls* (1933) (Paramount/the Kobal Collection).

Moreau destroys his ship so that Parker cannot leave the island. He then walks Parker towards the ship, and when Parker realizes that it is sunk, Moreau smirks and winks at Montgomery, revealing his part in the destruction. His behavior is sneaky and unsettling.

Because Parker does not know Lota's true nature as a Beast Woman, Moreau enjoys his superior knowledge as well as his accomplishment. When Moreau, while making tea, explains to Parker that Lota is one of his creations, Parker's response is to hit Moreau. The making of tea, the most civilized of activities, contrasts with the physicality of Parker and Moreau's "professional" activities. Parker is not a talker, but has a physical and primitive response when upset. This instinctive element of Parker's humanity indicates the interconnection between man and the beasts.

Moreau has created laws for the Beast Men, like not eating flesh, so that he can control their behavior. While stating the laws, followed by the question, "Are we not men?" the Beast Men appear to be participating in a religious ceremony; but this ceremony has been established by Moreau. Religion is shown to be "the opiate of the [Beast] people," imposed by Moreau in order to control his creations, to mask their instincts with rules and to impose restraint on their actions. Instincts in themselves are not evil, but Moreau tampering with living creatures *is* evil.

In Wells' novel, religion was able to mask the sexuality of the Beast Men, but not in Kenton's film. The Beast Men are sexually charged, which is first seen in their reaction to Lota and then even more so when Ruth, Parker's fiancée, reaches the island. She is blonde and wearing light-colored clothes, as opposed to Lota. While Ruth sleeps in her slip, one of the Beast Men, Ouran, watches her and then finds a way to open the bars on the window and come into her room. Moreau manipulates the sexuality of Lota and Ouran in order to further his experimentation. The actions of the Beast Men and Lota bring up the taint of interspecies sexuality, infidelity, and rape. Parker's attraction to Lota could lead to his infidelity to Ruth, while Ouran's interest in Ruth could lead to rape. If Ouran rapes Ruth it would serve Moreau's purposes just as well as encouraging the relationship between Parker and Lota. Moreau commits evil in creating the Beast People and consequently encourages them to take part in evil.

The Threat of the Monster

In *Island of Lost Souls* all of the evil starts with Moreau and radiates outward. The drunken captain of the *Covena* (and the subsequent drinking of Captain Donohue, who comes with Ruth to rescue Parker), the strange Beast Men, Lota's love for Parker, and Ouran's lust for Ruth all stem from the machinations of Dr. Moreau. Moreau brings out the worst in the people around him, and in tampering with nature, he creates something unnatural. Once off the island, the human characters will be safe.

In the novel *The Island of Dr. Moreau*, Dr. Moreau is the monster; but there is also the satiric realization of mankind's link with other animals. Even back in civilization, Prendick continues to see the bestial curled up within himself and others, waiting to come out. The potential is always there for monstrous behavior. Prendick sees the connection between man and beast with his own eyes but cannot allow himself to admit the monstrous within mankind. In *Island of Lost Souls*, Dr. Moreau is the main monster. While the Beast Men appear to be the monsters on this island, they are more like secondary monsters. They are frightening in appearance because they are unusual and not recognizable as either human or animal, but they are not responsible for their own behavior.

The Nature of the Evil

When isolated from the restraints of society, Moreau has allowed his own evil to run wild by creating the Beast Men. But he goes beyond that to order a Beast Man to rape Ruth and murder Captain Donohue. The Beast Men are initially kept under control by Moreau, but when they learn that Moreau does not obey the law, the Beast Men are given an impetus to follow their instincts and disregard the law as well. The Beast Men completely lose their layer of civilization when Moreau gives the order to commit murder, and Moreau's circle of evil increases.

Moreau asks Parker, "Do you know what it feels like to feel like god?" Like Frankenstein in the 1931 movie, Moreau is a mad scientist who compares himself to god. Yet Moreau is not completely successful as a creator, for his creatures do not retain their new shape. When Moreau states that he feels beaten by the stubborn beast flesh that keeps coming back, Lota starts to cry. Moreau laughs at the thought that he can use pain to rid her of her returning animal shape, and that Parker, who is already attracted to her, will continue to want her. Moreau realizes he has triumphed with Lota because she has human emotions. Animals, after all, do not cry.

Lota is a complicated character, and seeing her thoughts and emotions creates sympathy for her in the viewer. She is drawn to Parker, and is hurt at his rejection of her. Lota even goes beyond human behavior. She attacks one of the Beast Men as she, Parker, Montgomery, and Ruth attempt to escape the island, and sacrifices herself for the man she loves. Lota possesses what is best in mankind — love and devotion. Her behavior is exemplary and contrasts with the evil selfishness of Moreau.

The Monster Destroyed

When Captain Donohue is killed by Ouran, the Beast Men realize that all men can die. Ironically, Moreau orders the Beast Man to disobey the law, which leads to his own downfall. The Beast Men walk towards Moreau, saying, "Not Men. Not Beasts. Things." They become aware of their hybrid nature as something that is inexplicable. They take Dr. Moreau to his own House of Pain, crowding around him with scalpels in their hands while he screams. In subjecting him to the same torture which he used on them, the Beast Men provide him with a fitting end.

Montgomery has been Moreau's assistant, but when he learns of the threat to Ruth, Montgomery works to help Parker and Ruth escape from the island. By changing sides, Montgomery also isolates Moreau and suggests his singular situation. Even more than having created the Beast Men, having successfully ordered a murder, Moreau is outside of the pale of morality.

Normality Restored

With Moreau destroyed, the threat of the monstrous is over. The last scene of the film shows Montgomery, Parker, and Ruth in a row boat heading towards the ship that will take them back to civilization. Montgomery lights a pipe and says, "Don't look back." They are off the island and consequently safe and in a normal environment. The flame from the lighter that Montgomery has is small and controlled, providing a contrast with the fires raging on the island that will eventually destroy all trace of the monstrous.

On Moreau's island the primitivism of the island is equated with sexuality. At the end the island goes up in flames, and the tamed passion of the engaged couple, Parker and Ruth, survives. The threat of interspecies sexuality between Lota and Parker is averted, as well as the attempted rape of Ruth by Ouran. Back on the mainland, Parker, Ruth, and even Montgomery will be able to live normal lives. Away from the evil influence of Moreau they can marry and reproduce in the conventional manner.

The Island of Dr. Moreau (1977)

DIR.: Don Taylor. PERF.: Burt Lancaster, Michael York, Nigel Davenport, Barbara Carrera. MGM, 2001. DVD.

In each of the works under discussion in this chapter, Dr. Moreau has removed himself from England to an island in order to practice science in his own fashion, away from any laws or interference from others. The science that Dr. Moreau uses changes to keep up with the times when the films were made. In H. G. Wells' novel, Dr. Moreau is a vivisectionist, someone who performs painful and untried operations on living animals. In the 1933 film he is shown as a geneticist, experimenting with evolutionary ideas. By 1977 Dr. Moreau, as shown in Don Taylor's film, is involved with cell research. This progression shows the cultural evolution of science but does not make a real difference in the character of Moreau. But the science in itself is not the evil; the evil is how science is used. In Wells' novel, Moreau experiments with no ultimate goal and develops a way of life for his Beast Men that satirizes human society. Kenton's film, *Island of Lost Souls*, presents Moreau as a mad scientist who experiments on the Prendick character psychologically. Moreau's evil comes from within himself and is not shared by any of the other characters. Taylor's film shows Dr. Moreau tampering physically with a human being as well as with animals. Despite the fact that man is another animal on the evolution chart, this willingness to experiment on a human being marks Dr. Moreau as even more evil than the earlier Dr. Moreaus. Taylor's Dr. Moreau is a mad scientist, alone in his insanity and isolated on his island.

For H. G. Wells, the traits of all his characters exist in everyone. Wells saw every person as potentially wanting to play god, like Moreau, and also having the ability to stand back and allow evil to happen, like Montgomery, Moreau's assistant. Like Prendick, we are confronted by something we don't understand and at times don't know where to turn for help. By changing the central characters of the work even slightly, the film adaptations change the meaning of the film. Taylor's movie, like Kenton's before it, shows evil as emanating from Dr. Moreau, who uses science for his own purposes. In Don Taylor's film, Dr. Moreau is not at all like us, but he is a threat to our well-being. He is an evil force that could attack us and must be stopped, rather than a representative of part of ourselves or our society.

Montgomery has removed himself emotionally from the human race. In all of the works, Montgomery relies on alcohol to keep his emotions numb; however, his moral substance is dramatically changed in the different approaches. In the novel, Montgomery is killed while giving alcohol to the Beast Men; he seeks his own death rather than return to jail in England. In the 1933 film Montgomery helps the Prendick character escape and leaves the island with him. In Taylor's 1977 picture he is killed by Dr. Moreau as he tries to help Braddock. Montgomery is a better person in Taylor's film than in the other movies and less connected with Moreau, which makes Moreau even more alone in his evilness.

A monster who seems normal and rational: Dr. Moreau (Burt Lancaster) in Don Taylor's *The Island of Dr. Moreau* (1977) (A.I.P./the Kobal Collection).

The Prendick character (named Braddock in Taylor's film) is always played as something of an Everyman character, someone like everyone else. The fact that his name changes from film to film points to the difficulty of pronouncing "Prendick," the name H. G. Wells gave him, and the fact that what he is called doesn't matter. He doesn't learn or change over the course of the films. Andrew Braddock, the Prendick character in Taylor's 1977 movie is a little different than the other Prendick characters in that he, like Montgomery, is a better person than in the novel. Braddock does not fight in the lifeboat in Taylor's film. He sees a clear difference between man and beast and does not see the animal in the human, as

Wells' character does. There is something optimistic, rather than satiric, about Taylor's film, and this tone is brought out by the characters of Montgomery and Braddock. In this movie, mankind is capable of acting with dignity and kindness.

The World at the Start of Taylor's Film
The Island of Dr. Moreau

Andrew Braddock is representative of what is best in the normal world, and he brings something of the civilization of England with him wherever he goes. Even in a lifeboat or marooned on a tropical island, where life is precarious, Braddock remains a compassionate and kind man. Inside the lifeboat of the *Lady Vain*, Braddock enlists the aid of the other survivor to toss a dead body overboard. The two survivors arrive at an island, and Andrew Braddock goes to look for water while his fellow passenger rests in the shade. The island looks lush and beautiful, but mysteries abound. A shadow falls over the resting man; he screams and is dragged off through the jungle. While looking for water, Braddock feels someone looking at him, and then he is chased. As he runs for his life, Braddock falls into a large, camouflaged hole in the ground — an animal trap. This is the first time in the film that Braddock finds himself in the position of an animal rather than a man, and the first indication that the place of man and beast is confused on Moreau's island.

After falling into the trap, Braddock awakes in a bed to find Montgomery taking care of him. Montgomery lies to him and tells him his companion died of thirst and exposure, and assures him, "You're the lucky one." Montgomery helps Braddock by giving him food and shelter, but the lie about the fate of the other man is disconcerting; the viewer wonders why Montgomery lies. Like Braddock, the viewer is unsure of what is happening on the island. When Braddock becomes uneasy about the island, Montgomery attempts to reassure him by saying that he has gotten used to what happens on the island and states that Braddock will as well — not a very satisfying response. Taylor's film is more extreme in its portrayal of characters than Wells' novel or the earlier film: Braddock and Montgomery are better people than in the novel, while Moreau is worse.

Meeting Dr. Moreau, Braddock is confused by his reiterated statement, "It's truly amazing how the flesh reasserts itself." Braddock has difficulty understanding the context for Moreau's remarks. Having heard the sounds of animals, Braddock asks what kinds of animals there are on the island, and Moreau answers, with an uneasy laugh, "All kinds." Braddock and Moreau talk past each other: Braddock expects to be told of the tropical inhabitants of the jungle while Moreau hints of the odd nature of the humanimals he has created. Moreau appears enigmatic to Braddock but not yet evil.

The most intriguing person on the island is a beautiful young woman named Maria who walks an ocelot on a leash. Speaking of Maria to Braddock, Montgomery states, "That belongs to Moreau." Montgomery's statement that Moreau owns Maria suggests a sexual relationship between Moreau and Maria. Moreau explains that he brought Maria to the island when she was eleven after buying her in Panama City for the price of a dozen eggs. Despite Moreau's statement, Maria's origins remain unsettled. In Wells' novel there is no female character with a name; in *Island of Lost Souls* the woman Lota was created by Dr. Moreau. The viewer is left to wonder about Maria's origins and her relationship with Moreau.

Maria's compatibility with the ocelot hints at the possibility that they are sisters under the skin. Braddock tries to hold the cat, but it runs off into the jungle with Maria's handkerchief attached to the leash. She ends up finding the cat, while he finds the handkerchief. The scene is symbolic of his relationship with Maria in that Braddock retrieves and relates to the civilized and feminine part of Maria, her handkerchief, but does not connect with her feline attributes. Braddock never asks for more information about Maria from either Maria herself or Moreau. He keeps himself willfully ignorant of her situation for fear of what he might find.

Love between young people is natural and normal in the world, even in the midst of what is uncertain and deviant, and Taylor's film becomes a love story as well as a horror movie. Maria initiates a sexual relationship with Braddock, leaving Moreau's dinner table and going to Braddock's second floor bedroom. The sexual relationship, filmed romantically, is certainly normal for the late 1970s, when the film was made. However, the potential for horror is never far away. While Maria is with Braddock, the camera pans out of Braddock's window and down to the courtyard below to reveal Dr. Moreau looking up at Braddock's room, unseen by them. The viewer is left to wonder if Moreau has sent Maria to Braddock or if Moreau is jealous. Moreau's attitude toward Maria and Braddock becomes another mystery of the island. The developing love between a handsome young man and a beautiful young woman, however, is the only normal thing that has happened so far in the film.

The Monster Within and Without

By contrasting Moreau and Braddock's views of life, Moreau is shown to be a monster who is dissimilar from everyone else. Moreau seeks scientific answers for no definable purpose. Explaining his work on cells to Braddock, Moreau poses such questions as, "How does a cell become enslaved to a form? How can we change that destiny?" Braddock responds, "Should we?" Unlike Moreau, Braddock is concerned with the moral rather than the scientific approach. Braddock, a mechanic who works with machines, has a humane and

They look like a perfect couple, but is she completely human? Andrew Braddock (Michael York) and Maria (Barbara Carrera) in Don Taylor's *The Island of Dr. Moreau* (1977) (A.I.P./the Kobal Collection).

cautionary attitude towards living creatures that contrasts with the approach of Moreau.

For much of the early part of the film, Braddock does not know the nature of Moreau's experiments. When Braddock questions him about the inhabitants of the island, Moreau never answers directly. Yet Braddock becomes suspicious of Moreau's research. When Braddock sees that the servant M'Ling looks facially heavier and hairier than he did previously, Braddock asks Moreau, "What have you done to him?" Moreau replies that he is trying to help M'Ling, who is "a special kind of human being." Braddock is left to assume that Moreau is turning humans into animals.

Having been chased by creatures through the jungle once again, Braddock screams, "What were they?" Not receiving a satisfactory answer, he explores the buildings in the compound and finds cages of animals. In one room an animal, now partly human, is awake and strapped to an operating table. Braddock confronts Moreau, "What in the name of God are you doing here?" But, of course, Dr. Moreau is not operating "in the name of God." He has made himself into a god. When Moreau explains that he is making a bear into a human being, Braddock responds, "God almighty.... Why?" Moreau has several answers, including that he is seeking to control heredity, to end deformities, to avoid pain, and that the possibilities of good coming from his experiments are endless. Moreau states that his work is being used for the benefit of humanity; however, Moreau supplies no evidence that any benefits have emerged from his research. Nothing becomes of the endless possibilities Moreau claims to have unearthed. Once the humanimals are created, they are used as servants or set loose on the island. The animals suffer during the operations, and the humanimals often become murderous as they revert to their animal origins. They are a threat to the humans on the island, as they are unnatural creatures who are neither completely animal nor completely human. They are not caged like dangerous animals, nor are they in their natural habitats. Consequently, they are an outside threat, but not an evil. They cannot, after all, be blamed for acting like animals even when they look like monsters.

The monster of the film is Dr. Moreau. He is a threat to everyone on the island and will destroy anyone who questions his research efforts. The tag line for Don Taylor's 1977 film is, "The Doctor Is In-SANE!" For the first half of the movie, Burt Lancaster, as Dr. Moreau, seems a model of reason, as he is calm and deliberate in his actions. He has none of the insidious menace shown by Charles Laughton as Dr. Moreau. Moreau's behavior radically changes midway through the film, however, when he begins experimentation on Andrew Braddock himself, turning Braddock from a man into an animal. The monstrousness of Dr. Moreau indicates that the evil on the island comes from Moreau himself, a force separate from the normal world. His insanity suggests his individuation.

Braddock feels a kinship with the humanimals on the island and seeks to bring out their best rather than suppress and control their worst instincts. Braddock himself is kind to others and is induced to violence only to spare pain to another or to save his life. Although Braddock recognizes the human in the humanimals, Moreau sees the animal within Braddock. For Moreau, Braddock is just another animal for experimentation. The evil shown in this film does not come from any characteristic common to mankind or animalkind or society. Only Moreau, someone who takes control of the lives of others, is the source of evil.

The Threat of the Monster

Although Moreau only shows himself to be a monster half-way through the movie, it is clear he has been a monster his entire scientific life. Moreau keeps strict control over the behavior of the humanimals, both in his laboratory and on the island; he reacts with violence and anger if his desires are countered. When Moreau shows a bear to the Bearman, the Bearman responds positively. Moreau beats him because he is frustrated that the Bearman identifies with the animal rather than the human. The humanimals outside of the human compound inhabit a cave where they live by the laws that have been given them by Moreau. The laws, something like the ten commandments, have been designed to keep the humans safe by keeping the humanimals from hunting, from shedding blood, and from eating the flesh of another animal. The laws go against the instincts of the animals, as they are required to drink like men, to walk like men, and to eat a vegetarian diet. If any humanimals break the law, they must return to the House of Pain where Moreau will experiment on them further in order to correct them, to make them like he wants them to be.

Because of his optimistic view of the world, Braddock cannot understand the need for this system of laws. He believes the humanimals are human enough for those things which mankind exemplifies in his world view: "pity, consideration, and feelings." Moreau replies that the humanimals are touched with the noble virtues: "rage, anger, hatred, homicidal hatred." His ironic response indicates that Moreau's opinion of mankind is much bleaker than Braddock's. Braddock looks upon the positive traits that should be encouraged, while Moreau sees the negative traits that need to be controlled. When Braddock comes upon one of the humanimals that has broken the law, the creature begs him for death rather than to be returned to the House of Pain. Braddock acts with compassion and pity by shooting the creature, but Braddock has broken the law, and his act of mercy has repercussions.

The incident with Braddock leads the humanimals to question what they have been told. They see that one of the masters has broken the law. One yells in defiance of the laws, "Better an animal, strong, proud." One says, "The human law is not ours, but his." The Sayer of the Law believes in the law: "It is our law. Are we not men?" But this time he gets no response from the other creatures. The humanimals are under a system of government which is similar to that within human society. They do not understand the hypocrisy of those they consider their masters. Seeing the masters break the rules, the humanimals become convinced that they do not have to act as men but can act on their own instincts. Their system of government, artificially imposed from above, falls apart at a contradiction.

Man, in Taylor's film, has a capacity for both great evil and great good. The natural goodness of man is evident in Montgomery and Braddock, while the evil is evident in the insane behavior of Moreau. The humanimals, although they become threatening, are not responsible for their behavior. Those that have "homicidal hatred," as Moreau states, are aware of what Moreau has done to them in the House of Pain. Indeed, it is under the influence of Moreau's tampering with him that Braddock comes to show "homicidal hatred." Mankind may be capable of the evil of Moreau or the murderous anger shown briefly by Braddock, but these are rare states in any but the insane and not a normal part of human behavior.

The Nature of the Evil

Moreau thinks the evil is the obdurate flesh in the case of the humanimals—or in the case of Braddock, the obdurate mind. But the real evil is Moreau, who believes he can change and control man and beast. In an attempt to get rid of Braddock and do research, Moreau devises an experiment to examine the line between the human and the animal. In a way, Moreau punishes Braddock for disobeying his laws by sending him to the House of Pain. Moreau surprises Braddock with an injection, saying, "I hope you will forgive me. You will become an animal and you will bring that back to me." The science of Moreau suggests a clear delineation between man and beast, and he plans to turn Braddock from a man into an animal. Braddock wakes up with heavy-looking facial features and screams at Moreau, "What are you doing to me you bastard? Let me go."

Moreau anticipates having access to the brain of an animal through Braddock. Seeking to understand how an animal thinks, Moreau questions Braddock to see if he has lost control of his human aspect, if Braddock has crossed the barrier from human to animal. In response, Braddock screams at him, "You're the animal." For Braddock, to be human is to be kind and compassionate, which Moreau is not. In an attempt to force Braddock to behave like an animal, Moreau brings Braddock live rodents to eat after he hasn't eaten in two days. Braddock refuses to eat like an animal and starts to tell Moreau the story of his life. He announces in triumph, "I remember it all," although Braddock frequently has trouble retrieving words. Frustrated by Braddock's ability to hold onto the human, Moreau replies, "Damn you. Let go, let go." Moreau seeks to know more about the failure of his experiments by learning the difference between man and animal through the inside of Braddock's mind as it becomes an animal mind. But Braddock refuses to go along with Moreau; Braddock holds onto his humanity. Moreau is sadistic and is playing god by interfering with the species of animals, as well as the human within Braddock.

Wells wrote his novel to explore the connection between the species, positing that man is just one of many animals on earth and does not have dominion over the other species. Moreau states in this film, "In order to study nature, you must become as remorseless as nature." Nature, in the form of dehydration and exposure at sea, kills one man on the lifeboat. Braddock kills out of pity and in order to save his own life. On the other hand, Dr. Moreau has become more remorseless than nature in his desire to act as god. He has tortured and killed the humanimals, tortured Braddock, and shot Montgomery (who attempted to rescue Braddock from Moreau's experiment). Moreau kills so that his inhumane experiments will not be stopped, so that he can continue to behave selfishly.

The Monster Destroyed

Looking at the dead body of Montgomery, the Sayer of the Law sees Moreau's hypocrisy. He does not understand how Moreau could tell the humanimals not to kill while he kills. When the humanimals confront Moreau with his hypocrisy, Moreau starts whipping them. As they surround him, Moreau justifies himself by saying, "I created you." Like Dr. Frankenstein, he believes that because he created something, he also has the right to destroy it. Instead, the humanimals kill Moreau, and then they are frightened by their action. Looking at the blood on his hands, the Sayer of the Law says, "We have killed, we have broken the law." Although the Sayer of the Law believes that the humanimals must have laws, the others insist, "No more laws." They seek destruction and anarchy.

Even as he dies, Moreau does not repent. Seeing Braddock, Moreau's last words before death are, "You are an animal." After being released from his cage by Maria, Braddock takes a lesson from Moreau on how to stay alive and announces to the humanimals, "He is not dead. You cannot kill Moreau. He sees you now, but you cannot see him. Fear him. Obey his law." Braddock lies in order to save Maria and himself. He then hoists up the body of Moreau, using a rope under his arms; but it doesn't take long for the humanimals to see through this ploy. They continue to attack the compound, smashing everything and setting it on fire. They destroy and open the pens to set wild animals loose.

Braddock commits murder as an act of self–preservation and to protect Maria. One humanimal comes after them as they attempt to escape in the lifeboat, and they fight and kill him. Once again Braddock has killed, but this time to save their lives. His behavior, like Montgomery's attempting to save him, contrasts with the evil of Moreau. Moreau behaves like a monster. He causes fear and destruction that is of no benefit to anyone and harmful to all.

Normality Restored

As Maria and Braddock make their way away from the island, the screen shows the dead Moreau, suspended before his burning and collapsing compound. The humanimals will revert to their natural form. Moreau's reign is over, and Braddock, with his compassion and kindness, has survived. Braddock is safer in the lifeboat, adrift in the ocean, than on Dr. Moreau's island.

The camera shows the boat floating on the water, just as at the start of the film — Taylor's film begins and ends in the lifeboat of the *Lady Vain*, a tiny spot in a seemingly endless expanse of water. We don't yet know the fate of Braddock and Maria. Braddock wakes up, slowly lifting his head to show the viewer his face and hands, normal and human once again. He has no superfluous flesh or animal hair. The human flesh has reasserted itself. Seeing a ship in the distance, Braddock yells for help. Maria is looking away, but she slowly turns her head toward the camera. The viewer wonders if she has started to revert to being an animal or if she was always human. Maria's face is shown for only a few seconds: it is tear-stained, showing her humanity, since animals do not cry.

According to one scholar, Don Taylor's *The Island of Dr. Moreau* was shot with alternate endings. In one ending, Maria lifts up her head and shows that she has reverted to being a panther. This would indicate that she was one of Moreau's creations—a successful creation that Moreau passed off as human. Moreau must have enjoyed the thought of Braddock's relationship with her and wondered, as Moreau does in the earlier film directed by Kenton, if she can procreate. Maria's human face in the version I saw indicates that Moreau did adopt her as a child, indicating that he was once a kind person but that somehow over the years on the island he changed. But without any indication of why or when he changed, we cannot know where his evil came from.[21] Maria's human face indicates the triumph of the young couple over the insanity and inhumanity of Moreau. Away from the island, with Moreau dead, the world can return to normality until the next monster appears.

The Island of Dr. Moreau (1996)

DIR.: John Frankenheimer. PERF.: David Thewlis, Fairuza Balk, Ron Perlman, Marlon Brando, Val Kilmer. New Line Home Video, 1997. DVD.

The novel *The Island of Dr. Moreau* is a satire that connects Prendick with all mankind, and connects mankind with other animals. The evil within Dr.

Moreau is not limited to him but evident elsewhere. In the 1933 film *Island of Lost Souls*, there is no satire or lesson to be learned. The island inhabited by the insane Dr. Moreau becomes a nightmare from which the Prendick character must escape. Once off the island he and his fiancée will have a new life unthreatened by the monster, Dr. Moreau. In Don Taylor's 1977 film the Prendick character also escapes the island at the end, this time in the company of Moreau's adopted daughter, and in doing so they are free of the monster and the monstrous. Like the novel, the 1996 film finds more connections between life on and off the island. Back in civilization, Edward Douglas, as the Prendick character is called in Frankenheimer's 1996 film, is still haunted by his experience. Although the movie attempts to make connections between the Beast People and ordinary people, they are never fully developed. Ultimately the film does not present a clear and consistent point of view from which an analysis of its world, or what it wants to say about that world, can be made. However, the presentation of the more passive of the Beast Men is haunting.

John Frankenheimer's 1996 *The Island of Dr. Moreau* has some excellent aspects, as well as some failings. The movie was nominated for awards by the Academy of Science Fiction, Fantasy & Horror Films in the categories of Best

A serious Nobel Prize–winning scientist? Dr. Moreau (Marlon Brando) in John Frankenheimer's *The Island of Dr. Moreau* (1996) (New Line/the Kobal Collection).

Science Fiction Film and Best Make-Up, but failed to win. It was also nominated for several Razzie Awards for Worst Supporting Actor, Worst Director, and Worst Screenplay; Marlon Brando won the Worst Supporting Actor award, as well as the Worst Screen Couple award with that "Darn Dwarf." As shown by these nominations and awards, the film has both vociferous supporters and detractors. Although some aspects of the movie excite the viewer, most of the film suggests the unrealized potential of the actors and material. The picture had difficulties during production, which may explain the lack of a unifying underlying theme. The original director, Richard Stanley, was fired after four days of shooting, and John Frankenheimer was hired to replace him. Franken-heimer stated, "When I came on the film it was obvious that the screenplay was weak. No one seemed to know what kind of film they wanted: science fiction, a parody, a tale of horror, a condemnation of science fiction?" (Pratley 266). Frankenheimer stated that he decided to make a moral fable after rereading the novel; however, the moral is not ultimately clear.

The film is overwhelmed by its stars and special effects. Marlon Brando's Dr. Moreau is similar to the character he played in *Apocalypse Now* (1979); he is a cultured man who behaves in unusual ways but never seems insane, much as in the novel. He treats the Beast Men as his children and reigns over them like a god. Val Kilmer's Montgomery, on the other hand, is unpredictable and difficult to understand. Since his actions lack motivation, he appears to have been corrupted by the influence of Moreau and to share Moreau's goals. The Beast Men are shown as both better and worse than in the other adaptations. They fall into two extremes of behavior — namely, those who are pacific and those who are aggressive. Aissa, the female created by Moreau, is seemingly without fault, as Moreau intended her to be. However, many of the Beast Men engage in madness and mayhem rendered in special effects that overwhelm the larger meaning or point of view of the film. The overall message meant to be conveyed by the movie is never comprehensive, yet the strands that do come together reveal that evil, like goodness, comes from within. All people contain the possibility of behaving like monsters and rely on outside agencies, such as religion or even the United Nations, to control their behavior.

The World at the Start of Frankenheimer's Film
The Island of Dr. Moreau

The first scene of Frankenheimer's film reveals many of the difficulties in attempting to interpret the movie as a whole. At the start of the film Edward Douglas, who was heading towards a peace-keeping mission for the United Nations when his plane crashed, is in a lifeboat in the midst of the South Pacific Ocean. As Douglas watches, the two other men in the lifeboat begin to fight over the last thermos of water. He watches them tumble into the water and comments in voiceover, "They fought like beasts, not men." This is the first mention of the thought that beasts are prone to violence while men are not, although man is certainly shown to be just as capable of violence in this film. As one man in the water tries to get back into the lifeboat, Douglas hits him with an oar until he is knocked back into the ocean to become food for a shark. Later in the film, Montgomery comments that for someone working on a peace settlement, there was a lot of blood in the raft. In his backhanded way, Montgomery suggests that Douglas is a murderer. Douglas might have taken a chance and taken this man back on the lifeboat; but on the other hand, the man had tried to kill someone else in the lifeboat and might have tried to kill Douglas as well. However, it is not clear what the viewer is to think of Douglas; what is apparent is that Douglas, while thinking ill of the behavior of others, acted in his own self-interest.

In no previous rendition of *The Island of Dr. Moreau* is a reason given for why Prendick is on the *Lady Vain* to begin with. By making him a peace-keeper for the UN, this film hints at his moral superiority in that he is actively engaged in something to help mankind. Although Douglas comments on the violence as being "like beasts," he also engages in violence. He clearly believes that men are different from animals, yet his action in the lifeboat is more violent than that engaged in by the other Prendick characters in the novel or other films. This ambiguity of killing someone and saying beasts are violent leaves the viewer to wonder how to react: the presentation of Douglas is paradoxical, as he is both more sympathetic and less sympathetic than other Prendick characters.

The Monster Within and Without

Each man in Frankenheimer's film has the potential for evil within him, an evil which comes forth in extreme situations. Life on the lifeboat is an extreme situation, but so is life on Dr. Moreau's island. Montgomery, once a brilliant neurosurgeon, was sought out by Moreau to be his assistant because of a promising paper that he wrote. But on the island, Montgomery has been diminished to being Moreau's policeman. Unlike Wells' Montgomery, he does not have the excuse for being on the island that he would be put in jail were he to return to England. The viewer is never informed as to why Montgomery remains on the island, but clearly Montgomery has been influenced for the worse by his relationship with Moreau.

Montgomery plays a larger role in this film than in the novel, and he is a more malevolent character than in the novel. Frequently he makes ironic jokes that possess a double meaning not readily apparent to either Douglas or the viewer. When asked by Douglas if he is a doctor, Montgomery replies, "More like a vet." When Douglas comments that Aissa, the panther woman, is beautiful, Montgomery responds, "She's a pussy cat," hinting at her feline origins.

Sometimes his actions are at the expense of Douglas' emotions. For example, after leading Douglas to reminisce over his fondness for pet rabbits and to kiss a rabbit on the head, Montgomery breaks the rabbit's neck. Montgomery uses words and actions to confuse Douglas, seemingly for his own amusement. Making Montgomery a negative character darkens the picture of mankind presented by the film.

As a sign of the times in which the film was made, Montgomery self–medicates with drugs as well as alcohol. Montgomery is frequently high in scenes and recommends the taking of "Jimi Hendrix–style" narcotics. Distributing pills to the female Beast People by delivering them from Montgomery's mouth to theirs suggests inter-species sexuality. Montgomery acts as a nihilist, not caring what he does or what happens to him. Towards the end of the film, after Moreau's death, Montgomery dresses like Moreau and goes out to party with the Beast People. Montgomery is shown as a lesser Moreau, a point emphasized by his looking like Moreau. In the spreading violence and disorder, he seeks his own end.

Montgomery even behaves like Moreau, undertaking experiments on his own. Douglas finds containers of his blood and a study of his DNA in Moreau's lab, and learns that Montgomery has been experimenting on him from the start of their relationship. The viewer never knows if Douglas is in danger from these experiments; yet, just taking blood from him without informing him represents a violation of his person. Montgomery, who has been corrupted by the spreading evil of Moreau, throws his life away rather than return to civilization with Douglas.

This film shows all men as being capable of evil behavior. Moreau may be worse than some, but he is not isolated in his evil. Moreau's evil is reflected in the behavior of Douglas, Montgomery, a captain who threatens Douglas, and even the Beast People. Some of the Beast People embody a capacity for the enjoyment of killing for its own sake. They are more responsible for their behavior than the Beast Men in the other adaptations, as they free themselves of controls and actively seek total destruction. Even those Beast People close to Moreau, who remain faithful to the masters in other adaptations, take out their frustration by killing Aissa and shooting Montgomery. However, a few Beast People, such as Aissa and the Sayer of the Law, are without the capacity for evil that exists within man. Moreau was successful in his experiments with them, but the meaning to be gathered from this success is never clear.

The Threat of the Monster

Dr. Moreau states that in his experiments he is working towards the betterment of man. Douglas discovers that before Moreau retired to his island he had won the Nobel Prize, establishing his seriousness as a scientist. He is a cultured man who frequently plays the piano.[22] Although his character seems empathetic and kindly, Moreau has set himself up as a god on his island and forces his creatures to endure pain and suffering. He makes them into unnatural beings who are neither men nor beasts. Instead of just experimenting for the sake of experimentation, as in the novel, Dr. Moreau's experiments have a clear goal. According to Moreau, the Devil causes mankind "to destroy and abase," and he has seen the Devil in the genes. Through the destruction of the evil elements at the molecular level, Moreau seeks to create a being incapable of malice. Dr. Moreau seems to have been successful with Aissa, and she may be the acme of creation; however, she cannot retain her human form.

Dr. Moreau believes that as a force for good he acts to relieve the Beast Men of evil. Moreau drives out, like the pope in his popemobile, to attend to his followers. He rides among them, sitting high, dressed in robes. Because of a sun allergy, he covers his immense body with fabric, wears a white chemical on his face, and sports strange headgear. When one of the creatures asks him, "What am I?" he answers, "You are all my children." He has created them as Beast People, and he sees himself as their father, much as the pope is the father of his faithful flock. Moreau wants to be thought benevolent, but he maintains his position by force.

Moreau, as a monster, acts as god. He has a means of dealing with the unfaithful or disobedient that contrasts with the whip used by Dr. Moreau in the other versions. Around his neck Moreau wears a necklace contraption that allows him to press a button and remotely shock the Beast People by triggering a device implanted in their bodies. The implants suggest that the pain comes from nowhere, enforcing the idea of punishment by god (Smith 51). The scene satirizes man's tendency to worship what he cannot understand, and the desire of a dominating person to keep his followers in line through structure and punishment. In this way, the film connects the Beast People with mankind and satirizes Moreau as a god. Whatever his initial intentions on the island, Moreau has fallen victim to the desire for power and become a monster.

The Nature of the Evil

Moreau has sought to make the society of the Beast People dependent on him as a kind of pope or god. Although he is the primary evil, evil has crept into some of the Beast People themselves. A wild animal cannot be held responsible for his violence, but the Beast People are no longer wild. The Beast People in this film are both male and female, and they do reproduce. Early in the film Douglas witnesses some of the Beast People operating on a hideous-looking woman who gives birth to a malformed child. Because of their ability to evolve, the Beast People learn from their experiences and each other. Moreau's creations are varied: some are civilized and pacific, while others are rebellious, bestial, and predatory. In their variety, the Beast People resemble humans, and once they lose their external controller, most of them find pleasure in destruction. A few of those closest to Moreau, like Aissa and the Sayer of the Law, attempt to keep their civilization going after the death of Moreau, but the great majority of the Beast Men are bent on mayhem and destruction.

Frankenheimer reveals his dark view of mankind in his portrayal of the Beast Men. In the novel by H. G. Wells, Prendick must live with the Beast People after Moreau's death, and they save his life. The majority of Wells' Beast Men live quietly, and only one poses a real threat to Prendick. In this film, the majority of the Beast Men become violent after Moreau is killed. All creatures, except for those who have been successfully altered by Moreau, have a propensity for evil that needs to be controlled.

The Monster Destroyed

Following the death and cremation of the Leopard Man, the Hyena Man discovers an implant among his ashes, and consequently locates and removes his own implant from his chest. Moreau will no longer be able to control him with his necklace. Aroused by their new freedom, a group of Beast Men break into Moreau's compound where they are met by Moreau, who offers to share milk and cookies with them in a strange parody of a family situation. When one of them hits the piano, Moreau explains atonal music to them. He then plays some Gershwin on the piano, attempting perhaps to soothe them with music. Moreau seems to ignore the reality of the situation, but perhaps he believes his best chance of remaining alive is to be calm until he can reach his necklace.

The Beast People seek an answer to their identity. They ask Moreau, "Father ... we are not like you. What are we?" And Moreau says, "You are all my children," but that is only defining them through himself. He does not provide them with a separate identity. When Moreau grabs hold of his necklace, he attempts to shock the ring leader, but his weapon is no longer effective. Without the implant the Hyena Man imitates Moreau by acting as a god and pronouncing that there is no more pain, and consequently that there is no more law. Although Moreau responds that there is always law, the Hyena Man proceeds to give the new law: to walk on all fours, to slurp up drink, to eat flesh, and to act as animals because they are not men. The Beast Men have gone from living a life in the wild as beasts, to behaving as men under threat of electric shock, to delighting in following their instincts. They develop a new law for themselves which allows them to tear Moreau apart and enjoy the feast of flesh and blood — a different kind of communion.

The Beast People divide into two camps, one of rebels who live by the new law and one of adherents to the old law. The rebels delight in the disobedience and violence. The other group, headed by the Sayer of the Law, attempts to keep control. The Sayer of the Law, who looks like Charlton Heston as Moses, wears a long, tan, flowing robe and carries a staff. He has internalized religion and states that Moreau is not dead, but that his spirit is watching them. In the novel, Prendick declared that Moreau was not dead as a means of controlling the Beast People. It is not something that Prendick believes, but something he uses to save his life. Prendick attempted to keep the Beast Men believing in Moreau's law in order to save his life. In Frankenheimer's film, the Sayer of the Law does not knowingly lie as Prendick did; he believes in what he says. There is something touching about the Sayer of the Law keeping up his beliefs even without his god.

Seeking to help Aissa, Douglas tries to find the serum that will keep her human, but Montgomery has destroyed everything scientific. Out of frustration, Douglas physically attacks Montgomery. Seeing Douglas' anger and desperation, Montgomery responds by saying, "Who is the animal?" Montgomery has not objected to the goings on of Moreau, but he taunts Douglas for fighting him. He suggests that Douglas is an animal, a point that he also made about the murder in the lifeboat. Montgomery does not hold himself out as a god like Moreau, but he does not believe in anything else either — Montgomery has lost his purpose in living, if he ever had one, and he seeks to make everyone as miserable as he is.

The Beast People continue on their rampage, led by the Hyena Man. Many sport commando-style weapons and drive vehicles. They repeat the negation of the law, that they are not men, and, indeed, in their runaway destruction the Beast People become monsters. They enjoy their capacity to hunt and kill, fueled by an increased intelligence and human weapons. Moreau had wanted them to be human in terms of being non-aggressive and cultured, but instead they have taken on the worst traits of humans. In a way, they are something like Edward Hyde in Stevenson's *Dr. Jekyll and Mr. Hyde*, as they are the worst part of mankind and completely without control.

Montgomery stimulates the Beast Men further with drugs. Talking about the instincts of the dog, Montgomery says he wants to go to doggy heaven — and then he is shot by the Dog Man. It was the Dog Man that was Prendick's faithful companion to the end in the novel, and he gave his life to save Prendick. In this film, the Dog Man is faithful to Montgomery in that he takes Montgomery's life as Montgomery requests him to do. The scene is unsettling, and no discernible point is made through the characters and action other than Frankenheimer's belief that in the end everyone is capable of hysteria and violence.

The Hyena Man wants to become a god like Moreau. He looks to Douglas as a leader and demands Douglas tell all of the Beast Men that the Hyena Man is the new god. Douglas states that there can be only one number one god, and it could be the Hyena Man or another Beast Man. By pointing to other Beast

Men, Douglas encourages the Hyena Man to kill the other contenders. Indeed, Douglas has the best chance of surviving if the most violent Beast Men kill each other. As the violence proceeds, it is impossible to distinguish among the different Beast Men on the screen or to care what happens to them. At this point the murder, violence, and special effects seem to take over the film itself. Or perhaps the movie itself becomes a monster, happy to go on the rampage without worrying about meaning.

As Douglas finally makes his escape from the compound and finds a boat on the pier, the more pacific of the Beast People crowd around him. The Sayer of the Law puts his arm around Aissa to comfort her. When Douglas says he will come back with medicine to help them, the Sayer of the Law states, "We have to be what we are — not what the father tried to make us." They will revert to animals rather than the combination of human and animal that Moreau has made them. The Sayer of the Law is accepting of what comes in a manner that suggests his is the correct attitude towards a law that is larger than Moreau. Only Aissa, the most evolved of Moreau's experiments, wants to continue as a human, perhaps because of her love for Douglas. The Sayer of the Law shows a morality in his resignation and acceptance not seen in any of the other characters. If the majority of the Beast Men are more violent than humanity, the Sayer of the Law is better than the majority of people.

Aissa (Fairuza Balk) saves the life of Edward Douglas (David Thewlis), and he will try to keep her human in John Frankenheimer's *The Island of Dr. Moreau* (1996) (New Line/the Kobal Collection).

Normality Restored

Douglas leaves the island vowing that this is a true record of what he saw, told "as a warning to all who would follow in Moreau's footsteps." Moreau was not able to change nature and was killed in his attempt to do so. While trying to create a perfect species, Moreau has only added to the pain and misery of himself and others without changing anything in a lasting way. Moreau was a monster in behaving selfishly. However, the lesson is not clear on how to prevent this from happening again. Not to act as a god was part of the lesson of Mary Shelley's novel *Frankenstein*, and Robert Walton was left alive to tell the story of his survival by not taking the path of ambition that Frankenstein traveled. No human alternative to Moreau is indicated in Frankenheimer's film.

Douglas returns to civilization but finds that it is not civilized. In voiceover, he reflects that sometimes "I look about me at my fellow man and I am reminded of some likenesses to the Beast People, and I feel as though the animal is surging up in them and they are neither wholly animal nor wholly man, but an unstable combination of both, as unstable as anything Moreau created. And I go in fear." Frankenheimer finds an analogy for mankind in the Beast Men, as they are composed of both good and bad; while some rebel and kill, others accept life as they find it. However, it is a grim view of man indeed.

Dr. Moreau created both the good and the evil; he divided man's violent and passive sides, much as Dr. Jekyll attempted to do. But whereas Robert Louis Stevenson ultimately suggests that man cannot split his tendencies but must accept the bad as well as the good, Frankenheimer's portrayal of the Sayer of the Law indicates that Moreau's experiment has in some way worked, and this is the part of man which we should all emulate.

The Sayer of the Law is correct in stating that each animal must be as originally created and act in accord with his own nature. But that means that man must accept his own propensity towards violence, which we never see happen in the film. Douglas must have been somewhat aware of man's bestial nature from the start, as he was a peace-keeper for the United Nations, and he committed murder in the lifeboat. He then should not be shocked by seeing the animal in others, and he should have a fear of mankind even before his experiences on Moreau's island. Ultimately, the Sayer of the Law's voice feels as though it is the most trustworthy, as he sees and accepts a higher law than that created by Moreau.

5

Vampire and Victim

Dracula, by Bram Stoker (1897)

Often considered the scariest of monsters, the vampire is also the most popular in recent years. Based on an historical character,[23] as well as the traditions of folklore, vampires have been portrayed in many different ways. Recently, in the works of Anne Rice and in such series as *True Blood* and *Twilight*,[24] vampires have become representative of social misfits and exude sexuality. These romantic and sensual vampires are a long way from the repulsive monster of Bram Stoker's novel *Dracula*. Yet people have always been simultaneously attracted to and repulsed by the idea of vampires. When asking my students about vampires, I am surprised by how many claim they would become vampires in order to gain eternal life.

Although other works involving vampires had been published in English,[25] Bram Stoker started the tradition of the sophisticated vampire who preys on beautiful women, does not cast a shadow or appear in a mirror, cannot eat or drink in the traditional manner, cannot cross a threshold without an invitation, has the ability to shift his shape into a wolf or bat or motes, and sleeps in a coffin equipped with his native soil. Of all the works Bram Stoker wrote, only *Dracula* has remained popular, both because of the nature of the topic and his dramatic means of presenting his story. *Dracula* has been a best-seller from the time it was first published and the basis for many adaptations. Interest in the "real" Dracula and in the adaptations of Stoker's novel has added dramatically to awareness of the novel.

In this chapter I will discuss Bram Stoker's Count Dracula as a monster who is intimately connected with his victims and their society instead of a monster who destroys from without, devastating everything in his path. The universal desire for immortality is only part of the means by which Stoker's Count Dracula can be seen as a monster whose roots are within his victims; in addition, the monster enlivens elements of sexuality repressed within Victorian society. Stoker's novel shows the fear experienced by many men at the time it was written of the New Woman — the independent woman who didn't need a man — and the fear of syphilis. In this chapter I will also examine the film *Nosferatu*, directed by F. W. Murnau (1922); *Dracula*, directed by Tod Browning (1931); and Francis Ford Coppola's *Bram Stoker's Dracula* (1992) because of the different aspects of the vampire they reveal. In the film *Nosferatu*, Dracula is a repulsive danger from without, a plague from the East who threatens the families of Germany. Dracula is also a menace from without in Browning's film *Dracula*, although in this picture Dracula is sexually attractive. Francis Ford Coppolla's *Bram Stoker's Dracula*, however, exaggerates aspects of the novel to show the Count as a monster from within who takes advantage of the not-so-secret desires of his victims.

Bram Stoker's novel *Dracula* is an adventure tale in the Gothic tradition, with two beautiful women and four heroes, as well as a Christian allegory or chivalric romance. The men are fighting the Great Serpent or dragon for their women and for their souls. Because of its mystical theme and dramatic structure, these elements add to the epic feel of the novel. Many readers have been fascinated by the sexual symbolism of the vampire's acts. Brian Aldiss, a modern critic, writes, "My own theory is that in fact Dracula is only metaphorically about vampirism. Its real subject is that obsession of the fin de siècle, syphilis. Dracula is the great Victorian novel about VD, for which vampirism stands in as Stoker's metaphor" (144). A reading such as Aldiss' is plausible because of the epic but general nature of the struggle involved. In several recent adaptations, including the film by Francis Ford Coppola, the curse of the vampire has been seen as an allegory for AIDS. Dracula started his reign at the end of the nineteenth century, at a time of rapid transformation. Victorian society was exposed to sudden and dramatic changes in areas as different as transportation, medicine, and the role of women. Dracula takes advantage of his victims' concealed desires. He finds his way into England because of the repressed desires of the characters, and achieves power because of the changes in the position of women at the end of the nineteenth century. Ultimately Dracula is defeated by the combined efforts of a group of the good and true, led by Abraham Van Helsing, a character who acts as Dracula's nemesis.

The World at the Start of Stoker's Novel Dracula

The novel begins as Jonathan Harker travels into Transylvania to complete a real estate transaction for his client, Count Dracula. Harker, eminently British, describes his impressions of the foreign land in his journal, and recounts his interest in his unusual surroundings:

JONATHAN HARKER'S JOURNAL — (Kept in shorthand.)
3 May. Bistritz. — Left Munich at 8:35 p.m., on 1st May, arriving at Vienna

early next morning; should have arrived at 6:46, but train was an hour late. Buda-Pesth seems a wonderful place, from the glimpse which I got of it from the train and the little I could walk through the streets. I feared to go very far from the station, as we arrived late and would start as near the correct time as possible. The impression I had was that we were leaving the West and entering the East; the most western of splendid bridges over the Danube, which is here of noble width and depth, took us among the traditions of Turkish rule [9].

Harker records a series of contrasts, marking the differences between the West and the East. With his precise habit of journal keeping, Harker reports the unpunctuality of the trains in shorthand, allowing him to write quickly to keep pace with his travel and in a means known to few. Harker keeps careful track of times and dates, points that lose their meaning and become petty and insignificant when contrasted with the eternal lifespan of Count Dracula, whom Harker will soon meet. As he approaches his destination, Harker notices the wonder of Budapest and the bridge indicative of leaving the ordinary and expected and entering the mysterious "traditions of Turkish rule."

Harker ponders the strangeness of his situation as he thinks to himself, "Was this a customary incident in the life of a solicitor's clerk sent out to explain the purchase of a London estate to a foreigner?" (21) Concerned with doing his job well so that he can become a partner in a prestigious law firm, Harker is anxious over the notion of visiting Count Dracula in Transylvania, something definitely unusual and even exotic for a citizen of the United Kingdom in the late 1800s. On his trip, Harker eats different food than he has ever encountered and witnesses mysterious behavior which he cannot understand; for example, the passengers make a sign to protect him from the evil eye when he tells them he will be visiting Count Dracula. Although the countryside is beautiful, it has been a place of siege, famine, and disease. The animals reflect the unease of the people — the horses act up and the wolves howl. Harker, a modern middle-class professional, is out of his element in the elegant and traditional home of an aristocrat, Count Dracula. In traveling from the West to the East, Harker has entered unknown and dangerous territory.

The Monster Within and Without

Although today we would know not to go at night to the home of Count Dracula in Transylvania, readers in 1897 did not have our knowledge of vampires. Harker describes many signs of the vampire that are familiar to the reader, which he does not recognize: Dracula's great strength, the lack of mirrors in his home, his black dress, his strange appearance, his inability to eat or drink, his nocturnal hours, and his ability to scale the walls of his castle like a lizard. The Count delights in hearing the wolves howl ("The children of the night;

what music they make!" [28]), hinting at his closeness to the wolves. After a few days Harker becomes alarmed by his situation and feels as though he is a prisoner in the castle. Disobeying the Count by sleeping in a room other than the one prepared for him, Harker refuses to be his willing victim.

Harker is drawn to a room in the castle where he feels a female presence and falls asleep there. At a later time Harker records the events following his sleep. The passage is rather lengthy but titillating in showing Harker as a willing victim for the female vampires. He is their victim because of his own sexual desires:

> I was not alone. The room was the same, unchanged in any way since I came into it. I could see along the floor, in the brilliant moonlight, my own footsteps marked where I had disturbed the long accumulation of dust. In the moonlight opposite me were three young women, ladies by their dress and manner. I thought at the time that I must be dreaming when I saw them, they threw no shadow on the floor. They came close to me, and looked at me for some time, and then whispered together. Two were dark, and had high aquiline noses, like the Count, and great dark, piercing eyes, that seemed to be almost red when contrasted with the pale yellow moon. The other was fair, as fair as can be, with great masses of golden hair and eyes like pale sapphires. I seemed somehow to know her face, and to know it in connection with some dreamy fear, but I could not recollect at the moment how or where. All three had brilliant white teeth that shone like pearls against the ruby of their voluptuous lips. There was something about them that made me uneasy, some longing and at the same time some deadly fear. I felt in my heart a wicked, burning desire that they would kiss me with those red lips. It is not good to note this down, lest some day it should meet Mina's eyes and cause her pain, but it is the truth. They whispered together, and then they all three laughed, such a silvery, musical laugh, but as hard as though the sound never could have come through the softness of human lips. It was like the intolerable, tingling sweetness of waterglasses when played on by a cunning hand. The fair girl shook her head coquettishly, and the other two urged her on. One said, "Go on! You are first, and we shall follow. Yours' is the right to begin."
>
> The other added, "He is young and strong. There are kisses for us all."
>
> I lay quiet, looking out from under my eyelashes in an agony of delightful anticipation. The fair girl advanced and bent over me till I could feel the movement of her breath upon me. Sweet it was in one sense, honey-sweet, and sent the same tingling through the nerves as her voice, but with a bitter underlying the sweet, a bitter offensiveness, as one smells in blood.
>
> I was afraid to raise my eyelids, but looked out and saw perfectly under the lashes. The girl went on her knees, and bent over me, simply gloating. There was a deliberate voluptuousness which was both thrilling and repulsive, and as she arched her neck she actually licked her lips like an animal, till I could see in the moonlight the moisture shining on the scarlet lips and on the red tongue as it lapped the white sharp teeth. Lower and lower went

her head as the lips went below the range of my mouth and chin and seemed to fasten on my throat. Then she paused, and I could hear the churning sound of her tongue as it licked her teeth and lips, and I could feel the hot breath on my neck. Then the skin of my throat began to tingle as one's flesh does when the hand that is to tickle it approaches nearer, nearer. I could feel the soft, shivering touch of the lips on the super sensitive skin of my throat, and the hard dents of two sharp teeth, just touching and pausing there. I closed my eyes in languorous ecstasy and waited, waited with beating heart [41–43].

The act of the vampire woman is described in a sexual way, as though she were moving her mouth down his body in order to perform fellatio on Harker. Attracted to the women's scarlet lips and red tongue, Harker experiences a strange combination of feelings: fear, longing, and worry about fidelity to his fiancée. Indeed, Harker believes his desire to be "wicked," yet it is "burning." The women are voluptuous, "both thrilling and repulsive." As one woman comes towards him, Harker sees her as a woman and an animal. Her breath is sweet and offensive. Harker reveals that one woman, who is so sexually attractive, is somehow familiar to him and connected with a "dreamy fear." Is this an innate fear of vampires or rather a male fear of powerful women? Harker is intrigued by what on the surface seems beautiful and desirable, but underneath is vile and wrong. Harker cannot escape from them, so that in his state of sexual arousal he is forced to be their victim. Harker is hypnotized or mesmerized by the power of the vampires. In describing this scene, Stoker has intentionally sexualized this passage so that the reader may experience Harker's desire and fear. Although the scene feels as though it will result in the ejaculation of Harker's semen, the women are after his blood. One woman says, "There are kisses for us all," and yet they are not seeking to kiss him but to use their lips and teeth to draw blood from his vein. In this novel, describing blood becomes another way of discussing semen. Stoker complicates the meaning of the blood early in the story in order to prepare for the revelations later on. As the wives have taken advantage of Harker's unexpressed sexual urges, so Count Dracula will feast on his wife, Mina Harker.

In this dramatic and sexy scene, Harker has rebelled against the orders of the Count. Harker, who was so punctual and concerned with his career, has done something unexpected. His immediate worry is that his fiancée, Mina, will find out he was attracted to other women and has "done something" with them; yet, later he realizes this is no longer important. The rules of polite society have been broken, and Harker must act to save all of Western civilization. By learning about the Count's women, Harker develops a first-hand knowledge of what could become of his fiancée, Mina, and her friend Lucy Westenra, were they to become subject to the Count. His ability to distinguish between the pure lady and the impure woman will change as the women he knows become tainted by Count Dracula. Although the surface may be lovely, what cannot be seen is offensive, as Dracula's women are rotten at the core. In this early passage in the novel, an ordinary person is shown to have a desire for a vampire; vampires cannot be resisted because of the attractiveness of the vampire and the vampire's ability to hypnotize a victim.

When the Count stops the women from feeding on Harker, they accuse the Count of never having loved, of not having sexual desire. In response, the Count indicates that he loved them in the past. But his is a perversion of Christian love and marriage bonds. In this conversation love equals sexuality, but their relationship is a perversion of the traditional idea of love. In place of Harker, the Count gives them a young child to feed on. Women are supposed to take care of children and suckle them, but in a travesty of womanhood, the situation is reversed with the vampire women. Feeding on a child is a perversion of the love of a parent for a child. The vampire ladies feast on a baby in a reversal of the way that a child would take sustenance from its mother; here the women take sustenance from the child, killing it in the process and keeping themselves not alive but undead. Evil gets passed along from the Count to the women and the innocents who are their victims.

Harker himself becomes something of a double to Dracula, another way in which the monster is connected with him. As we have seen, Harker has an intimate relationship with the Count's women. In addition, the Count wears Harker's traveling costume to make other people think that Harker has left the castle, while Harker goes down the castle wall as he has seen Dracula do. Later the Count will take Harker's place with his wife, Mina. The Count and Harker are intricately connected, and Harker has the potential to become as monstrous as Dracula.

The Threat of the Monster

Dracula is clearly the monster of this novel, yet we never know his origin. He speaks of the history of the Draculas but never reveals the events that made him a vampire. Dracula initially contacted Harker's firm because of his determination to come into England and make converts there. Dracula moves from the East to the West, from Transylvania to England. One of his first victims will be Lucy Westenra, whose name contains an anagram of Western. Harker, seeing the Count in his dirt-filled coffin, remarks, "This was the being I was helping to transfer to London, where, perhaps for centuries to come he might, amongst its teeming millions, satiate his lust for blood, and create a new and ever-widening circle of semi-demons to batten on the helpless" (53–54). By developing an ever-widening area of operation, Count Dracula will create semi-demons and destroy his victims. All the time they will be spreading their own disease to their victims. Overwhelmed with the desire to kill the Count, Harker hits him in the face with a shovel, wounding him on the forehead but not stopping him.

Arriving in England, Count Dracula seeks out Harker's fiancée, Mina Murray, and her friend, Lucy Westenra. Lucy has entertained three marriage proposals in one day before accepting the Hon. Arthur Holmwood, who, within the course of the novel, becomes Lord Goldalming. In an unconventional moment for a Victorian woman, Lucy wishes she could have three husbands. To some extent, Mina and Lucy are New Women, who at the end of the nineteenth century changed the role of women by leading self-determined lives. While Lucy questions the marriage laws, Mina is employed and adept at using modern machines, such as the typewriter. New Women were much written of in the late 1800s because of their independence and spirit, but many men also feared that the New Woman would no longer need men. Their independence makes Lucy and Mina vulnerable to the Count.

In order to obtain access to Mina, the Count has established contact with Renfield, who is housed within Dr. Seward's sanitarium. Renfield resembles an anti–John the Baptist, as he makes the way for the greater person who is coming — Satan or the Antichrist in this case. Although Renfield calls the Count his master, there doesn't seem to be any previous contact between them. Renfield is not a vampire, but Seward classifies him as zoophagous: he eats live bugs and then larger animals. The Count satisfies Renfield's desire for the lives of animals with promises. Later on in the novel, his own behavior disturbs Renfield, as he comes to feel responsible for the souls of the creatures he has eaten. Renfield is useful to the Count because the Count cannot enter into an area unless he is invited to do so. Renfield allows Dracula into the sanatorium where Mina is staying so that he can begin his attack on her. Renfield's death soon follows, as he is no longer of use to the Count. While dying, following an attack by Dracula, Renfield calls out the name of God, indicating his desire for salvation in the final moments of his life.

At first the evil of this novel appears to be contained in Count Dracula, and then Harker learns of the vampiric wives of the Count. Slowly, the evil moves from the isolation of the Count's castle to spread through England. As the Count travels, the evil comes with him and takes up lodging in the bodies of his victims. What seems clearly foreign arrives in the midst of English society, English women, and English marriages.

Bram Stoker's Count Dracula is a foreigner who brings a new type of evil into England. His threat would seem to be a threat from without, as he comes from abroad. But Dracula is a threat from within because he plays upon the desires of his victims. They are not willing victims in that they are not attracted to Dracula in any way, and yet the Count uses Renfield's desire for blood, and Lucy's and Mina's desire for love, while his wives take advantage of Harker's sexual desires. Dracula imposes himself on his victims, killing some and changing women into strange and sexualized versions of their former selves.

Although distinguished looking, Dracula is not handsome. In Bram Stoker's novel, Jonathan Harker describes Count Dracula as "a tall old man, clean shaven save for a long white moustache, and clad in black from head to foot, without a single speck of colour about him anywhere" (21). Examining him closer, Harker reports:

> His face was a strong — a very strong aquiline, with high bridge of the thin nose and peculiarly arched nostrils; with lofty domed forehead, and hair growing scantily round the temples, but profusely elsewhere. His eyebrows were very massive, almost meeting over the nose, and with bushy hair that seemed to curl in its own profusion. The mouth, so far as I could see it under the heavy moustache, was fixed and rather cruel-looking, with peculiarly sharp white teeth; these protruded over the lips, whose remarkable ruddiness showed astonishing vitality in a man of his years. For the rest, his ears were pale and at the tops extremely pointed; the chin was broad and strong, and the cheeks firm though thin. The general effect was one of extraordinary pallor [23–24].

Count Dracula appears dry and unapproachable. Mina writes, "His face was not a good face; it was hard, and cruel, and sensual ... he looked ... fierce and nasty" (155). Frequently he is compared to an animal because there is something inhuman about his appearance. Indeed, Dracula affronts all of the senses of those near to him. The Count has hairs on his palms, long nails, and his breath stinks. There is a desire to pull away from him, to escape the presence of Dracula. His position as neither living nor dead causes revulsion when he comes near; for example, when the Count first approaches him, Harker shudders and is overcome with "a horrible feeling of nausea" (24). Like many of the other monsters we have looked at, he repulses those who come near him because there is something unnatural about his appearance. He subtly violates the norms of society with his looks. A casual glance does not reveal his difference from others in any but a superficial way. Yet on further study, Dracula's appearance suggests his evil nature: his mouth is described by Jonathan as "cruel-looking," and Mina calls him "fierce and nasty," although sensual as well.

The Nature of the Evil

Count Dracula's threat comes from the fact that not only will he kill his victims, he will prevent their immortal souls from reaching heaven. As Dracula brings his evil from the East to the West, he finds fresh victims who are unaware of the reality of the vampire and whose gentility and morality he can use against them. Dracula becomes an Antichrist or Satan, building up a band of supporters from his victims. Eventually Dracula could "convert" the entire world. He cannot be stopped by ordinary means; a force of good is required to oppose the force of evil. Van Helsing can lead the force of good because he is intimately connected with Dracula. Like Count Dracula, Van Helsing is not English. He functions as an alter ego or nemesis to Count Dracula.

Dracula has different ways of attacking his victims. He can kill them by draining them of blood, or he can make a female his wife by having her drink *his* blood. Even a victim who dies, however, will not find eternal rest, but will become one of the undead who will continue to feed on others. They will not just be dead, they will be condemned to eternal damnation. Having obtained the information from Harker that he needs to enter England, the Count begins his attack on the purest part of Victorian society — the unmarried women — focusing first on Lucy Westenra.

As Lucy becomes weak, drained of blood, Dr. Seward becomes fearful of what is happening to her and asks for the assistance of Professor Van Helsing of Amsterdam. After examining Lucy, Van Helsing states, "This is no jest, but life and death, perhaps more" (122). In the terms of this novel, whether Lucy lives or dies is not as important as whether her soul will be at peace in heaven for all eternity. Van Helsing alone recognizes the existence and the danger of Count Dracula and must make others come to see the situation as he does. The difficult is that people do not believe in vampires.

Lucy loses blood at night and requires several blood transfusions, which are performed directly: a healthy man lies near the comatose Lucy and blood is drawn from his vein through hypodermic needles and tubing into the vein of Lucy. After he donates his blood to Lucy, her fiancé states that he feels as though they are married. Blood being transferred between them is a symbolic form of semen. Of course, unbeknownst to her fiancé, Lucy has had transfusions from other men as well.[26] In this strange manner, Lucy has her wish granted and is married, via transfusions, to all the men. Despite the transfusions, through a series of wild events orchestrated by Count Dracula (a wolf breaks the window, Lucy's mother dies, Lucy faints, and the maids are drugged), Lucy is victimized for the final time and dies. Van Helsing says, "It is only the beginning" (169). After her death, Count Dracula battles the band of the good for Lucy's soul, just as they previously battled for her life.

Following the death of Lucy, a woman that children call the "Bloofer Lady," perhaps meaning beautiful and bloody, haunts the graveyard after dark. Lucy's tomb shows the effect of time:

> The tomb in the day-time, and when wreathed with fresh flowers, had looked grim and gruesome enough; but now, some days afterwards, when the flowers hung lank and dead, their whites turning to rust and their greens to browns; when the spider and the beetle had resumed their accustomed dominance; when time-discoloured stone, and dust-encrusted mortar, and rusty, dank iron and tarnished brass, and clouded silver-plating gave back the feeble glimmer of a candle, the effect was more miserable and sordid than could have been imagined. It conveyed irresistibly the idea that life — animal life — was not the only thing which could pass away [202–203].

Through the dead flowers and rusting features, Dr. Seward points out the contrast between life and death. Everything that is alive dies. Stone and metal change over time. The result is melancholy but a natural process. As each day ends with night, so each life ends in death. Decay is the natural end to life and a part of life — but Lucy is outside of that process.

As the doctors continue their death-watch, they observe Lucy feeding on a child:

> When Lucy — I call the thing that was before us Lucy because it bore her shape — saw us she drew back with an angry snarl, such as a cat gives when taken unawares; then her eyes ranged over us. Lucy's eyes in form and colour; but Lucy's eyes unclean and full of hell-fire, instead of the pure, gentle orbs we knew. At that moment the remnant of my love passed into hate and loathing; had she then to be killed, I could have done it with savage delight. As she looked, her eyes blazed with unholy light, and the face became wreathed with a voluptuous smile. Oh, God, how it made me shudder to see it! With a careless motion, she flung to the ground, callous as a devil, the child that up to now she had clutched strenuously to her breast, growling over it as a dog growls over a bone [188].

Lucy is no longer a virginal woman, but a "thing," "callous as a devil." She is someone to be compared with animals and the Devil. While alive, Lucy was very modest, although her joke about marrying three men betrays a bit of gameness or coquetry. But now her face becomes "wreathed with a voluptuous smile," the word "voluptuous" being one that Harker used to describe Dracula's wives. Proper Victorian women were not to be overtly sexual in any way. Becoming a vampire has made Lucy into an impure woman.

Lucy, with "something diabolically sweet in her tones," calls to her fiancé, "Come to me, Arthur. Leave these others and come to me. My arms are hungry for you. Come and we can rest together. Come, my husband, come!" (188). She attempts to entrap her fiancé by appealing to his sexual desire for her. Nothing of the living Lucy remains, and in order to bring peace to her soul, the men kill Lucy by driving a stake through her heart, cutting off her head, and putting garlic in her mouth.

With Lucy's death, Mina becomes the center of Dracula's attention. Dr. Van Helsing gives Mina the ultimate Victorian praise: "She has man's brain — a brain that a man should have were he much gifted — and a woman's heart" (241). All of the men respect her, but they do not treat her as an equal. Although she arrives at the idea that they should pool all the information they have about Count Dracula, and physically performs the transcription and typing necessary to make it possible, the men attempt to keep her innocent of their activities going forward. They seek to protect her by not involving her or informing her of their plans. And yet by doing this they leave her open to the penetration of the vampire. By letting Mina sleep without the protection of a cross, communion wafers, garlic, or male presence, they leave her open to the advances of Count Dracula. Suddenly realizing she is in danger, Dr. Seward enters her room to find this scene:

> On the bed beside the window lay Jonathan Harker, his face flushed and breathing heavily as though in a stupor. Kneeling on the near edge of the bed facing outwards was the white-clad figure of his wife. By her side stood a tall, thin man, clad in black. His face was turned from us, but the instant we saw we all recognized the Count — in every way, even to the scar on his forehead. With his left hand he held both Mrs. Harker's hands, keeping them away with her arms at full tension; his right hand gripped her by the back of the neck, forcing her face down on his bosom. Her white nightdress was smeared with blood, and a thin stream trickled down the man's bare breast which was shown by his torn-open dress. The attitude of the two had a terrible resemblance to a child forcing a kitten's nose into a saucer of milk to compel it to drink [252].

Rather than retreating, the Count has responded to the men's attempts to deprive him of his natural earth resting places by attacking Mina Harker. This leaves the men in a weak and pursued position, but more than ever determined to defeat the Count in order to save their own Mina, a representative of the best of Victorian womanhood. The events of this night change the status of Mina among their band and make her the focus of their attention as they attempt to save her from becoming one of the vampire wives of the Count. Mina recollects how the Count comes into her room while her husband Jonathan sleeps, saying that if she makes a sound he will "dash his brains out before your very eyes." If she doesn't allow the Count to bite her in front of her husband, he will destroy the husband in front of the wife. The Count then sucks from her neck for what he announces is the third time; indeed, he tells her that she shouldn't protest because he has done this before. She goes into a half swoon while he sucks, and this may be linked to the hypnotic power of the Count. He takes away "his foul, awful, sneering mouth," and she sees it drip blood. He has over-sated on her. He enjoys both the refreshment and the sadism of the occasion.

The Count mocks Mina for playing her brain against his and helping the men fight him:

> And you, their best beloved one, are now to me, flesh of my flesh; blood of my blood; kin of my kin; my bountiful wine-press for awhile; and shall be later on my companion and my helper. You shall be avenged in turn; for not one of them but shall minister to your needs. But as yet you are to be punished for what you have done. You have aided in thwarting me; now you shall come to my call [252].

The Count addresses Mina with words from the Bible, as Adam described his closeness with Eve, suggesting they are married. She will become a vampire wife to him, in some ways a brutal mockery of the Biblical role of the wife. And he announces that later she will be with him happily as both companion and helper; she will be by his side and on his side. She will then take revenge on the human men. In the meantime, he is going to use her for revenge by making her come to him as he wants. For this purpose he forces her to drink from a vein in his breast. He holds her hands and forces her lips to the wound "so that I must either suffocate or swallow some of the...." — something that she is too humiliated to name. Again, blood has been substituted for semen. He has, in effect, raped her. He has forced her to do his bidding by having her ingest his bodily liquid in order to defeat her resistance and to aid in his escape from the men. He has done this in front of her husband, showing his power over both Mina and Jonathan. In a mockery of the wedding ceremony and the relationship of husband and wife, he will force Mina to do his bidding and be his helpmate.

The events of this night happened because the men were trying to protect Mina from worrying about the Count and consequently did not share their knowledge with her. They treated her as a Victorian woman rather than the intelligent and independent woman she shows herself to be. Their attempt to keep her innocent has backfired. She has been tainted physically, emotionally, and spiritually. She asks, "What have I done to deserve such a fate, I who have tried to walk in meekness and righteousness all my days" (288). But more than being an innocent victim of the Count, as Lucy has been, she is now going to be used by him as a weapon against those who would destroy him. Their one attempt to save her by putting a eucharist wafer on her forehead to purify her results in Mina's being branded. She is now marked both externally, on her forehead, and internally, in her blood, as the Count's own, as well as having her mind controlled by him. She is a constant reminder of his presence and his power among the men who would save her from the Count.

Strangely, Mina may still be a virgin. After all, she married her husband when he was still in a hospital so that they would be able to travel together. Since returning to England, their world has been upset by the deaths of many of their relatives and friends, followed by the attack on her by the Count, after which she will not allow her husband to touch her because she is "unclean." She seeks an intimate relationship with her husband, but instead has suffered one with Dracula. The blood on her bed following the Count's attack may be symbolic of the loss of her maidenhead. The Count has interrupted her marriage to Harker with a strange wedding ceremony of his own.

The Monster Destroyed

The Count's destruction begins with the coming together of the good people of the novel — Dr. Seward, Prof. Van Helsing, Jonathan and Mina Harker, Quincey Morris, and Lord Godalming — to form the Crew of Light to fight for the life and soul of Mina. This Crew of Light is on the side of Christ, religion, and the sanctity of marriage and family, and is allied against the forces of Satan and darkness. Their previous relationships as suitors of Lucy, friends, and professional acquaintances are subsumed into their work together. Mina began the fight against Dracula by bringing together all their letters, journals, and articles; and putting them in order; and copying them so that everyone is informed about their enemy in order to understand the behavior and motives of Count Dracula. In this way the various "normal" thoughts of the characters, as well as the reader, are brought to bear on extraordinary occurrences.

Dr. Van Helsing tells everyone what he knows about vampires and their powers. He explains what would happen if they do not succeed: "But to fail here, is not mere life or death. It is that we become as him; that we henceforward become foul things of the night like him — without heart or conscience, preying on the bodies and the souls of those we love best. To us for ever are the gates of heaven shut; for who shall open them to us again?" (209). Having warned them about the consequences of failure, Van Helsing encourages them to do what is right. With a cross on the table before them, this small band holds hands and makes a solemn compact. The warriors go forth not just to save Mina, but to save the world from the spread of vampirism.

Together the group hunts the boxes that allow the Count to live in England and destroys most of them by putting communion wafers in the soil. They then follow the Count to his own ground in the old country where there is a final confrontation between the forces of good and evil. In Transylvania the members of the party come towards the Count from different directions, their movements forming the pattern of a cross. The Count dies from a knife wound in his throat from Jonathan and another to his heart from Morris. Sadly, in the struggle Morris dies as well. As the sun sets, the men witness the stain on Mina's forehead disappear, and all say "Amen." They acknowledge the presence of God in the defeat of one associated with the Devil.

Normality Restored

The novel ends with a final note by Jonathan Harker talking about the seven years since the death of Count Dracula. Harker and Mina have a son, Quincey, whose "bundle of names links all our little band of men together" (326). The new life represents a new generation of the pure, rather than the tainted, that has come from the fight against evil. They note that nothing remains in Transylvania at the place of their struggle, although the castle still stands above "a waste of desolation" (327). They look at their papers and note that they contain no authentic documents and consequently no proof of their story. Van Helsing states that they want no proof, as the Harkers' son "will understand how some men so loved [his mother], that they dare much for her sake" (327).

The band of Christians destroys Count Dracula, making the world safe for the next generation, as symbolized by the child of the Harkers. The birth of this child suggests the ultimate purity of his parents despite their experiences with the Count and his wives. The papers of the group have been published so that the history "may stand forth as simple fact." Although those present can attest to its truth, nothing can be proved.

The monster has been killed, and their brush with the monstrous is over. Yet Harker was involved with the Count's wives through his desires, and Mina was tied to him through his blood. Count Dracula succeeded in briefly infiltrating England and changing Lucy, turning her into a voluptuous woman who used her beauty to attract children and her sexual wiles to draw men to her. While blood was exchanged, this represented semen and became a kind of penetration. Vampirism could have been spread like a venereal disease among the "teeming millions" of England. To be rid of the monster took almost super-human force because the evil was not only in Count Dracula but secretly in his victims and the repressions of Victorian society. Ultimately, goodness has prevailed and made the world a place where an untainted child can be born and live and believe.

Nosferatu; eine Symphonie des Grauens (A Symphony of Horror) (1922)

Dir.: F. W. Murnau. Perf.: Max Schreck, Alexander Granach, Gustav von Wangenheim, Greta Schröder. Alpha Video, 2002. VHS.

There are hundreds of films in which Count Dracula makes an appearance, but most are loose adaptations of Stoker's novel wherein the character of Count Dracula is used without the situations from the novel. Many of the films have kept the character of Van Helsing as a nemesis for Dracula. While the novel conceives of the vampire as bringing out the sexuality hidden within his female victims, and consequently as a threat from within the characters and society, the films most frequently present the vampire as a threat from without. Dracula preys on victims with whom he has no connection.

The movies provide an opportunity to give Dracula a unique physical image, and Dracula appears physically different from the rest of the characters, as he looks, dresses, and talks in an opposite manner. The Dracula from F. W. Murnau's 1922 film *Nosferatu* is one of the strangest-looking ever filmed. Dracula, although young in this picture, has nothing attractive about him. His looks are disconcerting to the characters and the viewer. Dracula's looks exemplify his unnatural state much in the way that Frankenstein's Creature's exterior did as well. No one else is like either the Creature or Dracula. Dracula is tall and emaciated, and has unusual facial features. His nose is hooked, while his eyes are circled with black, and his teeth are thin and pointed, like those on a dangerous snake. His hands seem to have the ability to reach beyond the area in front of them. His long fingernails grow even longer during the course of the

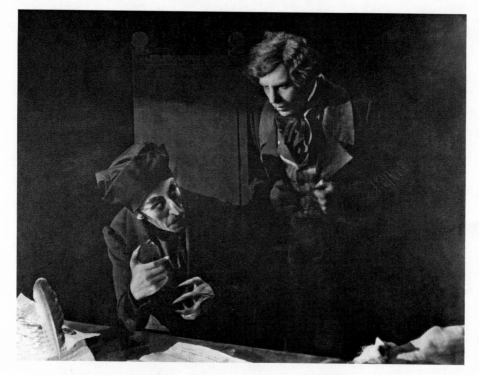

Count Dracula (Max Schreck) examines a picture of the wife of Harker (Gustav von Wangenheim) and plans to make both his victims in F. W. Murnau's *Nosferatu* (1922) (Prana-Film/the Kobal Collection).

film. Dracula has the strength to easily maneuver his own coffin, as well as the ability to command items without touching them. Count Dracula is not an ordinary human being and can only appear so when seen by someone like Harker, who focuses on doing his job and being polite. The Count is not living, nor is he dead. He is undead, nosferatu. Max Schreck, an actor whose last name means "terror" in German, plays Count Dracula, who in this film is known as Graf Orlok.[27] *Nosferatu* haunts the imagination of the viewer today in large part because of Schreck's performance and the unusual images created by the cinematography.

Nosferatu, directed by F. W. Murnau, is a silent film that is infused with beauty and mystery through the use of the film technique called German Expressionism, which conveys meaning through metaphor. Even the subtitle of the picture, "A Symphony of Horror," suggests the poetic aspects of the film, as the musical term "symphony" brings out the unusual nature of this movie. Because of its poetic, allusive nature, the film is complex. Incorporating stylized sets and bold ideas, the style would be used to a lesser extent in both *Dracula* (1931) and *Frankenstein* (1931).

The movie advances through connections between characters and action, and contrasts of light and shadows. The action of the film moves forward through crosscutting between characters that interconnects and contrasts the characters of the film. By showing the similar placement of characters, parallels and contrasts are made. This technique adds to the viewer's growing feeling of unease as the character of Count Dracula moves towards Bremen. In addition, framing characters with windows and doors also connects the characters in this film. Frequently surreal buildings and passageways, such as bridges, windows, and doorways, reveal the contrasts between characters as they move from place to place. These filmic devices show the monster as an outsider who nevertheless is able to insinuate himself within the lives of the characters.

Although Murnau's film was based on Bram Stoker's novel *Dracula*, the names of characters and towns, as well as several plot elements, were changed in making the film. The word "nosferatu" is spoken by the character Abraham Van Helsing in Stoker's novel, describing what people in Eastern Europe call the undead. Despite the changes made in the movie, Stoker's widow brought a successful lawsuit for copyright infringement against the film company. All copies of the picture were ordered destroyed. Subsequently, different editions of the film have surfaced, but with some variation in the names of characters and the words on the intertitle cards. In the version I have watched, the intertitle cards have been translated into English, and the characters have been given some approximation of their original English names. Thus, Ellen Hutter, as she was known in Murnau's original film, is called Nina (rather than Mina) Harker. Because of the confusion of the names, I will refer to the characters by their names in Stoker's novel while discussing this film, although I will mention the town of Bremen, Germany, where many of the characters reside, rather than Whitby, England, as in the novel.

Nosferatu, set in 1838, reveals the coming of a plague to Germany. Its message is geared to the Germany of 1922, when the film was made, a time of uncertainly as Germany attempted to recover from having lost World War I and to discover where its future lay. National Socialism had begun in Germany in 1920, and among its tenets were anti–Semitism, racism, and pan–Germanism. Count Dracula represents a force that Germans fear will corrupt its young people. He is Eastern European, mysterious, and seeking to make his way into the center of Germany by destroying the fabric of German society and the future of German families, starting with the Harker family.

The World at the Start of Murnau's Film Nosferatu

In *Nosferatu*, vampirism is shown to be connected with the plague, but other meanings are suggested by the vampirism as well. Written on an intertitle card, the first words of the film, supposedly put forth by the historian Johann

Cavallius, announce the subject of the movie as the plague in Bremen in 1838. Cavallius asks, "Did Nosferatu bring the plague to Bremen?" and then remarks that the innocent couple, Harker and his wife, were at the center of the start and the climax of the epidemic. The plague is a disease brought into Germany by the rats associated with Count Dracula, a threat from without. Thus the vampirism is both a means in itself of infecting the innocent and symbolic of the spread of a real disease. Dracula's aristocratic origins and his foreignness suggest that he, and the plague, began as a threat from beyond Germany's borders. A member of the aristocracy from Transylvania, Dracula has come to Bremen to prey upon the middle-class people of Germany. In addition, the Count has been thought to be representative of the Jews, the repression of the government, and the fear of homosexuality. The film *Nosferatu* suggests many possible meanings for vampirism because of its symbolic resonances, without committing anything to words. The musical imagery of the subtitle of the film, "A Symphony of Horror," reinforces the associative nature of the themes of this movie — that the horror does not consist of just one thing but of many possibilities.

The plague upsets the normal world presented at the start of *Nosferatu*. This world, before the arrival of Count Dracula, contains the possibility of love and happiness, but also suggests an ever-present menace. The film first focuses on a young, handsome married couple, the Harkers. There is a montage at the start of the picture showing their innocence: Jonathan dresses, gathers flowers, and presents them to his wife, while Mina plays with a cat. Finding delight in each other, they are associated with growing, life-filled things. Once outside his house, however, Harker comes face to face with the impossible reality that *Nosferatu* embodies: an unknown man, later shown to be Van Helsing, says to Harker, "You can't escape destiny by running away." A sense of negative fate and mysteriousness hangs over Harker and the atmosphere of the film itself.

The mystery started with Harker's encounter with Van Helsing continues with the words introducing Harker's boss, Renfield. An intertitle card reads, "The agent Renfield was a strange man, and there were unpleasant rumors about him." The viewer never learns the substance of those rumors. Perhaps they have to do with Renfield's connection to the Count, his insanity, or his possible homosexuality or Jewishness. Renfield reads a letter from Dracula which has been written in mysterious symbols, which Renfield alone can decipher. Renfield and Dracula share this private language and perhaps other secrets as well. As a consequence of the letter, Renfield sends Harker to Transylvania to help Count Dracula secure a home in Bremen right across from where the Harkers live. His last words to Harker add to the sense of unease created by the journey: Renfield points out that as Harker is young, "what matter if it costs you some pain — or even a little blood?" Renfield seeks to bring the world of Count Dracula and the world of the Harkers together.

The normal world of *Nosferatu*, shown by the montage of the life of the Harkers, is a world in which Renfield and Count Dracula are out of place. The connection between Renfield and Dracula is secret and unhealthy, unlike the bond between Harker and his wife. How Renfield became a confederate of Count Dracula is never explained. Renfield sends Harker to Count Dracula knowing that Harker himself, and indeed all of Germany, will be hurt by the vampirism of the Count. While Harker is away in Transylvania, Renfield is locked in an insane asylum, showing that those around him recognize and can deal with insanity. But with Count Dracula they will be dealing with a more powerful and deadly force.

The Monster Within and Without

Everything evil emanates from Count Dracula. He is a force of evil that destroys whatever is in his way in order to work his will. There is no evil within Harker and his wife, as they are innocent and good of heart. They are healthy, fun-loving people who are caught in the horror of the nosferatu via the corrupted Renfield. In his innocence, Harker gets closer and closer to the evil, exposing himself and also his wife to Dracula. The feeling that disaster awaits the unwary German suggests the era in which the film was made.

Harker is, if anything, too naïve; he has no defense against the evil of the world. Indeed, Harker attempts to throw away the one thing that may help him in his plight — a book called *The Book of the Vampires*. While staying at an inn in Transylvania, Harker starts to read this book which he finds on his night table. This book contains much information, but Harker does not read it all, and little is shown to the viewer. We do learn that the first nosferatu was born in 1443, but no more about how that happened. Attempting to throw away *The Book of the Vampires*, Harker gives it a toss, but it lands in his suitcase. He cannot escape vampires, and knowledge of vampires follows him.

Although Harker is innocent, his wife, Mina, has a psychic connection with the Count. Despite the fact that she remains in Germany, she is more aware of what happens in Transylvania than Harker. Yet the evil is not in Mina, she is just more atune to it than her husband. The evil resides within Count Dracula and within Renfield (in that he elects to sacrifice Harker for the benefit of the Count).

The Threat of the Monster

Count Dracula first appears as his carriage arrives to pick up Harker on the road in an area which a concerned local has termed "the land of phantoms." The carriage looks like a hearse, as the carriage itself and the horses are covered with sheets. The film is speeded up so that it appears that the carriage travels at an unnaturally quick speed; one of the travelers quotes the words from

Stoker's novel, "For the dead travel fast." It appears as though Harker rides in his own hearse, with death as the carriage driver; indeed, he is in mortal danger.

There are changes in Harker soon after his first contact with Dracula. Harker's deteriorating condition can be traced through his repeated morning rituals. He begins his stay in Transylvania with a healthy sleep in a hotel. In the morning sunlight comes through the window, falls onto his face and enlivens Harker. As will be seen later in the film, this use of sunlight contrasts with the need of the vampire to be hidden away during the light of day. Harker wakes up and stretches happily, feeling strong and in control of himself. This is his waking routine, but during the course of the film he is seen rising with less and less gusto.

Once inside Dracula's home, Harker becomes wary of the Count's behavior and with good reason. Items within the Count's home symbolize his state. For example, a skeleton on a clock strikes the hour of midnight. Seeing Dracula reading strange symbols—the same type of symbols that Renfield had been studying—Harker becomes nervous and cuts himself with a knife he is using to slice bread. Dracula is so attracted to the "precious blood" that Harker becomes frightened and backs away from him. What happens next is not shown. In the morning Harker wakes up slightly concerned, and immediately checks on his cut finger and then finds a mirror to look at the hurt in his neck. His morning ritual is less cheerful than it had been, but he is not seriously impaired. Indeed, he is delighted to see the daylight and happily eats, writes a letter to his wife, and surveys the castle. Although alarmed at everything that has happened, Harker continues his business transaction with Dracula.

The following night Dracula's behavior becomes a threat not only to Harker, but to Mina as well. Seeing a picture of Mina, Dracula exclaims, "What a lovely throat," suggesting his future intention with respect to Mina. Back in his own room Harker opens *The Book of Vampires* and reads that the vampire drinks from his victim's neck, confirming his suspicions of his situation. As the clock once more strikes midnight, Harker attempts to escape. He opens the door to his room but sees Dracula coming towards him. Without a hat, Dracula is bald, and his ears appear huge. His appearance suggests a rat, the animal he is associated with onboard ship and that traditionally carries the plague. As Dracula enters Harker's room, Dracula is framed by the door as if in a coffin, reminding the viewer of his undead state. Harker is trapped. There is no lock on his door, so he cannot even try to keep the evil out. He cannot climb out the window, as he is many stories above the ground, and he ends up hiding under his sheets like a child in desperation.

Back in Germany, Harker's wife feels the danger to him. By means of cross-cutting the scenes of Harker and the vampire with scenes of Mina reacting from afar, the film reveals the intimate connection between husband and wife, as well as the connection between Mina and Count Dracula. Seeing Mina teetering on the edge of a railing, Mina's friend finds her in a "somnambulistic dream" and rescues her. But her danger continues, as well as Harker's. Back in Transylvania, the shadow of the vampire falls across Harker, and in Germany, Mina screams. Her doctor says she has a fever, but the intertitle card announces that she senses the danger of the nosferatu. She herself is aware of the movement of the Count and the threat to her husband, but is helpless to assist him. At the same time, a connection is being forged between Mina and the Count.

After his encounter in his bedroom with the Count, Harker awakes the next morning without his usual enthusiasm. He puts his hand to his head, no doubt suffering the after effects of being drained of blood by Dracula. Exploring the castle and seeing Dracula in his coffin, Harker faints and then wakes to observe Dracula feverishly and single-handedly piling his coffins onto his carriage. In an impossible action, Dracula then climbs into the top one and places the cover on it from within. The horse and wagon move off with the load of coffins, but without a driver. The nosferatu is starting on his journey, moving towards Bremen. The threat of the evil of the Count is moving beyond Harker to the wider sphere of Germany. Dracula's coffins, which are necessary to provide him with his own soil for sleeping, will later contrast with the coffins in Bremen that suggest the number of dead from the plague. The impossibility of the Count's movements allows him to seem superhuman and consequently unstoppable, as he needs no one else to help him with his accoutrements.

The Nature of the Evil

Dracula's greatest threat is his spreading evil. He can destroy individuals and perhaps will destroy the inhabitants of the city of Bremen as he makes an inroad into the country of Germany. Because he can control creatures outside of himself, like rats, Count Dracula has the capacity to do what and go where he likes.

According to Van Helsing, the vampire is allied to other strange phenomenon. Giving a lecture on the secrets of nature and their strange correspondences to human life, Van Helsing compares vampirism to other strange "freaks" of nature. Van Helsing understands the evil of the vampire as being similar to the workings of the Venus flytrap and the polyp. Harker, like a fly in the Venus flytrap, has been caught in Dracula's trap. Renfield also appears as a freak of nature as he waits for his master and eats bugs like a carnivorous plant.

Crosscutting of scenes in the film underscores the relationship between the vampires and the rest of the world. During his lecture, Van Helsing shows a polyp with claws, a "phantom" as he calls it, which is a word used by the locals to describe Dracula. Unlike in later Dracula movies, Van Helsing does not play an active role and is not compared with Dracula. Van Helsing's lecture is crosscut with a scene of Mina on the dunes, amid a graveyard, waiting for her husband to return. Although Dracula has not come near Mina, she is already associated with death. Scenes of the Count's voyage are intercut with Harker's struggle to return home. Mina states that "he" is coming and she must go to him, but because we have been viewing scenes of both Harker and the Count moving towards Bremen, it is not clear as to whom she is referring. She loves her husband but feels the Count's power, although they have never met. These scenes suggest a contrast between Harker and the Count, as Harker represents life and the Count brings death. They have entered into a contest for the soul of Mina. Ultimately she will be both the victim of the vampire and the cause of his death.

The sway of Count Dracula appears to be increasing, as Renfield reads a newspaper article describing a plague in Eastern Europe — the victims have been found to have two bites on their necks. Thus Count Dracula is connected both with phantom living creatures and the plague itself. The evil of the nosferatu is spreading. Onboard the ship that Dracula sails on, the sailors fear foul play as the crew is killed one by one. As the first mate investigates the situation by removing the lid of a coffin, the Count stands straight up from his coffin without bending his knees. The scene is eerie, as the movement is impossible for a human being. As performed by the Count, it is a reminder of the fact that he is undead. A sailor realizes the seriousness of the situation and jumps overboard to avoid having his soul taken by the Count.

Mina, an ideal of the feminine, sews a cloth that says "I love you" in German. But her model femininity will lead her to make the ultimate sacrifice. Harker has returned home but cannot save Mina from her fate. Mina has promised her husband never to open *The Book of the Vampires*, which he has brought back with him. This is a misguided attempt to keep Mina out of harm's way by keeping her ignorant. Like many mythic women who cannot resist the forbidden, she is drawn to the mystery of the book. From her reading she learns the Count can only be defeated by a woman who is pure of heart, who offers her blood to him freely, and who keeps him with her until the cock crows. Evil can only be destroyed by surrender of the self for the good of others.

The Monster Destroyed

As Mina has psychic knowledge of the action of the Count, so does Renfield. Renfield's fate, like that of Mina, is tied up with that of the Count. In many ways Renfield's behavior reflects the Count's behavior. While the Count was within the ship, Renfield was institutionalized. The Count's arrival in Bremen is crosscut with Renfield's escape from the insane asylum after he strangles his keeper. As the Count secures a rendezvous with Mina, Renfield escapes and is chased by a mob. The people of Bremen long for an answer to the cause of the sickness that destroys the lives of their loved ones. Although they cannot cure the plague, they can control Renfield's behavior. Renfield is caught and imprisoned once again as the Count, Renfield's master, breathes his last. Later, Renfield, tied up with rope, announces that his master is dead.

Once the Count arrives in Bremen, people start to die from the plague. Many shots in the film frame both Mina and the Count in windows and doorways, connecting them with each other and showing their movement. The evil of the Count approaches, and at the same time, his psychic connection with Mina increases. The Count has entered into new territory by journeying to Bremen; Mina is also about to enter into new territory in her relationship with the Count. In the final scenes of the film, the Count looks out from his window directly into the Harkers' apartment. While sleeping, Mina feels him looking at her through the window and awakes with terror. She sends her husband out to seek help. Then, holding her hand over her heart, Mina considers what to do. Looking from her window, she sees a long line of coffins being carried in the narrow street below. Mina walks to her window that faces the Count and opens her window, giving Dracula permission to enter.

Dracula starts making his way towards her, invited to cross the threshold into her home. We see his shadow coming towards her door, and it appears huge and hideous. The shadow of his hands gropes towards her apartment and then across her body. In a travesty of sexual intercourse, the shadow moves up from between her legs to clutch her heart. Her femininity and her sexuality are taken advantage of by the Count. She looks so beautiful and is afraid that she cannot fulfill her important role, while he seems completely grotesque. The heroine of pure heart sacrifices herself to destroy the nosferatu. We see only his head on the far side of her bed, drinking from her neck. Mina looks like a lump on her bed; she is no longer an individual. Her face is not shown, and she has passed out. His act is a matter of life and death for both of them. She lets him feed on her until the cock crows. Hearing the noise, and seeing the sunrise through the window, the Count puts his hand to his heart

The evil has spread to Bremen as Count Dracula (Max Schreck) looks across to where Mina Harker lives in F. W. Murnau's *Nosferatu* (1922) (Prana-Film/the Kobal Collection).

and then to his face. He repeats the gestures Mina made when she first saw him at the window, realizing that he will die just as she prepared herself for her death. The sun falls on him, and then all that can be seen is some smoke rising from the floor. The way that the sunlight falls on the Count's face contrasts with the healthy way that sunlight fell on Harker when he first was in Transylvania before he met the Count.

Normality Restored

Throughout the film Murnau crosscuts scenes and images to connect and contrast one character of the film with another. The interconnection does not indicate the doubling of characters so much as their contrast. The evil that exists in the Count is not found in Mina or Harker, despite their connections with him. He is a threat from outside of them and to all of Germany. Harker returns with Van Helsing too late to save Mina. He holds his wife as she dies. Harker's embrace of her in death contrasts with their first embrace together during the initial montage scene of the film. Everything has changed for the Harkers from the start of the picture.

Mina dies along with the Count, but her sacrifice is not in vain. According to the last intertitle card, "The stifling shadow of the vampire vanished with the rising sun." The plague is at an end. Daylight has returned to the land. With Count Dracula dead, life can return to normal. Germany has been diminished through the death of Mina, but life will continue because of her sacrifice. Using the characters created by Bram Stoker, Murnau built a symphonic film that symbolically reveals the need for Germany to face the evil from without that threatens to destroy the country.

Dracula (1931)

DIR.: Tod Browning. PERF.: Bela Lugosi, Helen Chandler, David Manners, Dwight Frye. Dracula: The Legacy Collection, 2004. DVD.

Many Hollywood versions of Dracula have been filmed, but Tod Browning's 1931 *Dracula*, starring Bela Lugosi, is the best known.[28] Although the film is not well edited and unclear in aspects of its story line, it has remained a cultural touchstone, influencing all Dracula films made subsequently. The movie conveys many evocative images and what have become traditional moments, including when the Count announces, "I never drink ... wine." Several of these iconic moments involve the relationship between Van Helsing and Dracula, such as when Van Helsing identifies Count Dracula as a vampire by seeing that

Dracula does not produce a reflection in a mirror, and when Van Helsing keeps Dracula at bay by holding a cross in front of his face. As in the novel, it takes Dracula's nemesis to recognize the evil represented by the Count and to lead the group of good men to fight him.

But this Count Dracula, unlike the one in Stoker's novel, is predominantly a force of evil from without, one who comes from the exotic locale of Transylvania and begins destroying British virgins. In Browning's film Count Dracula is contrasted with the wholesomeness of British and Christian values. In 1931, when the picture was made, America and England (although the subject is English, this film was made by an American director in the United States) had xenophobic foreign policies that made citizens fearful of people from such exotic locales as Transylvania. Citizens felt the need to shore up their society against any foreign aggression. In 1931 the fear was not that a vampire may be among us, nor that he might take from us that which we hold most dear, but that our innocent women might go eagerly to his arms and become his willing victims.

With his sleeked-back black hair and broad face with handsome, even features, Bela Lugosi makes a sophisticated, sexually attractive Dracula. He is middle-aged rather than old, and clean shaven. His approach is stiff, melodramatic, cold, and commanding. His Hungarian accent and mellifluous voice are instrumental in marking him as foreign and setting him apart from the other characters. His clothes are elegant, suggesting Dracula's aristocratic origins. Lugosi, as Dracula, wears a tuxedo, white shirt, medal, and cape at all times. Lugosi's performance is one of the pleasures of viewing this film, as his attractive foreignness adds a new dimension to the story. Because Lugosi's Dracula possesses a sexual charm that makes him appealing to women, his female victims have some complicity in their own destruction. Lucy Western is enthralled by Dracula even before she is mesmerized by him.

In Stoker's novel, Dracula was intimately connected with the characters and the repressive society; vampires brought out the sexuality of Harker and the British women. But in this film, Dracula is primarily a threat from without. With his sexual charm and mesmerizing power, Dracula seduces the women of England. However, there are a few indications in the film that Dracula is also partly a threat from within, that he appeals to the repressed sexuality within a woman like Lucy because he is so different from anyone they know. At one point in the movie Dracula expresses his emotions, and this makes him sympathetic in the eyes of the characters and the viewer. Also, Dracula and Van Helsing are shown to be alter egos as they face off in a battle of wills for the well-being of the women of England.

Dracula, like many filmed versions of novels, is shortened and simplified by the removal of characters and locations. The film was not based directly on the novel, but rather on Hamilton Deane's stage play. In this movie it is Renfield who goes to Transylvania to meet with Count Dracula rather than Jonathan Harker, as in the novel. Renfield then arrives back in England where he is incarcerated in

Count Dracula (Bela Lugosi) welcomes Renfield (Dwight Frye) to his castle and traps him in his web in Tod Browning's *Dracula* (1931) (Universal/the Kobal Collection).

Dr. Seward's sanatorium. John Harker, rather than Jonathan Harker, is the fiancé of Mina, here in Browning's film Dr. Seward's daughter. As Dracula has bought Carfax Abbey, located right next to the sanitarium, the players all have reason to be in close proximity with each other.

The World at the Start of Browning's Film Dracula

At the start of this film, Renfield, seeking to meet Count Dracula in Transylvania, is outside his element. Acting in a responsible, logical British manner, he cannot understand the reaction of the people around him. When Renfield explains to his fellow passengers riding through the Carpathian Mountains on Walpurgis Night that Count Dracula's carriage will be meeting him at Burgo pass at midnight, all cross themselves and attempt to convince him to stay the night at an inn. By cutting from Renfield's travels towards the Count's castle and the activities within that castle, a contrast is formed between the safe, everyday world and the vampiric world of Count Dracula.

While the villagers watch the sun going down and begin to prepare for their evenings at home, the inhabitants of Dracula's castle come to life. In the basement of the castle a coffin opens and a hand tests the air, an opossum sits in a niche, and a bug crawls out of a hole. From another coffin a female hand appears, and then her pretty but pale and emotionless face. A casket opens and another woman emerges. A rodent comes out of a coffin containing a skeleton. Finally, the camera focuses on a frontal image of Dracula, centering on his eyes. His eyes can mesmerize and have power over all who look at them. Three women in the background move towards him while Dracula slowly walks up the winding steps of his castle stairs. The activities in Dracula's castle are like a reverse of the normal world, in which people sleep at night. The coffins indicate that they are already dead and are brought back to life at night. The nocturnal animals and people present a frightening alternative world not only to the world of the peasants that Renfield has met in Transylvania, but to Renfield's British sensibility as well.

Already nothing is as expected. Although he finds his surroundings confusing and potentially dangerous, Renfield insists on behaving as though he were playing by British rules. Renfield's approach is sincere and trusting; he attempts to act like a gentleman, rather than one fearful of the unknown and the unusual. The result will be disastrous for him. Although Dracula appears to be a gentleman, his looks are deceiving.

The Monster Within and Without

Evil takes many outward forms in this film, but they all stem from Dracula. Renfield sees Dracula in two variant forms during the carriage ride to Dracula's castle. As Renfield rides in the Count's coach to his castle, he looks out the window to see the driver. The viewer knows something that Renfield does not know: the driver is Count Dracula. Although Dracula is dressed differently from the first scene in which he awakes, the Count's eyes remain the same! At another point, Renfield looks out the carriage window and sees that there is no driver for the carriage, only a bat flying above the heads of the horses. Dracula and his wives frequently shape-shift into bats and wolves, allowing them access to areas they otherwise might not be able to enter. But even though they can change their outward appearance, they remain evil at the core.

When Renfield arrives at Count Dracula's home, the great doors of the castle creak open to admit him. The set is huge, dwarfing Renfield. Candelabra in hand, the Count descends the staircase to greet his confused guest. Count Dracula's elegance and formal manner mask his intentions. Renfield, following the Count back up the staircase, has to think about how to get through a huge spider web that blocks the entire stairway. Count Dracula has no problem negotiating the spider web — he steps right through it. Renfield breaks the web with his cane and then steps through, momentarily disturbing a large spider. Dracula explains, announcing his intentions quite clearly, "A spider spinning his web for the unwary fly. The blood is the life, Mr. Renfield." As with the spider, the blood of others supplies life for Dracula, and Renfield has been successfully caught in the Count's web.

In Stoker's novel there is a connection between Harker and Count Dracula in that there is a confusion between their identities; in Browning's film, Count Dracula is completely foreign to Renfield. While looking through the legal documents he has prepared for Dracula, Renfield receives a papercut on his finger, and the blood from the wound arouses Dracula. Renfield misinterprets Dracula's response and believes that he is squeamish about blood. As Dracula moves towards him, Renfield is saved for the moment when the cross he has been given by a peasant falls out of his shirt. But then Dracula holds Renfield with his eyes by mesmerizing him, and this allows the Count to feed on his blood. Dracula is the source of the evil in this film, and his monstrousness quickly spreads to other characters. In the novel, Dracula needs Renfield in order to provide the means by which Dracula can enter the sanatorium and gain access to Mina. In this film Renfield supplies a meal for Dracula and functions as a kind of early warning system for those in England, showing that association with Dracula leads to insanity or death. Yet because Renfield becomes insane, his words are not believed.

The Threat of the Monster

Renfield is vulnerable to Count Dracula because of his education, his system of government, and his good manners. His intelligence, breeding, and politeness are no defense against the ancient evil of Dracula. Along with other English attorneys and businessmen, Renfield secures the purchase of English property and safe passage for Count Dracula from Transylvania to England. As Dracula's ship comes into port and is boarded by officials, crazy laughter is heard. When the hatchway door is opened, all that can be seen is the deranged Renfield standing at the bottom of the stairs, laughing hysterically. It appears that Renfield alone has survived the trip. But Renfield is completely changed from his earlier self. By making himself agreeable and abiding by the rules of polite transactions, Renfield has allowed the Count to feed on him and render him insane. Yet Renfield still has moments of clarity.

By sending him visions, Dracula promises Renfield lives in the form of insects and rats; consequently, Renfield has an allegiance to Dracula. Dracula bends the bars of his windows and allows Renfield to escape from the sanatorium, but at other times Dracula threatens Renfield with death and does ultimately kill him. Occasionally Renfield's pre–Dracula existence comes to the fore and he tries to stop Dracula from hurting others. When he is most lucid, Renfield justifies his behavior with a glimmer of his old intelligence: he knows that Dracula is after Mina and at times warns the others to beware. But because of his association with Dracula, Renfield's warnings are not taken seriously.

Dracula is a complete outsider, a foreigner invading British soil. He looks, dresses, and sounds different from everyone he meets. In London, Count Dracula soon finds a victim: a lower-class flower seller who is held by his eyes so that she never resists. Dracula's attacks center on young women of an age to marry and procreate. He upsets the natural order of their lives by mesmerizing them and seducing them; consequently, he puts the future of England at risk. The institutions that should protect the women — their religion, their legal and medical systems— as well as their men, are seemingly helpless in the face of the advancing evil. In addition, the sanatorium, the symphony, and the ships of the harbor all allow evil to come into their midst. Dracula succeeds in making inroads into England because the British characters act politely even when they feel that something is wrong. Only an outsider, Van Helsing, is effective in locating and tackling the source of the evil.

The Nature of the Evil

Count Dracula poses a threat to the lives of everyone he has contact with. He has the capacity to kill his victims, but more horrible than that, to make the female victims his wives, dependent on the blood of others in order to remain undead. They cannot die a natural death but must eternally make victims of others. Yet Count Dracula is not completely repulsive. Through his charisma and his emotions, the characters and even the viewer gain some sympathy for him.

Count Dracula quickly adapts to life in London and makes himself charming and accepted into society through the use of his title (everyone wants to know a Count), his accented English, his formal manners, his elegant clothes, and his manipulation of the politeness of others. He assimilates into the English culture and takes advantage of the rules of society. When the Count attends the symphony, he is dressed just right for the event. There, with a contrivance involving the hypnotism of an usher, the Count meets Dr. Seward, his daughter Mina, Mr. Harker, and Lucy Western. Dracula can then focus on the small group of people staying with Dr. Seward in his sanatorium, where Renfield has been taken and which is located right next to Carfax Abbey, the property the Count has purchased.

Meeting Count Dracula in their box at the symphony, the women quickly engage him in conversation. Lucy quotes from a poem that she is reminded of by the decayed state of Carfax Abbey: "Quaff a cup to the dead already! Hurrah for the next who dies!"[29] Dracula replies in a way described by the script as "half-dreamily, a deeply tragic note underlying his words": "To die — to be really dead — that must be glorious." Dracula hints at the unique aspect of his own situation — that he longs to die. The viewer becomes aware of the hopelessness and endlessness of his condition in a way that never occurs in the novel. In this film Dracula speaks no words about love, but his longing for death reveals emotion not otherwise indicated. The showing of emotion in this scene humanizes Dracula and makes him more attractive and mysterious to Lucy. Yet he has also revealed how different he is from all humans. The next day Mina mocks his accent and emphasis on death, but Lucy announces that she finds him fascinating. The Count knows the impression he has made on Lucy; consequently, Dracula intends to make her his next victim.

While Dracula makes inroads into English society, Van Helsing works feverishly to stop him. Van Helsing announces that the deaths he has investigated are the work of a vampire, as he sees the same two marks in the necks of the victims. He arrives in London to study Renfield and hopes to prove that "the superstition of yesterday can become the scientific reality of today." Thus the ancient force of darkness is confronted by modern science.

Dracula and Van Helsing are introduced in the home of Dr. Seward. Until this point, the difference between Dracula and his victims in terms of his clothes, manner, accent, and taste has been emphasized. But Van Helsing is different as well. When first shown on the screen, the camera focuses on his eyes, just as it had focused on Dracula's eyes when he first appeared. Like Dracula, Van Helsing, is foreign and speaks English with an accent. By exaggerating the similarities between Dracula and Van Helsing, they become worthy opponents. The connection between Van Helsing and Dracula makes them alter egos or doubles who engage in battle against each other. Whereas the English are bound by the rules of polite society, Dracula is not; for example, he hypnotized the usher and created a false phone call in order to be introduced to Dr. Seward.

Van Helsing, suspecting a vampire in their midst, also exceeds the rules of polite society.

Dracula plays the role of neighbor and guest, taking advantage of the hospitality of Dr. Seward. Good manners should be a sign of predictable behavior, but Dracula does not behave in predictable ways. It takes another outsider, Van Helsing, to confront Dracula. Both Dracula and Renfield have a habit of walking into rooms unexpectedly, just as they are being discussed. As Prof. Van Helsing gets Mina to reveal the marks on her neck, he asks, "What could have caused those?" Immediately the maid appears and announces the arrival of their neighbor, simultaneously providing the correct response to Van Helsing's question: "Count Dracula." Van Helsing's question is answered, but he cannot prove his conjecture. Opening a silver cigarette case, Van Helsing notices that the Count casts no reflection, evidence of his lack of a soul. Van Helsing shows him the mirror and the Count knocks it to the floor. Dracula realizes what he is up against: "For one who has not lived even a single lifetime, you are a wise man." Van Helsing recognizes that he still cannot prove that Dracula is a vampire, as he says, "The strength of the vampire is that people will not believe in him." No one wants to believe that which seems impossible.

Dracula's evil has spread so that a dead English virgin has become someone who preys upon children. He has turned Lucy into an animal, someone no longer human, doomed for eternity. Having worked his will on Lucy, Dracula now centers his attention on Mina. Through his night visits to Mina's room, Count Dracula causes her to change her opinion of him. Mina becomes excited when she sees the Count, and her chest heaves. At the same time, through dreams and visions, Mina knows that Lucy has become one of the undead who threatens children, and she fears a similar fate for herself. Mina seems changed, distant, and fixated on the neck of her fiancé, John. Disturbed by the relationship between Count Dracula and Mina, John wants to rescue her by taking Mina away. John doesn't understand the evil that threatens Mina, although she explains to him what has happened to her. He believes they can escape the Count by going elsewhere. Van Helsing knows that Mina needs to stay and face the source of the problem so that he can bring Count Dracula's destructive sway to an end.

The Monster Destroyed

The good people of Browning's film gather together at Seward's sanatorium. Van Helsing must start the process of defeating Dracula by convincing everyone that Dracula is a vampire and that ordinary means cannot be used to defeat him. This leads to a scene in which there is a standoff between Dracula and Van Helsing; the forces of evil and good confront one another. Both are concerned with Mina, and both are foreign. Dracula advises Van Helsing to go

Van Helsing (Edward Van Sloan) and Count Dracula (Bela Lugosi) are alter egos in
Tod Browning's *Dracula* (1931) (Universal/the Kobal Collection).

back to his own country. Van Helsing replies that he wants to protect those
Dracula would destroy. Dracula says it is too late, that his blood flows through
Mina's veins. As Van Helsing threatens Dracula, Dracula says, "Come here,"
and tries to hypnotize Van Helsing. Van Helsing's will resists Dracula, and ultimately Van Helsing picks up the Christian symbol of the cross to counteract
Dracula's power. Van Helsing is safe for the moment, but Mina is not. Women,
confronted by the handsome Count, do not have the willpower to resist his
hypnotic eyes.

Count Dracula gains access to Mina once again when wolfbane falls away
from her neck and he is able to hypnotize the nurse watching her. He takes her
with him to Carfax Abbey. As they enter the basement of the Abbey, Renfield
appears, and John and Van Helsing are waiting. Renfield suspects that the Count
believes he has brought Van Helsing to the Abbey, so he begs Dracula not to
kill him. Renfield fears for his soul, as the lives of many creatures are on his
conscience and blood on his hands. But Dracula kills Renfield anyway. Dracula
and Mina walk down the staircase as though descending to hell. The Count

believes he is triumphant. As the dawn comes, Van Helsing discovers Dracula in his coffin and drives a stake through his heart. Mina turns out not to be in the second box, but her screams, as she suffers from the stake that kills Dracula, reveal her hiding place — as well as the physical connection between herself and Dracula. Having imbibed his blood, Mina can only be restored to life by Dracula's death.

Normality Restored

In the final scene of Browning's 1931 film, Mina and John mount the stairs of the Abbey as though ascending to heaven — a reversal of her previous walk with Count Dracula. The sound of church bells resounds. It looks like a wedding in reverse and suggests that a wedding will be forthcoming. With Count Dracula dead, Mina returns to her previous state; her soul is pure once more. She is away from the clutches of Count Dracula and ready to be married to John Harker. Only with the Count's death can Mina — and all English women — be safe.

Van Helsing has led the men from the sanatorium next door to Carfax Abbey to defeat Dracula; they need not return to Transylvania as in the novel. The final battle does not result in the death of one of their member, and there is no coda about the couple and their child. Mina and John are restored to each other's arms, and that is enough. Through the combination of twentieth-century science and age-old staking, the force of good has defeated Count Dracula. Van Helsing announces, "Dracula is dead forever." No reminder of him would seem to remain, and yet there has been no end to Dracula's reappearances. Hundreds of vampire movies have been made since Browning directed this one, each influenced by Browning's vision but also changing the presentation of Dracula to accord with the ideas, beliefs, and values of the age in which it was made.

Bram Stoker's Dracula (1992)

DIR.: Francis Ford Coppola. PERF.: Gary Oldman, Winona Ryder, Anthony Hopkins, Keanu Reeves. Columbia/Tristar, 1997. VCR.

In the hands of director Francis Ford Coppola, Bram Stoker's tale of the forces of good battling the evil of Count Dracula becomes a love story. Dracula is not a plague that rampages through Germany, as in *Nosferatu*, nor a force from abroad who attracts the innocent women of England, as in Browning's film; rather, Dracula clearly has two sides, the human and the monstrous. Coppola's film, incongruously named *Bram Stoker's Dracula*,[30] shows how Count Dracula, who has survived for centuries following the suicide of his wife, seeks to be reunited with her. In Coppola's film, Mina is pulled between her remembered love for Dracula and her vows to her fiancé and husband, Jonathan Harker. Love, rather than goodness and religion, becomes the dominant theme of the film. In this treatment of the story, the gothic horror tale becomes the story of a Prince seeking to be reunited with his lost love. Coppola's product goes the furthest of any film to date in presenting the evil as coming from within Count Dracula's victims rather than as a force from the outside.

That the evil is within Count Dracula's victims is seen first with Lucy Westenra whose sexual precociousness provides an opportunity for the Count. Mina becomes his willing victim because of her desire for passionate love and her remembered love for the Count. The reactions of the characters to the Count indicate that they are eager recipients of his evil, as he brings out their sexual passions. On the other hand, Van Helsing becomes more of a double for the Count than presented in any earlier film.

Count Dracula combines many opposite tendencies, including a superhuman capacity to love with a monstrous propensity to prey on other people. Like other monsters, he unites the human with the inhuman and unnatural. As played by Gary Oldman, Dracula's appearance changes so that he appears ancient and

Indulging in a private pleasure, Count Dracula (Gary Oldman) in Francis Ford Coppola's *Bram Stoker's Dracula* (1992) (Zoetrope/Columbia Tri-Star/the Kobal Collection).

hideous when seen by Harker in Transylvania, and young and handsome when first seen by Mina in London. In Transylvania his skin is dry and wrinkled, he wears flowing robes, and his long hair is elaborately arranged in a fashion similar to that of Princess Leia in *Star Wars*. There is nothing attractive about him or his surroundings, as even his castle seems haphazardly constructed. At other times he reveals the capacity to become a shockingly ugly batman and a wolf-man, with translucent skin stretched over bones and wings. Taking the form of the wolfman, he rapes Lucy. However, when Dracula arrives in London, he becomes visible to Mina as an elegantly dressed and handsome dandy. In addition, he can enter and leave rooms as rats and mist. Strangely, his repulsive shapes do not inhibit his sexual conquests. Disgust and attraction are entwined in the reaction of his victims.

At times the viewer can see Dracula's victims from his point of view, but only his human side evokes the sympathy of the viewer. When the viewer sees Dracula as an animal, it arouses fear in the viewer; when the viewer sees him as a human, the viewer wants him to succeed. As an animal, the world appears to Dracula in a manner that Coppola calls "pixilated." At these points the film speeds up, as though the eye of the camera were the eye of an animal focusing in on its prey. The picture projected on the screen is broken up into small pieces as the eye of Dracula seeks its victim; then the focus becomes clear as he latches onto the victim. The pixilation does not make the viewer identify with the Count because the viewpoint is not human but animal; the strange sensation creates fear in the viewer, a belief that at any moment the viewer could become his victim. However, in Dracula's search for love as a human, we see Mina from Dracula's human point of view. This aspect gives the viewer some sympathy for the Count as everyone wants to believe in a form of true love that defies death.

The World at the Start of Coppola's Film
Bram Stoker's Dracula

The film *Bram Stoker's Dracula* begins with a short picture of the world before the arrival of the monster, Count Dracula. In the backstory, Vlad Tepes becomes a vampire during a time of turbulence and war when the Christian world was threatened by Moslem invaders. The film begins in 1462 in Constantinople as the Roumanian knight Vlad Tepes, or Prince Dracula, impales hundreds of men. Thus he behaves as a monster before he actually becomes a vampire. His vampirism results from his outrageous behavior in other ways. After the battle, Dracula praises God but thinks of his wife Elizabeth, with whom he appears to have a form of mental telepathy. Believing he is dead, Elizabeth commits suicide and leaves a note saying, "May God unite us in heaven." The remainder of the film seeks to answer the question of whether Dracula and Elizabeth will be reunited in heaven.

The priests raise an obstacle to the reuniting of the Prince and Elizabeth by saying she is damned, and so her soul will not go to heaven. Dracula defies Christianity by renouncing God and stabbing the cross with his sword. The cross bleeds, leading Count Dracula to announce, "The blood is the life," as he drinks the blood. The film suggests that Count Dracula is born through this Satanic ritual, that Count Dracula envelops himself in his own monstrousness. His cursing of God brings out the evil that is already within him, separating him from everyone around him — except those he forces to become like him.

The backstory is immediately connected to the principle story of the film through the doubling of roles for the actors. Winona Rider plays both Elizabeth and Mina Harker, underlining that Mina is the reincarnation of Dracula's wife. The head priest is played by Anthony Hopkins, the same actor who plays Van Helsing, emphasizing the later combat between Van Helsing and Dracula. Both characters played by Hopkins are on the side of God and opposed to Dracula.

The majority of the film takes place in the late 1890s, four centuries after the death of Elizabeth, as Jonathan Harker arrives in Transylvania, the characters make their way to England, and then go back again to a final battle with Count Dracula in Transylvania. Renfield had previously ventured to Transylvania to assist Count Dracula with his real estate transaction but returned insane. At Carfax District Lunatic Asylum, Renfield crouches on the ground, then stretches up his body and his hand until he looks huge, suggesting the rising power of Dracula, as Renfield announces that preparations are in order for his master.

Scene transitions are frequently accomplished through the connection of images in this film. Jonathan Harker leaves for Transylvania, kissing his fiancée Mina goodbye in a very careful manner. He appears to be a passionless man, although Mina longs for love. A peacock feather fan politely separates them from the view of the audience, and then the eye of the peacock feather becomes a tunnel for his train as he travels from the West to the East. The shape of the peacock feather connects the two scenes, linking societal proprieties with sexual suggestiveness. In the East, Harker will be tempted to sexual pleasure in a way he never anticipated. But what happens in the East does not stay in the East.

The Monster Within and Without

The connection between Dracula and his victims is not immediately apparent. A guest at Dracula's castle, Jonathan Harker attempts to be civil and treat Dracula with respect, however frightened he is by Dracula's manner and appearance. After Harker cuts himself while shaving, the Count licks the blood off the razor's blade, an action seen by the viewer but not by Harker. The Count proceeds to shave Harker himself, showing that he controls the life and death of this man. Scared by the strangeness of everything, Harker remains passive. Dracula also exposes his human side by revealing his unhappiness to Harker. Speaking of his wife's death, he says, "She was fortunate. My life at its best is … misery." Although Dracula presents his feelings honestly and makes a bid for sympathy, his elaborate costumes, make-up, and evil intentions distance him from Harker and from the viewer as well.

We are repelled by Dracula because he is different than we are. Dressed like the pope, with a long red train behind his robe, Dracula suggests an anti-religious figure; yet he never has the Satanic dimension given in the novel in the sense that the tale plays out a contest between the eternal forces of good and evil. In Coppola's film, Dracula's inability to be seen in a mirror and his lack of an ordinary shadow align him with evil and indicate that he lacks a soul. The movement of Dracula's shadow, which is not reliant on the movement of his body, reflects an alternative reality. So, for example, after Dracula has seen Harker's picture of his fiancée Mina, who is the embodiment of the Count's dead wife Elizabeth, Dracula doesn't react, but his shadow moves to strangle Harker, showing what Dracula desires to do.

The repression of Victorian society plays a large part in this film. Harker is undone by his sexual desires, which are revealed through the women in Dracula's castle. Because of his repressed desires, Harker is vulnerable to the openly sexual. Dracula makes use of the sexual desires of Lucy and Mina as well. Coppola emphasizes how Dracula latches onto something that is already within his victims, which then changes them in an unanticipated fashion.

Even before her encounter with Dracula, Lucy seeks sexual intimacy with her suitors. Lucy teases Quincey Morris with sexual double entendre. Putting her hand near his waist and saying suggestively, "Please let me touch it; it's so big," she pulls out his knife. Her lack of repression in a repressed age makes Quincey, Jack Seward, and Arthur Holmwood fall in love with Lucy. Although Mina is shocked by Lucy's sexuality, Mina also seeks more than her society offers and is capable of arousing and being aroused in unconventional ways. Thus the way is prepared for Dracula by Victorian society, which does not allow sexual outlets for its young men and women.

The Threat of the Monster

The monster, Dracula, has created himself by defying God after learning that the Church will not allow him to bury his wife because she committed suicide. Dracula becomes the source for all other vampires. He can turn women into his brides by letting them drink his blood, or take their blood and render them undead, feeding from beyond the grave like Lucy. The evil of the film stems from the Count's monstrosity, his need to drink the blood of his victims. But it also arises from his humanness, his desire to make Mina his bride in order to regain Elizabeth. He is selfish in his willingness to destroy others to feed himself, not just killing them but damning their souls as well.

Within Dracula's castle, Harker's world literally turns upside down: he opens a bottle of perfume, and the drops rise up. He doesn't know how to react, as he has no experience of such a phenomenon. His experience becomes sexual when three women vampires appear and become the aggressors. At first he is a not-unwilling victim; but then, as he feels his lack of control, he becomes afraid. In Coppola's film, Harker is definitely bitten and feasted on by the women. He survives because he climbs out the window before he is bled dry. Mina receives a letter from Harker, written at the command of Dracula, that is signed, "Ever faithful." The complimentary closure brings out both Harker's repression, as he is not expressing love to Mina, and the fact that "ever faithful" is not accurate — he has been somewhat unfaithful with Dracula's brides.

The crosscutting of scenes acts both to connect and contrast the affairs of different characters as Dracula invades England. By crosscutting between scenes of Harker in Dracula's castle and scenes of Lucy, Mina, and Renfield in England, Coppola displays Dracula's avenues of attack as he makes his way to the West. The viewer watches Lucy and Mina, two single Victorian women in England, acting in immodest ways, ways that will make them vulnerable to Dracula's attack. Mina, while writing to Harker, looks at pictures of sexual intimacy in Richard Burton's *Arabian Nights* (a book originating in the East that was brought back and published by a westerner). Mina has a curiosity that Lucy encourages, but that finds little other expression. Lucy, when she sees what Mina has been looking at, says that she did that last night — in her dreams. According to Mina, Lucy is a virtuous girl but has a free way of speaking; indeed, she speaks more like a twentieth-century woman than a nineteenth-century one. Lucy is a flirtatious virgin and not a fallen woman, and yet her flirtatiousness, although innocent, opens her to attack by Dracula. By crosscutting between events in Transylvania and England, Coppola's film connects the events, showing the similarity of the attacks on all of Dracula's victims and recording his increasing dominion over the West.

In several ways the attack on Harker parallels what happens to Mina. Both Mina and Harker are drawn to and experiment with sexuality, although they are reserved in their sexuality and in their expression, and both keep their experiences to themselves. Harker is mesmerized by Dracula's wives, while Mina feels Elizabeth's love for Dracula. Later in the film Harker will maintain that he is to blame for the activities of the Count, while Mina will claim it is her fault. Because of their suppressed desire for the unknown, Mina, Lucy, and Harker are open to vampires. Thus, since his victims are so open to the experience, the means of converting the human population to a vampire population seems fairly easy and straightforward — all the world could be vampires and monsters before long. Although Dracula's victims are drawn to the sexuality of the experience, they do not yet know what it means to be a vampire.

The Nature of the Evil

Dracula kills his victims by draining them of blood, forcing them to become vampires and prey on other people; or he forces them to drink his blood and become like his wives. Although they are not consciously willing victims, their own repressed desires have made them available to the vampire. By taking advantage of his victims, Dracula spreads his evil, turning them into monsters by sapping their bodies of blood and life and denying the possibility of heaven to their souls.

Blood itself becomes a major symbol of the movie. From Dracula's curse to Renfield's reiteration that "the blood is the life," blood achieves a significance that goes beyond its connection with semen in the novel. In Coppola's film, through the symbolism of the blood, vampirism is made analogous to syphilis and AIDS. The transference of blood between vampire and victim suggests not only sexual intercourse but also contagion through sexually transmitted infections. The viewer observes changes happening on a cellular level, as images of blood cells are projected onto the screen. The film evokes the fear during the time it was made of AIDS contagion through the transfer of blood by portraying the fear of syphilis during the time the story takes place.

Mina's willingness to become a vampire is suggested by the ease with which she steps outside of Victorian moral conventions, in addition to her interest in passionate sex. This propensity continues when Count Dracula tries to pick her up on the streets of London. As Dracula is new to England, so movies are new to the world, and Coppola brings the images together. In doing so Coppola shows the ability of Dracula to propagate vampires as quickly as the moving picture gained status and popularity. As the now young Dracula walks in London, we see it as a movie, the scene having been filmed as though with an early, hand-held camera. Dressed as a young dandy with cool blue glasses, he introduces himself as Prince Vlad. At first Mina resists, but then she goes with him to the cinema. She is drawn to the new experience where she will be reminded of her past life, for at the theater she sees hints of the life of Elizabeth.

The fates of Lucy and Mina are entwined through the crosscutting of scenes. The evil has now made inroads towards Lucy's demise and also through the awakening of Mina's remembered passion as Elizabeth. The Count condemns Lucy to a living undeath, as the film crosscuts scenes of her death with the marriage of Harker and Mina. As the young couple kiss, a symbol of their love, the Count, in the form of a wolf, ravages Lucy. Later, while being fitted for her wedding gown, Lucy tells Dr. Seward she is changing. Indeed, soon she will be buried in this dress. The dress is a parody of the Queen Elizabeth style so that Lucy becomes a symbol of England and virginity in her clothes. Count Dracula has further sexualized Lucy by making her frail and helpless and consequently more attractive to the men in her life. Although she has received a blood transfusion, she still has little blood. The question among the men is: Where did the blood that went into Lucy go? The viewer is shown the answer when the camera captures the Count in his coffin with blood dripping from his mouth. Like crosscutting, using images to change the scene emphasizes the connection between Lucy and Mina. For example, the camera focuses on the two holes in Lucy's neck. These holes fade to become the eyes of a wolf at the cinematograph. By encouraging her to pet the wolf, Dracula causes Mina to trust him. Later, while dancing with Prince Dracula, Mina feels like a princess; while dressed in her white wedding dress in her glass coffin, Lucy appears as Snow White. The Count has killed Lucy and seeks to be reunited with Mina.

Mina goes beyond nineteenth-century propriety by meeting Dracula alone at a restaurant for supper. This would be improper for a Victorian woman and indeed unacceptable for an engaged woman in any era. She plays a very dangerous game of infidelity. She is intrigued by the Count in part because he reminds her of her past life. While dining, they imbibe in the pleasure of drinking absinthe, an aphrodisiac that "wants her soul," according to the Count — a description that fits the Count himself. The screen shows the label of the bottle, focusing on the letters spelling "sin" within the word "absinthe." A closeup of Mina's blood shows absinthe changing Mina's blood much as a vampire's bite would. "What of the Princess?" Mina asks while they both see visions of her; here again they can communicate without speaking, as his visions of his wife answer her questions. Mina's mind is not where it should be, for while she is becoming closer to Dracula, crosscutting reveals Harker trying to escape from the Count's castle. Mina should be thinking of her fiancé.

Just as the evil is advancing, the forces of good receive a boost through the appearance of Van Helsing. The viewer first sees Van Helsing giving a lecture on civilization, syphilis, and bats. Van Helsing appears in the novel as a type of doppelgänger for Dracula, and this doubling is present in Coppola's film as well. Both men are foreign, and both are attracted to Mina. Van Helsing lacks social skills, speaking bluntly and to the point, much as Count Dracula does. He says of Lucy, shaking up the men who love her, "Lucy is not a random victim attacked by mere accident, you understand me? No — she is a willing recruit, a follower, I daresay — a devoted disciple. She is the devil's concubine" (107). When Van Helsing meets Mina, he dances with her just as the Prince did. It is as if he knows what she has been up to. When Mina asks Van Helsing about Lucy's death, he laughs and licks his fingers, which are coated with the bloody

Opposite: Mina Harker (Winona Ryder) and Count Dracula (Gary Oldman) — he is a dandy on the outside, but a monster within — in Francis Ford Coppola's *Bram Stoker's Dracula* (1992) (Zoetrope/Columbia Tri-Star/the Kobal Collection).

juice from a roast beef, and sadistically replies, "Then we cut off her head and drove a stake through her heart and burned it" (123). Like Dracula, he takes delight in the shocking.

Although Mina is engaged first and then married, she flirts with the Prince, as he is called here, going to the cinematograph and dining and dancing alone with him. She recognizes him in a subconscious way and is comforted by him without really knowing why, although the audience knows that she appears to be the reincarnation of the Prince's tragically lost wife, whose suicide led him to become the "undead." He behaves romantically towards Mina, telling her that he has "travelled across oceans of time" for her. Finally he comes to her when she is alone at night. The atmosphere is peachy and dimly lit, soft and warm. His story is a human love story, and yet the viewer cannot forget his monstrous aspect. Only his eternal love for Elizabeth, expressed by his handsome and human form, evokes sympathy. The scene shifts back and forth from the vampire hunters performing an exorcism and destroying the coffins with Dracula's native soil in Carfax Abbey — the vampire hunters doing their work in the name of God — with the view of green particles coming into the room where Mina sleeps alone. The Prince acts both out of love and as a vampire, seeking Mina's soul. Despite the fact that Mina relates to the Count's human aspect, Mina and the Count are initially at cross purposes, as she believes he has come to have sex with her, but his thoughts are elsewhere. When she reaches to be kissed, he pulls away and looks at her neck. He explains with his face ashamedly turned from her, that he is a vampire. Dracula is literally not able to face his love to tell her what he has done and what she would have to do to stay with him.

Count Dracula uses sex to seduce Mina into death. His bite to her neck is a forceful and difficult penetration, making her call out momentarily; this is not the hypnotically-induced desire that Lucy experienced, but a substitute for sexual intercourse and the breaking of her hymen. He then opens the vein in his breast and says, "Mina, drink and join me in eternal life." As she starts to drink, he seems to have an orgasm, but then he pulls her face away and says that he cannot let her do it because he loves her too much. Ultimately the Prince turns to the screen with a surprised look on his face for just a moment before the door opens and we see what Mina's husband and the other men see as they enter the room. From their viewpoint, Mina wears a little nightgown and kneels on the bed, enraptured but alone. She looks small and silly, no longer the center of the universe as she was when alone with her Prince. As the Count leaves (having gone from young, handsome prince to hideous batman to dozens of rats), Mina holds onto her husband, Harker, saying, obviously about herself, "Unclean." Although it appeared that she chose to remain with the Prince, she has now returned to her husband. She seems to stay with whomever she is with at the moment without making the choice between forever with the Count or a human life span with Harker.

The Count's evil has spread to Mina: he has telepathic powers over her, as well as a bond of love. When she is with him, she wants to become a vampire so that she can be with him forever. This is the evil of the Count, that he can induce passion and eternal love in his victims. Mina is torn between the Count and the forces of good.

The Monster Destroyed

At the end of the film, all prepare for the final battle between good and evil. Van Helsing hypnotizes Mina so that they may follow Dracula's movements back to his castle, yet Dracula can also read her mind, so he knows what they are doing. Mina temporarily seduces Van Helsing, who then attempts to cleanse her with a communion wafer, but instead the wafer burns her, showing how close she is to evil. She is in league with the women who were after Harker, as they now approach Van Helsing. Eventually Van Helsing cuts off the heads of the three women and throws the heads into the river.

The ultimate battle becomes a contest for the souls of both the Count and Mina. The Count calls to Mina and races against the sunset, for when the day is over Dracula will be safe. Mina helps the Count until he is stabbed, at which point his power over her is lost, and yet she uses her strength to save his soul. As Quincey dies, Van Helsing says, "We have all become God's madmen," meaning that in order to fight for what is right, they have had to behave as if insane. Mina holds off the men with a rifle in order to go into the chapel with the Count. Even though he is dying, her future is unsure — will she die with him or stay with Harker?

Normality Restored

The final scene of the film takes place in the chapel where Count Dracula renounced God. While four hundred years ago the Count and Elizabeth were separated, now they will be joined. "It is finished," says the Count, talking about his life, vampiredom, and the film. As he lies in the chapel, light radiating from the skies above touches his face, making him young and handsome again, and suggesting his soul will be saved. Mina kisses Dracula and then frees his soul by driving a stake into his heart and cutting off his head. The last shot of the film focuses on the painted image of Elizabeth and the Count, forever young, on the roof of the chapel as though they will be together in heaven. The happy ending of the film is provided not by her child with Harker, as in the novel, but her union with Dracula.

Rather than good men banding together to protect England and its women, a female reincarnation of Dracula's wife has given her husband peace after four hundred years. No longer will the world be bothered by vampires, but, more importantly, as it seems in this film, the souls of the happy couple will be reunited in heaven.

In Bram Stoker's novel, the Count uses Mina to take revenge on the men seeking to destroy him. She plays an important role in the story because of her intelligence, her manner of collating the pieces of the story for the education of the characters, and for the birth of her child. This child is a physical reminder of the Crew of Light that fought Dracula, a means of bringing together their names, an emblem of the consummation of her marriage, and a hope for the future. The birth of the Harkers' child indicates the complete end of their experiences with vampires. The novel's ending shows them as stable adults with a working and healthy relationship with each other. Coppola's film, *Bram Stoker's Dracula*, has no similar resolution, and reveals the elemental change in emphasis from the 1890s to the 1990s. Eternal love has become more important than the morality of good over evil, and the power of Dracula has increased because of the desires within his victims. They became his willing victims. Although the situation around them has returned to normality, the Harkers are not yet integrated into society. Their experiences mark them as apart from the others. Their willing surrender to sexual experiences outside of their relationship makes the viewer wonder if they can ever forgive each other and come to terms with their past. The introduction of the love theme between Count Dracula and Mina raises certain other problems for the future. On earth Mina has been torn between her allegiance to her husband and her passionate love for the Count. Mina seemed happier with the Count than with her husband; will she be happy with her husband for eternity?

Conclusion

When I first thought about British horror fiction in the nineteenth century, I was struck by the large gap between the writing of *Frankenstein* in 1818 and the writing of *Dr. Jekyll and Mr. Hyde* in 1886. These are the works of horror fiction that are most frequently read, discussed, and available today. Yet many other works were popular during the Victorian era. The horror genre was alive and well for all of that century. Monsters abound. They were not just limited to the horror novel itself; monsters were also a vital part of the mainstream literature of the time. Monsters were explored in novels, short stories, poetry, and plays throughout the era.

The Horror Tradition in British Nineteenth-Century Literature

Nineteenth-century horror works popularized many different kinds of monsters. The vampire and other horror traditions continued throughout the century. *Wagner, the Wehr-Wolf* was created by G. W. M. Reynolds in 1847. Later in the century Martians and other scientific monsters were developed by H. G. Wells. Ghost stories were extremely popular throughout the century; authors as diverse as Grant Allen, Mary Elizabeth Braddon, Rhoda Broughton, Wilkie Collins, Amelia Edwards, Elizabeth Gaskell, Thomas Hardy, Henry James, M. R. James, Rudyard Kipling, Sheridan LeFanu, George MacDonald, Dinah Maria Mulock, Edith Nesbit, Charlotte Riddell, Robert Louis Stevenson, Bram Stoker, and Mrs. Henry Wood all wrote ghost stories. Charles Dickens made use of the tradition of ghost stories in several works, including *A Christmas Carol* (1843). In that novel, inspired by his similarities to his dead and tormented partner, Ebenezer Scrooge examines the misspent aspects of his life. From his experiences, Scrooge realizes the errors of his ways and changes. Through identification with the ghost, Scrooge becomes a better and happier person. For Dickens, the monstrous is within mankind, and man has the capacity to change when he recognizes the error of his ways.

Many nineteenth-century authors focus on human monstrosity, although the monstrous character does not always go through a positive metamorphosis. Elements of the monstrous show up in such diverse places as William Make-peace Thackeray's description of the Becky Monster in *Vanity Fair* (1847–48; ch. 64) and in the character Heathcliff in Emily Brontë's *Wuthering Heights* (1847). Christina Rossetti's "Goblin Market" (1862) uses monsters in the form of goblin-men who threaten the human characters. Even works written for children used the monster tradition. Many fairy tales from France and Germany were translated during the nineteenth century, and modern versions of fairy tales by Anne Thackeray Ritchie and other authors were published. Monsters also appear in the fantasy works of George MacDonald, in Charles Kingsley's *The Water Babies* (1864), and as the Jabberwock in Lewis Carroll's *Through the Looking-Glass* (1872).

The idea of horror was deeply imbued in nineteenth-century literature. However, while the monstrous was often a threat to the society depicted in a work of fiction, the evil was not always a reflection of the hero or heroine of the work. Yet frequently monsters do contain aspects of the main characters and are often doubles of those characters. Evil comes from within the individual, seeping outward to destroy society. Two novels that are not horror novels themselves but contain elements of horror, and that have been explored many times in film, are *Jane Eyre* and *Great Expectations*.

Jane Eyre

Elements of the horror novel appear in many mainstream nineteenth-century novels. Charlotte Brontë's novel *Jane Eyre* (1847) concerns the heroine's search for love and religion beyond the constraints of Victorian society. She seeks to find her place in the world, and in doing so must learn to control her emotions. An adult who cannot control herself will suffer the fate of Rochester's wife, Bertha Mason, the fate of insanity and imprisonment. In the novel, Jane and Bertha are intimately connected. Bertha represents the angry, repressed aspect of Jane.[31] Jane has learned to control her passions, while Bertha cannot restrain herself. Bertha expresses the outrage that Jane would feel if she had a full picture of Rochester's motivations and behavior. As Jane tells Rochester about the woman who visited her room two nights before her wedding, she describes the woman as a monster. The face reminds her of "the foul German spectre — the Vampyre" (242). Rochester leads the witnesses from what was to be his wedding to Jane, to see Bertha Mason Rochester in her attic prison. Jane describes their view as they look through the door: "The maniac bellowed: she parted her shaggy locks from her visage and gazed wildly at her visitors. I recognized well that purple face — those bloated features" (250). Rochester stresses the differences between the two women, "'That is my wife, ... such is the sole conjugal embrace I am ever to know — such are the endearments which are to solace my leisure hours! And this is what I wished to have' (laying his hand on my shoulder): 'this young girl, who stands so grave and quiet at the mouth of hell, looking collectedly at the gambols of a demon'" (251). He views Bertha as a monster and someone very different from Jane. But Bertha represents that part of Jane that has not learned to control her rage.

The concept of two women similar in many ways, although one of them is mad, was brought out by Mary Elizabeth Coleridge in her poem "The Other Side of a Mirror" (1896):

> I sat before my glass one day,
> And conjured up a vision bare,
> Unlike the aspects glad and gay,
> That erst were found reflected there —
> The vision of a woman, wild
> With more than womanly despair.
>
> ...
>
> Pass— as the fairer visions pass—
> Nor ever more return, to be
> The ghost of a distracted hour,
> That heard me whisper: —"I am she!"[32]

Here a woman looks in her mirror and sees a woman who appears "wild," with "more than womanly despair." Although at first she tries not to recognize the reflection, ultimately she understands that this woman is herself. It is thought that Coleridge may have been influenced by the novel *Jane Eyre* when she wrote this poem. Many women, like Jane Eyre, have within them an angry or wild or monstrous part of themselves which must be repressed in order for them to be labeled as sane within a patriarchal society. All people must develop a civilized part of themselves to present to the world.

The film *Jane Eyre* (1944), directed by Robert Stevenson, contains elements of horror — but of a different sort than the novel. As the group mounts the stairs and opens the door of the attic, anticipation grows, as in a traditional horror movie. Like the guests, the reader looks past a perfectly dressed woman through a doorway into another world. Beyond the second figure the unknown waits. A figure rises up and puts its hands on Rochester's throat, and then the screen becomes all shadows. The differences between Jane and Bertha Mason are emphasized; no attempt is made to show the women as connected in any way.

Bertha appears very different physically in the same scene from the 1996 *Jane Eyre* directed by Franco Zeffirelli. The whole group climbs the steps to the attic and views Bertha just as the audience does. Bertha sits quietly at the fire, looking quite lovely with long, pretty hair, while Rochester says she is mad, the product of three generations of lunacy. She stares at Jane, and Jane stares at her before Bertha becomes hysterical. Bertha is beautiful on the outside and insane within, while Jane is plain outside but beautiful in her mind and soul. In both films Bertha is only the lunatic wife of Rochester, she is in no way made a double for Jane or for our own suppressed rage. In these film adaptations the monster is a threat from without and not from within, as in the novel.

Although none of the *Jane Eyre* movies allude to the similarities between Jane and Bertha, a recent play adapted from the novel by Polly Teale shows Bertha as a part of Jane Eyre from the beginning, so that the two actresses are on the stage together throughout the play. At times Jane manages to keep Bertha in the background, at other times she comes to the fore. The legacy of the connection between the protagonist and the monster continues.

Great Expectations

Jane Eyre, as a sensitive child, was subjected to terrors that were too great for her in an effort to curb what was seen as her wickedness. In order to survive, she learns to suppress her anger and behave in a calm and rational manner. Pip in Charles Dickens' *Great Expectations* (1861) is also a sensitive child who is subjected to terrors. For Pip, this is compounded by the fact that he feels guilty and cannot reveal his secret. Pip can only become a complete and adult human when he has both softened his heart and faced his demons.

There are many cases of the double in this novel. Dolge Orlick and Pip are doubles in that Orlick is a negative version of Pip, a kind of alter ego. Pip matures as he encounters the negative aspects of himself through his confrontation with Orlick. He continues to develop his heart and soul through his devotion during the decline and death of Magwitch, who seems at first to be the monster of the novel. In one sense, both Magwitch and Pip are monsters created by society. Late in the novel Pip discovers that in order to become a mature adult he cannot divorce himself from his roots and must reconnect with his past.

At the start of *Great Expectations* (1946), directed by David Lean, there is a very scary moment when Magwitch first jumps out at Pip in the middle of a graveyard. This is a horror movie moment which is enhanced with tension-heightening music, the waving limbs of a tree (resembling menacing arms), and the close proximity of a gibbet. Magwitch, played by Finlay Currie, physically resembles a monster, while Pip looks like a sweet and innocent child. The contrast between the two is clear, whereas in the novel many similarities are revealed. Lean changes the emphasis of the novel and does not include the character of Dolge Orlick, who represents the real monster within Pip. However, in this film Estella develops into a double of Miss Havisham, a double who has thrown away her life and denied herself love and happiness. But Pip is able to intervene in this travesty of Estella's life as he was not able to with Miss Havisham, and he rescues Estella from the living death of Miss Havisham. In the more recent *Great Expectations* (1998), directed by Alfonso Cuarón, the themes from the novel are transposed into a more modern era. Although the film is less successful as a movie than the earlier one because of the lack of character development of Finn and Estella, it is beautiful to watch. As in Lean's version, the emphasis is moved away from the development of Pip into a complete and integrated human being. As in many of the films examined above, the twentieth-century adaptations of *Jane Eyre* and *Great Expectations* do not show the monster as stemming from within the characters. Whereas novels written in the nineteenth century feature monsters that are connected with the protagonist, in the film adaptations of these novels, the monsters are a force from without.

Nineteenth-Century British Society and Today

Many other nineteenth-century novels also reveal the monster to be a part of the main character. In Oscar Wilde's *The Picture of Dorian Gray* (1890), Dorian Gray attempts to separate his body and soul, keeping himself young and handsome while his portrait shows his evil soul — a different kind of doppelgänger. The narrator, Marlow, of Joseph Conrad's *Heart of Darkness* (1899) is often connected with Kurtz, a man who has seen "The horror! The horror!" as he states when he dies. The horror that Kurtz has witnessed emanates from himself and the civilization he represents. Evil of one sort or another found its way into nineteenth-century novels, often in the form of monsters or monstrous characters who are deeply connected with the protagonist of the novel. In order to become a unified adult, the protagonist must come to terms with his or her own suppressed desires.

For the Victorians, characters must learn to control their desires and become productive members of society. This tradition can be seen in the great horror novels of the nineteenth century, including *Frankenstein, Dr. Jekyll and Mr. Hyde, She, The Island of Dr. Moreau,* and *Dracula*. But during the twentieth century, as shown in the movies, anything can be forgiven the character — even a monster like Dracula in Coppola's *Bram Stoker's Dracula*— who loves deeply. Our monsters no longer incorporate the evils we see in society, like selfishness and corruption. They are not similar to us; we do not share their weaknesses. However, there seems to be a tendency in this direction. Many recent horror movies, and even the films *Bram Stoker's Dracula* and *Mary Shelley's Frankenstein*, show a connection between the protagonist and the monster. Perhaps soon the identification will be increased to include the viewer, and once more horror will reveal its ability to change the way people think about themselves and their society.

Notes

1. Many, many people are involved in the making of a movie. I use the name of the director as a shorthand means of discussing the film, even though the director may not be responsible for the particular aspect of the film I describe.

2. There may be a trend in this direction, as recent movies such as *Hide and Seek* (2005) and *High Tension* (2005) portray an unusual relationship between the monster and the victim.

3. After the death of her first child, who was born prematurely, Mary Shelley wrote in her journal for Sunday, March 19, 1815, "Dream that my little baby came to life again; that it had only been cold, and that we rubbed it by the fire, and it lived Awake and find no baby. I think about the little thing all day" (Mary Wollstonecraft Shelley, *The Life & Letters*, by Mrs. Julian Marshall, London: Richard Bentley & Son, 1889, 1: 110). Shelley may have associated her desire to bring life back to her child with the creation of the unnamed Creature of her novel. The Creature states, "I, the miserable and the abandoned, am an abortion" (Shelley, *Frankenstein* 155).

4. Another connection between Mary Shelley and her characters is that she shares her initials, M.W.S., with Walton's sister.

5. The image of Frankenstein with this corpse connects him with the concept of reanimation, bringing the dead back to life. What he does in the novel is to create new life by putting together parts of different bodies. In many of the adaptations, however, Frankenstein wants to bring the dead to life again. Often the concepts are combined or indistinguishable.

6. Suppose you were to come home one day and have a stranger approach you and say that he had been watching you for a year from the apartment next door through a small hole in your wall and that he knew that you were a really good person and that he needed help and would like to get to know you. How would you react?

7. The actor who plays Fritz, Dwight Frye, specialized in bizarre characters. He also plays Renfield in the *Dracula* movie of 1931.

8. The only Frankenstein film to show Frankenstein taking an interest in his creation and reaching out to him is Mel Brooks' *Young Frankenstein* (1974). In this film, Frankenstein tells the Creature that he is "a good boy" and builds a bond with him. This attention helps Frankenstein as well as the Creature, as Frankenstein is able to assume his name and heritage following his connection with the Creature. However, his good will goes for naught after Frankenstein leads the Creature in performing a soft-shoe routine in public, a trained-seal type of act.

9. The Internet Movie Database, in its Trivia for this film, claims that Kenneth Branagh banned the term "Monster" on the set.

10. This scene is reminiscent of Miss Havisham, in Charles Dickens' *Great Expectations* (1861), burning herself up in her wedding dress. Elizabeth and Miss Havisham are both almost-a-bride forever.

11. The main character is a maid in Dr. Jekyll's house in Valerie Martin's novel *Mary Reilly* (1990), which was made into a film by Stephen Frears (1996). Both works equate addiction to alcohol with Jekyll's addiction.

12. For example, Florence Nightingale denied herself the pleasure of going to the theater, and Christina Rossetti stopped playing chess because of how much she enjoyed winning.

13. While unhappily seeking a profession, Stevenson wrote to his cousin, "What I should prefer would be to search dying people in lowly places of the town and help them; but I *cannot trust myself* in such places" (Harmon 61). Stevenson's statement sounds very much like the experience of Jekyll in this movie.

14. Hyde's looks worsen with each transformation, and his behavior becomes more violent. The viewer may find it difficult to believe that Hyde would not be recognized by Beatrix, Poole, and Lanyon as being Jekyll in disguise.

15. Creating fact out of fiction, Haggard had a clay sherd produced, measuring 10 inches by 7 inches, which replicates the Sherd of Amenartas and its various inscriptions as described in the novel *She*.

16. In England during the late Victorian era, women started to voice their desire for the right to vote and work. Several critics believe that Haggard's concerns shown in the novel with powerful women stem from his unease with the "New Women" in England.

17. Billali sinks to a new low when he appears before Ustane's father and says that he will give Ustane back to him — and then hands him a jar filled with her ashes. With this grisly joke, Billali furthers the cruelty of Ayesha.

18. The name *Lady Vain* and a few other references in the novel point to a negative estimation of women. For example, at the end of the novel, Prendick recounts that "prowling women would mew after me" (132). Perhaps, like H. Rider Haggard, Wells felt threatened by the New Woman and saw her as predatory.

19. To victimize the weakest man could lead to legal trouble if they survived, while the democratic approach of tossing lots would not.

20. This may be a reference to homosexuality, as Wells was very interested in the trials of Oscar Wilde.

21. In a rumored third ending, a pregnant Maria gives birth to a tiger kitten (Smith 43).

22. One of his creations, Majai, who is a little person, dresses the same as Moreau and plays a duet with Moreau — Moreau on a grand piano and Majai on a miniature piano. Majai is a precursor of the character Mini-Me, played by Verne Troyer, in Jay Roach's *Austin Powers: The Spy Who Shagged Me* (1999). The similarities between the characters of Moreau and Montgomery, as well as Moreau and Majai, also underscores the evil within each man.

23. Modern vampires are based on traditional Hungarian legends of Vlad the Impaler (1431–76), who would mount prisoners on sharp wooden posts and enjoy their agony while he dined. Vlad's home has become a tourist attraction, and some effort has been made to turn it into a theme park.

24. These works exist as novels and film or television series adaptations.

25. The first vampire tale in English, *The Vampyre: A Tale*, was created by John Polidori for the same occasion that led Mary Shelley to write *Frankenstein*. Polidori was Lord Byron's personal physician and among the young, talented group in Switzerland on that famous night in 1816 when they decided to create their own tales of horror.

26. Although blood transfusions were known at the time that Stoker wrote *Dracula*, blood types were not. Luckily for Lucy, the transfusions did her no harm, so all involved must have had compatible blood types.

27. The strange looks and actions of the actor became the subject of the 2000 film *Shadow of the Vampire*, a fictional account of the filming of *Nosferatu*, which posits that Schreck is so terrifying because he was actually a vampire. In *Shadow of the Vampire* the director of *Nosferatu*, Murnau, acts as an accomplice in supplying Schreck with a beautiful actress to feed on.

28. There are several connections between this film and the 1931 *Frankenstein*, also made by Universal. Bela Lugosi had been considered for the role of Frankenstein. Dwight Frye plays Frankenstein's assistant Fritz, as well as Renfield, and they are similarly insane. Edward Van Sloan gives an opening address and plays Dr. Waldman in *Frankenstein*, while in *Dracula* he plays Van Helsing. Both films are concerned with themes of extended life, danger from unnatural elements, and the banding together of a group to defeat a murdering intruder in their midst, an intruder who threatens to disrupt "normal" procreation.

During the same time that Tod Browning's *Dracula* was being filmed, the same script, costumes, and sets were used at night by Universal to shoot the Spanish-language *Drácula* (dir. George Melford; screenplay by Baltasar Fernandez Cué; starring Carlos Villarias and Lupita Tovar).

29. The poem Lucy quotes, "The Revel," was written by Capt. Bartholomew Dowling in India about 1845. He died shortly after writing it.

30. The early Frankenstein and Dracula films were connected by the time in which they were made and by the studio that made them. The later ones are connected as well: *Bram Stoker's Dracula* was filmed in 1992; *Mary Shelley's Frankenstein* was made in the same studio in 1994, in part because of the success of the earlier film. Both are big-budget films produced by Francis Ford Coppola; and both use the name of the author in their title but change the emphasis of the plot.

31. This connection between Jane Eyre and Bertha Mason was first developed at length by Sandra Gilbert and Susan Gubar in *The Madwoman in the Attic* (1979).

32. www.poemhunter.com. Web; October 15, 2009.

Bibliography

Primary Sources: Novels

Brontë, Charlotte. *Jane Eyre*. Ed. Richard J. Dunn. Norton Critical Ed. New York: W.W. Norton, 2001.

Dickens, Charles. *Great Expectations*. Ed. Edgar Rosenberg. Norton Critical Ed. New York: W.W. Norton, 1999.

Haggard, H. Rider. *She*. Ed. Daniel Karlin. Oxford: Oxford University Press, 1990.

Shelley, Mary. *Frankenstein*. Ed. J. Paul Hunter. Norton Critical Ed. New York: W.W. Norton, 1996.

Stevenson, Robert Louis. *Strange Case of Dr. Jekyll and Mr. Hyde*. Ed. Katherine Linehan. Norton Critical Ed. New York: W.W. Norton, 2003.

Stoker, Bram. *Dracula*. Ed. Nina Auerbach and David J. Skal. Norton Critical Ed. New York: W.W. Norton, 1997.

Wells, H. G. *The Island of Dr. Moreau*. New York: Barnes & Noble Books, 2004.

Primary Sources: Films

Bram Stoker's Dracula. Dir. Francis Ford Coppola. Perf. Gary Oldman, Winona Ryder, Anthony Hopkins, Keanu Reeves. 1992. Columbia/Tristar, 1997. VHS.

Dr. Jekyll and Mr. Hyde. Dir. John S. Robertson. Perf. John Barrymore, Charles Lane, Brandon Hurst, Nita Naldi. 1920. Kino, 2001. DVD.

Dr. Jekyll and Mr. Hyde. Dir. Rouben Mamoulian. Perf. Fredric March, Miriam Hopkins, Rose Hobart, Holmes Herbert. 1931. Dr. Jekyll and Mr. Hyde Double Feature, Warner Home Video, 2004. DVD.

Dr. Jekyll and Mr. Hyde. Dir. Victor Fleming. Perf. Spencer Tracy, Ingrid Bergman, Lana Turner, Donald Crisp. 1941. Dr. Jekyll and Mr. Hyde Double Feature, Warner Home Video, 2004. DVD.

Dracula. Dir. Tod Browning. Perf. Bela Lugosi, Helen Chandler, David Manners, Dwight Frye. 1931. Dracula: The Legacy Collection, 2004. DVD.

Frankenstein. Dir. James Whale. Perf. Colin Clive, Mae Clarke, John Boles, Boris Karloff. 1931. Frankenstein: The Legacy Collection, 2004. DVD.

Great Expectations. Dir. David Lean. John Mills, Valerie Hobson, Jean Simmons, Bernard Miles, Finlay Currie. 1946. Universal/the Criterion Collection, 1999. DVD.

Great Expectations. Dir. Alfonso Cuarón. Perf. Ethan Hawke, Gwyneth Paltrow, Hank Azaria, Chris Cooper. 1998. 20th Century–Fox, 2002. DVD.

The Island of Dr. Moreau. Dir. Don Taylor. Perf. Burt Lancaster, Michael York, Nigel Davenport, Barbara Carrera. 1977. MGM, 2001. DVD.

The Island of Dr. Moreau. Dir. John Frankenheimer. David Thewlis, Fairuza Balk, Ron Perlman, Marlon Brando, Val Kilmer. 1996. New Line Home Video, 1997. DVD.

Island of Lost Souls. Dir. Erle C. Kenton. Perf. Charles Laughton, Richard Arlen, Leila Hyams, Bela Lugosi. 1933. Universal, 1997. VHS.

Jane Eyre. Dir. Robert Stevenson. Perf. Orson Welles, Joan Fontaine, Margaret O'Brien, Peggy Ann Garner. 1944. 20th Century–Fox, 2007. DVD.

Jane Eyre. Dir. Franco Zeffirelli. Perf. William Hurt, Charlotte Gainsbourg, Joan Plowright, Anna Paquin. 1996. Koch Media GmbH, 2008. DVD.

Mary Shelley's Frankenstein. Dir. Kenneth Branagh. Perf. Robert De Niro, Kenneth Branagh, Tom Hulce, Helena Bonham Carter. 1994. TriStar, 2000. DVD.

Nosferatu; Eine Symphonie Des Grauens (A Symphony of Horror). Dir. F. W. Murnau. Perf. Max Schreck, Alexander Granach, Gustav von Wangenheim, Greta Schröder. 1922. Alpha Video, 2002. VHS.

She. Dir. Lansing C. Holden and Irving Pichel. Perf. Helen Gahagan, Randolph Scott, Helen Mack, Nigel Bruce. 1935. Commentary on DVD by Ray Harryhausen and Mark Cotta Vaz. Legend Films and Kino International, 2007. DVD.

She. Dir. Robert Day. Perf. Ursula Andress, Peter Cushing, Bernard Cribbins, John Richardson. 1965. Optimum, 2001. DVD.

Secondary Sources: Horror

Berger, Carole. "Viewing as Action: Film and Reader Response Criticism." *Literature/Film Quarterly* 6 (1978): 144–51.

Brennan, Matthew. *The Gothic Psyche: Disintegration and Growth in Nineteenth-Century English Literature.* Columbia, SC: Camden House, 1997.

Britton, Andrew, ed. *American Nightmare: Essays on the Horror Film.* Intro. by Robin Wood. Toronto: Festival of Festivals, 1979.

Carroll, Noël. *The Philosophy of Horror or Paradoxes of the Heart.* New York: Routledge, 1990.

Clarens, Carlos. *An Illustrated History of the Horror Film.* New York: Capricorn Books, 1967.

Cohen, Jeffrey Jerome, ed. *Monster Theory: Reading Culture.* Minneapolis: University of Minnesota Press, 1997.

Colavito, Jason. *Knowing Fear: Science, Knowledge and the Development of the Horror Genre.* Jefferson, NC: McFarland, 2008.

Desmond, John M., and Peter Hawkers. *Adaptation: Studying Film and Literature.* Boston: McGraw Hill, 2006.

Dryden, Linda. *The Modern Gothic and Literary Doubles.* New York: Palgrave/Macmillan, 2003.

Garrett, Peter K. *Gothic Reflections: Narrative Force in Nineteenth-Century Fiction.* Ithaca: Cornell University Press, 2003.

Grant, Barry Keith, ed. *Planks of Reason: Essays on the Horror Film.* Metuchen, NJ: Scarecrow, 1984.

Houston, Gail Turley. *From Dickens to Dracula: Gothic, Economics, and Victorian Fiction.* New York: Cambridge University Press, 2005.

Hutchings, Peter. *The Horror Film.* New York: Pearson/Longman, 2004.

Internet Movie Data Base. Imdb.com. July 31, 2009.

Jones, Darryl. *Horror: A Thematic History in Fiction and Film.* London: Arnold, 2002.

Jörg, Daniele. "The Good, the Bad and the Ugly — Dr. Moreau Goes to Hollywood." *Public Understanding of Science* 12 (2003): 297–305.

Kristeva, Julie. *The Powers of Horror: An Essay on Abjection.* New York: Columbia University Press, 1982.

Leibfried, Philip. *Rudyard Kipling and Sir Henry Rider Haggard on Screen, Stage, Radio and Television.* Jefferson, NC: McFarland, 2000.

McCracken-Flesher, Caroline. "Cultural Projections: The 'Strange Case' of Dr. Jekyll, Mr. Hyde, and Cinematic Response." *Narrative and Culture.* Ed. Janice Carlisle and Daniel R. Schwarz. Athens: University of Georgia Press, 1994. 179–99.

Olorenshaw, Robert. "Narrating the Monster: From Mary Shelley to Bram Stoker." *Frankenstein Creation and Monstrosity.* Ed. Stephen Bann. London: Reaktion Books, 1994. 158–176.

Pirie, David. *A Heritage of Horror: The English Gothic Cinema, 1946–1972.* New York: Equinox, 1974.

Rigby, Jonathan. *English Gothic: A Century of Horror Cinema.* London: Reynolds & Hearn, 2004.

Robins, Ruth, and Julian Wolfreys, eds. *Victorian Gothic: Literary and Cultural Manifestations in the Nineteenth Century*. New York: Palgrave, 2000.

Skal, David J. *The Monster Show: A Cultural History of Horror*. New York: Faber and Faber, 2001.

Tropp, Martin. *Images of Fear: How Horror Stories Helped Shape Modern Culture (1818–1918)*. Jefferson, NC: McFarland, 1990.

Tudor, Andrew. *Monsters and Mad Scientists: A Culture History of the Horror Movie*. Oxford: Basil Blackwell, 1989.

Twitchell, James B. *Dreadful Pleasures: An Anatomy of Modern Horror*. New York: Oxford University Press, 1985.

Waller, Gregory A. *American Horrors: Essays on the Modern American Horror Film*. Urbana: University of Illinois Press, 1987.

Wood, Robin. "An Introduction to the American Horror Film." Ed. Grant. 164–200.

_____. *Hollywood from Vietnam to Reagan — and Beyond*. Rev. ed. New York: Columbia University Press, 2003.

Secondary Sources: Frankenstein

Baldrick, Chris. *In Frankenstein's Shadow: Myth, Monstrosity, and Nineteenth-Century Writing*. Oxford: Clarendon, 1987.

Bann, Stephen, ed. *Frankenstein Creation and Monstrosity*. London: Reaktion Books, 1994.

Behrendt, Stephen C., ed. *Approaches to Teaching Shelley's* Frankenstein. New York: The Modern Language Association of America, 1990.

Botting, Fred, ed. *New Casebooks: Frankenstein*. New York: St. Martin's, 1995.

Branagh, Kenneth. *Mary Shelley's Frankenstein: The Classic Tale of Terror Reborn on Film*. New York: Newmarket, 1994.

Dixon, Wheeler Winston. "*The Films of Frankenstein*." Ed. Behrendt. 166–79.

Everson, William K. *Classics of the Horror Film*. New York: Citadel Press/Carol Publishing, 1990.

Forry, Steven Earl. *Hideous Progenies: Dramatizations of* Frankenstein *from Mary Shelley to the Present*. Philadelphia: University of Pennsylvania Press, 1990.

Friedman, Lester D. "The Blasted Tree." *The English Novel and the Movies*. Ed. Michael Klein and Gillian Parker. New York: Frederick Ungar, 1981.

Glutt, Donald F. *The Frankenstein Legend: A Tribute to Mary Shelley and Boris Karloff*. Metuchen, NJ: Scarecrow, 1973.

Grant, Michael. "James Whale's 'Frankenstein': The Horror Film and the Symbolic Biology of the Cinematic Monster." Ed. Bann. 113–35.

Heffernan, James A. W. "Looking at the Monster: 'Frankenstein' and Film." *Critical Inquiry* 24.1 (Autumn 1997): 133–58.

Hitchcock, Susan Tyler. *Frankenstein: A Cultural History*. New York: W.W. Norton, 2007.

Klein, Michael, and Gillian Parker, eds. *The English Novel and the Movies*. New York: Frederick Ungar, 1981.

LaValley, Albert J. "The Stage and Film Children of *Frankenstein*: A Survey." Ed. Levine and Knoepflmacher. 243–89.

Levine, George, and U. C. Knoepflmacher. *The Endurance of* Frankenstein: *Essays on Mary Shelley's Novel*. Berkeley: University of California Press, 1979.

Lupack, Barbara Tepa, ed. *Nineteenth-Century Women at the Movies: Adapting Classic Women's Fiction to Film*. Bowling Green, OH: Bowling Green State University Popular Press, 1999.

Margolis, Harriet E. "Lost Baggage: Or, the Hollywood Sidetrack." Ed. Behrendt. 160–65.

McMahon, Jennifer L. "The Existential *Frankenstein*." *The Philosophy of Science Fiction Film*. Ed. Steven M. Sanders. Lexington: The University Press of Kentucky, 2008. 73-88.

Nestrick, William. "Coming to Life: *Frankenstein* and the Nature of Film Narrative." Ed. Levine and Knoepflmacher. 290–315.

Nollen, Scott Allen. *Boris Karloff: A Critical Account of His Screen, Stage, Radio, Television, and Recording Work*. Jefferson, NC: McFarland, 1991.

O'Flinn, Paul. "Production and Reproduction: The Case of *Frankenstein*." Ed. Botting. 21–47.

Picart, Caroline Joan ("Kay") S., Frank Smoot, and Jayne Blodgett. *The Frankenstein Film Source-*

book (Bibliographies and Indexes in Popular Culture, Number 8). Westport, CT: Greenwood, 2001.

Schor, Esther. "*Frankenstein* and Film." Ed. Schor. 63–83.

Schor, Esther, ed. *The Cambridge Companion to Mary Shelley.* Cambridge: Cambridge University Press, 2003.

Senf, Carol A. *Science and Social Science in Bram Stoker's Fiction.* Westport, CT: Greenwood, 2002.

Tropp, Martin. "Re-Creating the Monster: *Frankenstein* and Film." Ed. Lupack. 23–77.

Secondary Sources: Dr. Jekyll and Mr. Hyde

Bell, Ian. *Dreams of Exile: Robert Louis Stevenson, a Biography.* New York: Henry Holt, 1992.

Geduld, Harry M. *The Definitive Dr. Jekyll and Mr. Hyde Companion.* New York: Garland, 1983.

Gray, William. *R. Louis Stevenson: A Literary Life.* New York: Palgrave Macmillan, 2004.

Harman, Claire. *Robert Louis Stevenson: A Biography.* London: Harper Collins, 2005.

Hubbard, Tom. *Seeking Mr. Hyde: Studies in Robert Louis Stevenson, Symbolism, Myth and the Pre-Modern.* New York: Peter Lang, 1995.

Jefford, Andrew. "Dr. Jekyll and Professor Nabokov: Reading a Reading." *Robert Louis Stevenson.* Ed. Andrew Noble. Totowa, NJ: Vision and Barnes and Noble, 1983. 47–72.

Lehman, Peter. "Looking at Ivy Looking at Us Looking at Her: The Camera and the Garter." *Wide Angle: A Film Quarterly of Theory, Criticism, and Practice* 5.3 (1983): 59–63.

Luhr, William, and Peter Lehman. *Authorship and Narrative in the Cinema: Issues in Contemporary Aesthetics and Criticism.* New York: Capricorn Books/G.P. Putnam's Sons, 1971.

Maixner, Paul, ed. *Robert Louis Stevenson: The Critical Heritage.* Boston: Routledge & Kegan Paul, 1981.

McNally, Raymond T., and Radu R. Florescu. *In Search of Dr. Jekyll and Mr. Hyde.* London: Robson, 2001.

Pinkston, C. Alex. "The Stage Premiere of Dr. Jekyll and Mr. Hyde." *Nineteenth Century Theatre Research* 14½ (1986): 21–44.

Prawer, S. S. *Caligari's Children: The Film as Tale of Terror.* Oxford: Oxford University Press, 1980.

Rose, Brian. *Jekyll and Hyde Adapted: Dramatizations of Cultural Anxiety.* Westport, CT: Greenwood, 1996.

_____. "Transformations of Terror: Reading Changes in Social Attitudes Through Film and Television Adaptations of Stevenson's Dr. Jekyll and Mr. Hyde." *Social and Political Change in Literature and Film.* Ed. Richard Chapple. Gainesville: University Press of Florida, 1994. 37–52.

Smith, Andrew. *Victorian Demons: Medicine, Masculinity and the Gothic at the Fin-de-Siècle.* Manchester: Manchester University Press, 2004.

Usai, Paolo Cherchi. *Silent Cinema: An Introduction.* London: British Film Institute, 2000.

Veeder, William, and Gordon Hirsch, eds. *Dr. Jekyll and Mr. Hyde After One Hundred Years.* Chicago: University of Chicago Press, 1988.

Wexman, Virginia Wright. "Horrors of the Body: Hollywood's Discourse on Beauty and Rouben Mamoulian's Dr. Jekyll and Mr. Hyde." Ed. Veeder and Hirsch. 283–307.

Woolf, Leonard. Author and ed. *The Essential Dr. Jekyll and Mr. Hyde.* New York: Byron Press/Plume/Penguin Group, 1995.

Secondary Sources: She

Brantlinger, Patrick. Introduction. *She*, by H. Rider Haggard. New York: Penguin Books, 2001. vii–xxviii.

Gilbert, Sandra M. "Rider Haggard's Heart of Darkness." *Coordinates: Placing Science Fiction and Fantasy.* Ed. George E. Slusser, Eric S. Rabkin, and Robert Scholes. Carbondale: Southern Illinois University Press, 1983. 124–38.

Gilbert, Sandra M., and Susan Gubar. *No Man's Land: The Place of the Woman Writer in the Twentieth Century.* Volume 2: Sexchanges. New Haven: Yale University Press, 1988.

Karlin, Daniel. Introduction. *She,* by H. Rider Haggard. Oxford: Oxford University Press, 1990.

Katz, Wendy. *Rider Haggard and the Fiction of Empire: A Cultural Study of British Imperial Fiction.* New York: Cambridge University Press, 1987.

Monsman, Gerald. *H. Rider Haggard on the Imperial Frontier: The Political and Literary Contexts of His African Romances.* Greensboro: ELT Press/University of North Carolina, 2006.

Murphy, Patricia. "The Gendering of History in 'She.'" *Studies in English Literature, 1500–1900* 39.4 (Autumn 1999): 747–72.

Sandison, Alan. *The Wheel of Empire: A Study of the Imperial Idea in Some Late Nineteenth and Early Twentieth-Century Fiction.* London: MacMillan; New York: St. Martin's, 1967.

Showalter, Elaine. *Sexual Anarchy: Gender and Culture at the Fin de Siècle.* New York: Viking, 1990.

Stiebel, Lindy. *Imagining Africa: Landscape in H. Rider Haggard's African Romances.* Westport, CT: Greenwood, 2001.

Young, Shannon. "*She*: Rider Haggard's Queer Adventures." *Straight Writ Queer: Non-Normative Expressions of Heterosexuality in Literature.* Ed. Richard Fantina. Jefferson, NC: McFarland, 2006. 134–44.

Secondary Sources: The Island of Dr. Moreau

Bozzetto, Roger. "Moreau's Tragi-Farcical Island." *Science-Fiction Studies* 20 (1993): 34–44.

Fried, Michael. "Impressionist Monsters: 'The Island of Dr. Moreau.'" *Frankenstein Creation and Monstrosity.* Ed Stephen Bann. London: Reaktion Books, 1994. 95–112.

Glendening, John. "Green Confusion: Evolution and Entanglement in H. G. Wells' *The Island of Doctor Moreau.*" *Victorian Literature and Culture* 30.2 (2002): 571–97.

Harris-Fain, Darren. Introduction. *The Island of Dr. Moreau.* New York: Barnes & Noble Books, 2004. vii–xiv.

McConnell, Frank. *The Science Fiction of H. G. Wells.* New York: Oxford University Press, 1981.

Pratley, Gerald. *The Films of Frankenheimer.* Bethlehem, PA: Lehigh University Press, 1998.

Renzi, Thomas C. *H. G. Wells: Six Scientific Romances Adapted for Film.* 2nd ed. Metuchen, NJ: Scarecrow, 2004.

Smith, Don G. *H. G. Wells on Film: The Utopian Nightmare.* Jefferson, NC: McFarland, 2002.

Straub, Peter. Foreword. *The Island of Dr. Moreau.* New York: The Modern Library, 1996. ix–xxix.

Secondary Sources: Dracula

Aldiss, Brian. *Trillion Year Spree: The History of Science Fiction.* New York: Atheneum, 1986.

Auerbach, Nina. *Our Vampires, Ourselves.* Chicago: University of Chicago Press, 1995.

Byron, Glennis. *Dracula: Bram Stoker.* New York: St. Martin's, 1999.

Coppola, Francis Ford, and James V. Hart. *Bram Stoker's Dracula: The Film and the Legend.* New York: Newmarket, 1992.

Dracula (The Original 1931 Shooting Script). Production Background by Philip J. Riley. Universal Filmscripts Series. Atlantic City, NJ: Magic Image Filmbooks, 1990.

Eisner, Lotte H. *The Haunted Screen: Expressionism in the German Cinema and the Influence of Max Reinhardt.* London: Thames & Hudson, 1969.

Glut, Donald F. *The Dracula Book.* Metuchen, NJ: Scarecrow, 1975.

Hogan, Patrick Colm. "Narrative Universals, National, and Sacrificial Terror: From Nosferatu to Nazism. *Film Studies* 8 (Summer 2006): 93–105.

Joslin, Lyndon W. *Count Dracula Goes to the Movies: Stoker's Novel Adapted, 1922–2003*. 2nd ed. Jefferson, NC: McFarland, 2006.

Senf, Carol A. *Dracula: Between Tradition and Modernism*. New York: Twayne, 1998.

Shepard, Leslie, and Albert Power. *Dracula: Celebrating 100 Years*. Dublin: Mentor, 1997.

Skal, David J. *Hollywood Gothic: The Tangled Web of* Dracula *from Novel to Stage to Screen*. New York: W.W. Norton, 1990.

Thomas, Ronald R. "Specters of the Novel: *Dracula* and the Cinematic Afterlife of the Victorian Novel." *Victorian Afterlife*. Ed. John Kucich and Dianne F. Sadoff. Minneapolis: University of Minnesota Press, 2000. 288–310.

Index